Transport, the Environment and Security

Transport, the Environment and Security

Making the Connection

Rae Zimmerman

New York University, USA

Edward Elgar
Cheltenham, UK • Northampton, MA, USA

Published by
Edward Elgar Publishing Limited
The Lypiatts
15 Lansdown Road
Cheltenham
Glos GL50 2JA
UK

Edward Elgar Publishing, Inc.
William Pratt House
9 Dewey Court
Northampton
Massachusetts 01060
USA

A catalogue record for this book
is available from the British Library

Library of Congress Control Number: 2012935273

ISBN 978 1 84980 020 4

Typeset by Servis Filmsetting Ltd, Stockport, Cheshire

Printed and bound by CPI Group (UK) Ltd, Croydon, CR0 4YY

Contents

Preface

Society is at a turning point in how it copes with the environmental problems and security threats that often play out in the transport arena. The ideas for this book combine the science of networks and the fundamental importance of connectivity that transport provides in the context of the environment and security. These areas are usually explored as separate concepts and this book provides a convergence. Combining these areas creates new ideas and directions that would be overlooked by focusing on any one of these areas separately.

The book is not meant to be an exhaustive treatment of these three areas but rather selects those parts of each area that provide meaningful interconnections with the others. Environment is broadly construed to encompass ecology, the urban environment, and social justice related to transport. Security primarily pertains to effects of terrorism and can also pertain to effects of other extreme events. Transport focuses on surface transport and primarily rail and road based transport rather than air and marine travel.

The book offers new insights in a number of areas that address very current problems, for example, how to reduce the sensitivity of ecological systems to transport activity through the use of wildlife corridors and use transport density as an advantage in reducing vulnerabilities posed by environmental hazards and security breaches.

Chapter 1 presents the concept of networks as a framework for integrating the three themes of transport, environment, and security. This is applied to the forces that connect, then disconnect and reconnect people to urban settlements. Chapter 2 then provides the context for road and rail transportation networks primarily in the US. This is followed by an in-depth analysis of transit systems nationwide that illustrates how they are networked and the attributes of those networks, primarily as they affect concentration of services and the environmental and security issues this may create. Chapter 3 begins the environmental component with an analysis of how transportation and climate change are interrelated. The dual relationship of how transport affects climate and climate affects transport is underscored along with how development continues to shape both of them. Some of the newer technologies for adapting to climate change are presented in light of heat and flooding. Chapter 4 provides solutions primarily in the form of reconfiguring transport networks and how institutional processes are organized to manage these changes. Chapter 5 extends the environment discussion in Chapter 3 from global climate change to some of the more traditional environmental areas that potentially influence transport networks, and also provides some unique network-based solutions to ecological problems. Chapter 6 introduces natural hazards and accidents that disrupt transport, and the role that transport in turn can play in alleviating some of the effects of these conditions. Chapter 7 brings in the third component, that of security, how transport has been a target, and what methods the US federal government has been implementing primarily in the form of funding to address these threats. Chapter 8 concludes with insights about future directions by taking advantage of network strategies to integrate the three areas.

The book provides some unique aspects of the transport, environment, and security nexus. It combines data on the environment and transport in order to obtain new insights into the relative ways energy is used. It also provides analyses of transit networks as a way of understanding their environmental and security dimensions. It provides unique analyses of new transport networks emerging in the form of fueling stations needed for new renewable fuels as well as environmental networks being created as ecological corridors to be compatible with transport networks.

The idea for this book came about over many years through separate research investigations in the environment, security and infrastructure, and a continuing interest in and fascination with network theory that dates back to my early studies in the natural and physical sciences. Since that time, the urban infrastructure domain through teaching, research and professional activities has provided an umbrella for continuing my work in the environmental field. That experience started with the first Earth Day and has evolved to encompass environmental justice, climate change, and the continuing catastrophes that overwhelm our lives. This book represents a beginning not an end.

Acknowledgments

The variety and breadth of the areas covered in this book inevitably draw from a considerable amount of research over many years. Innovative and invaluable grants were provided by the NYU Wagner School's Faculty Research Grant awards that enabled me to venture into new areas captured in this book and by the NYU Curricular Development Challenge Fund Grant for the development of a course on planning for emergencies and disasters and support of the underlying research for the course. I extend special thanks to those colleagues with whom I have published on transportation infrastructure-related topics, including Professor Jeffrey S. Simonoff, Dr Carlos E. Restrepo, and Dr Zvia S. Naphtali at NYU, Professor Vicki Bier at the University of Wisconsin (Madison) and Professor Michael R. Greenberg at Rutgers University. I am grateful to the many other colleagues I have learned from over the years through various professional venues and collaborations too numerous to list here. Colleagues who deserve special mention for the vision and guidance in many of the areas touched on in the book and with whom I have worked over the years include Dr James Peerenboom of Argonne National Laboratories, James L. Lammie, a former President and Chief Executive Officer of Parsons Brinckerhoff Inc., and Professor John Falcocchio of NYUPoly. I am indebted to the insights provided to me throughout my career by Dr Sigurd Grava whose untimely passing left a significant gap in the transportation profession. Colleagues at NYUPoly's Center for Interdisciplinary Studies in Security and Privacy under the direction of Professor Nasir Memon enhanced my thinking in the area of cybersecurity and its connection to infrastructure that is a part of Chapter 7. Discussions with colleagues in climate change research directed by Dr Cynthia Rosenzweig at Columbia University and Professor William Solecki at Hunter College were helpful as a foundation for connections between transport and global warming contained in Chapter 3 of the book. My colleagues at the Society for Risk Analysis, of which I have been a president, continue to shape much of my understanding of the intersection of transport, environment and security. I also want to thank the many scholars I have referenced in this work and organizations that provided me with publicly available data for the underlying research. Graduate student researchers over the years at New York University provided valuable support for my research in general, and I extend special thanks to the invaluable assistance of Elisabeth Wooton who assembled transit databases, Paul Salama for downloading alternative fuel station data, and Jennifer Hustwitt who I worked with on statistical analyses for portions of the transit data. My assistant Ann S. Lin provided critical assistance with the references. Most importantly I thank my family, Michael, Gabe and Alexa not only for their patience through this process, but also for providing many insights and support along the way.

1. Introduction

TRANSPORT, ENVIRONMENT AND SECURITY: COMMON OBJECTIVES AND SHARED STRATEGIES

The traditional purpose of transportation is to enable people to have access to goods and services and social support. Transportation, like other public services, is often taken for granted. It is assumed to be available when needed and effortless with the main purpose of overcoming distance. Yet, relationships between transportation and the values and needs encompassed by the environment and security influence how transportation infrastructure and its services are configured. The environment is multidimensional, including both physical and social dimensions, encompassing for example, climate, air and water quality, land resources and social equity. Security acknowledges the growing incidents worldwide, and vulnerabilities, consequences and concerns regarding terrorism. Accidents and natural hazards bring their own set of environmental and security problems. The rationale for combining transport, environment and security is that they share much in common, such as common outcomes. As such, these phenomena can often be managed in ways that are synergistic or at least consistent.

Synergies often arise as co-benefits. Precedents exist for co-benefits for transportation, environment, and security. Air quality and climate change goals, both of which relate to transportation, have co-benefits when pursued simultaneously (ApSimon et al. 2009). Social benefits arise from improved health by reducing air pollutants and greenhouse gases. For example, the US Environmental Protection Agency (EPA) program for common strategies to integrate climate change, air quality, health and the economy implies co-benefits (US EPA 2009). Holland (2008, p.3) identified co-benefits between air quality and health, estimating reductions in lives lost, hospital admissions and other health factors from reductions in fine particulates, sulfur oxides and nitrogen oxides (components of some transportation emissions) and greenhouse gases (GHG). Co-benefits of air quality and GHG reduction were also analysed in Asia by Huizenga and Ajero (2005) using transportation as a key component, and Bollen et al. (2009) examined similar co-benefits in the Netherlands.

Co-benefits emerge in areas not directly involving transportation but the strategies are nevertheless applicable to the environment – transport synergies, for example, by Elbakidze and McCarl (2004, 2007) and Pattanayak et al. (2005) who evaluate co-benefits of GHG mitigation and water quality improvements.

Thus, combining objectives is not new, but the combination of transport, environment and security is less well-studied or studied in more limited ways. For example, while transport has commonly been considered with air quality issues, another dimension for integrating transport and the environment is ecological or wildlife corridors which are a popular means of achieving environmental and transport objectives simultaneously. Chapter 5 addresses this.

Climate. Health. Sprawl. Disasters. Security. Economy. Environment. Transport has been the field in which these competing interests have played out for well over a century, and longer, when humans first relied on wheels to move faster. It is over a hundred years since major transportation technologies emerged to meet the needs of an enlarging and often decentralizing population.

When decision choices are framed separately, they often compete, leading to expanding budgetary demands. Recognition of the interconnectedness of the many demands that are made on transport is crucial for meeting competing goals. The environment, including climate change, and security are posing new challenges especially where several of these objectives have to be met simultaneously. While these multiple needs have been around a long time it is their combination that presents new challenges. Even if synergies are not possible, compatibility or co-existence is an important option.

Transport and the choices people make about it involve a design that is often unseen and ad hoc but is reflected in networks. Networks are an organizing principle that can combine often disparate needs into a common set of goals. Transport has been extensively explored as a network, and incorporating environment and security builds on that concept.

Networks connect transportation to disasters, environmental protection, renewable resources, and security, recognizing interdependencies and co-benefits. A network approach provides the interconnections to explore multiple priorities and policies.

There is a sense of urgency in addressing these areas together. There are some wake-up calls that disasters have called attention to, where transportation behavior plays a key part in survival. People who perish in natural disasters often do so in their cars. Accessibility to the means of egress during disasters is often socially, culturally, and politically determined.

Disadvantaged people in hazard-prone areas have less access to the means of travel whether it is car ownership or accessibility to public transit (Bullard 2007).

The connections between environmental benefits and transportation provided by renewable energy, for example, often arise unexpectedly. Solar energy for vehicles provides environmental benefits, addresses climate change, and can provide backup power in emergencies where solar panels are used directly on emergency vehicles (CH2MHill 2009, p.7). Electric vehicles equipped with batteries were used to enter devastated areas following the Japan earthquake in March 2011; they were able to use backup power, they could be charged using ordinary outlets or fast charging stations, they did not rely on gas stations which were out of service, and could move easily over debris given their lightweight construction and tire structure (Belson 2011). According to Belson's account, they were used for a wide range of services including transporting supplies, serving doctors, and supporting inspections. Moreover, steel-encased batteries in electric vehicles (the Nissan Leaf) were able to withstand the destructive force of the tsunami though the cars suffered damages (Bunkley 2011). Countless disasters have spawned new disasters with escalating consequences because essential services were disrupted. Important co-benefits are realized if strategies such as renewable energy can fill the gap for transport and other services, even if just in the short term.

TRANSPORT AS A NETWORK

Transport as a network is a valuable approach for understanding the linkages among transport, environment and security and the consistency of transport and production of co-benefits with the environment and security. The network concept is briefly introduced, borrowing from network science – what it is and how it shapes choices and institutions. Then network concepts are applied to the forces that connect, disconnect and reconnect transport services. Major drivers of these forces are presented primarily in terms of population – its size, density, distribution, and rate of change – that often frame transportation choices and the means to integrate transport, environment, and security. The utility of the network concept is that transport, environment, and security follow similar network principles, which enables a common language to be created among them that allows comparisons and an understanding of their interactions.

Network Theory in Brief

Networks are in their simplest construction nodes (often called vertices) connected by links (also called edges) (Newman 2010, p.1), and the concept is well-developed throughout the literature in multiple disciplines (Barabasi 2002). Activity flows and transfers occur across networks and physical contexts influence their form or structure and behavior. Although the behavior of networks is highly contextual a few principles have become apparent. These are meant to be examples rather than exhaustive. The degree to which they have been tested and agreed upon varies considerably. Emphasis is placed on what aspects of a network provide strength or make it vulnerable in the face of internal and external influences.

Important properties of networks are relevant to the study of transport networks. These include centrality and the related concepts that define centrality – degree, betweenness, and closeness (Newman 2010; Wasserman and Faust 2009). Bohannon (2009, p.409) summarizes these concepts for terrorism (citing Krebs 2001): Degree measures the extent of activity, betweenness is control over network flows, and closeness is the accessibility of a given node to others in the network. Taking a closer look at the concepts, centrality as the overarching concept is a measure of the importance of a node and in the social network theory literature it is equated with its visibility or prominence (Wasserman and Faust 2009, p.172) and can occur at various scales in a network – the node, link or sub-groupings of the network (Wasserman and Faust 2009, p.170). Newman (2010, p.169) defines the degree centrality of a node as the extent to which the nodes have edges attached, which is the same as the definition of degree (Newman 2010, p.133). Betweenness is related to centrality and Newman (2010, p.185) defines betweenness centrality as whether a particular node or vertex is between other vertices along a path and can be a measure of its influence (Newman 2010, p.186). Closeness centrality is a measure of distances among vertices (Newman 2010, p.181). These concepts very much depend on the network structure, for example, whether the structure is star-shaped, circular or linear (Wasserman and Faust 2009, p.171).

Network flows can have direction or not, and be weighted or not. Summarizing these concepts again (adapted, for example, from Newman 2010):

- Centrality signifies importance
  - Degree is the number of links connected to a node (control);
  - Betweenness is the extent to which a node lies between other nodes along a path (influence);
  - Closeness is the proximity of nodes to other nodes (accessibility).

Network-related concepts other than those related to centrality are also important for transport, environment and security linkages:

- Concentration pertains to spatial and functional distributions;
- Remoteness refers to outliers or nodes connected to a single node or link in only one direction, potentially indicative of isolation;
- Flexibility and adaptability refer to the ability to serve more than one function or support activity in more than one direction. Redundancy can provide flexibility but not always.

Certain specific principles arise from the literature on network theory and its applications to transport that are relevant to how transport systems relate to the environment and security. Network structure has been related to vulnerability (Taylor and D'Este 2007). Holme et al. (2002) and Grubesic and Murray (2006), for example, observe that network structure changes as important nodes and edges are removed, and how they are removed affects vulnerability.

Some key principles are common themes throughout the book, presented below in terms of how network properties influence transport.

(1) Network structure, number of connections, flows and network vulnerability:
- More complex and diverse networks are more susceptible to intrusion than simple networks. Stefanini and Masera (2008, p.35) point out that those infrastructure networks that are more networked and highly distributed need to consider more diverse threats than simpler or single systems.
- Networks can be multidimensional with interconnections defined as occurring among the dimensions. Some have characterized this as "metanetworks" (Bohannon 2009).
- The greater the number of links, nodes and interconnections among them, the more vulnerable the system becomes to intrusion, since potential flows can increase and the degree of control can decrease (Aderinlewo and Attoh-Okine 2009).
- Measures of importance related to centrality are distance (among nodes), or how long it takes to move from one node to another, as well as clustering or tightness (Newman 2010, p.10).
- Motter and Lai (2002) argue that where loads or activity flows can occur freely in a network, cascading effects can occur, and the disruption of a single node where it has a large load can have dramatic effects.

- The size of a node or link can reflect how concentrated the flows are.
- Network boundaries can be dynamic and unstable where the number and location of nodes and links are expandable (Wasserman and Faust 2009, pp.30–33).
- Network structures may not be uniform in influence. In fact certain levels may contribute to the stability of the entire network. That is, the placement of certain features of a network can be critical. Deutsch (1966, pp.154–5) theorized that the "middle level of command" in government and other organizational structures enables a network to keep in touch with its parts especially when resources are scarce. He defined the "strategic middle level" as being close to both the rank and file and higher echelons defined in terms of the vertical structure of an organization (Deutsch 1966, p.154).

(2) Network adaptability:
- Networks can adapt if loads can shift from one node or link to another. This implies heterogeneous and dynamic structures. The ability to reconfigure is key to adaptation. Motter and Lai (2002), however, argue that when networks can shift their loads around among different nodes, instabilities can occur that contribute to cascading effects and can ultimately destroy the network. Their concept involves the size of nodes, and they argue that where small nodes are removed the effect may not be as great as if larger ones are removed. Moreover, they argue that homogeneous networks are more stable than heterogeneous ones.
- The capacity of networks to isolate portions of their structure is one aspect of adaptability.
- Networks are more adaptable where subgroupings or subnetworks exist, enabling the network to fall back to relatively stable units after an intrusion or disruption. The Herbert Simon (1966, pp.90–92) parable of the watchmakers illustrates that clearly; where the watchmaker that built in subunits into the watches would not have to start from scratch every time there was an interruption.

Networks and Transport, Environment and Security

Transportation systems consist of nodes, links and user activity that constitute flows. A number of studies use networks as a foundation for describing and analysing the behavior of transport systems (Rodrigue et al. 2006, 2009; Nagurney and Qiang 2009; Levinson and Krizek 2008) and specifically to address behavior in the context of disruptions, vulnerability and security (Murray-Tuite 2008; Murray-Tuite and Fei 2010).

As indicated earlier, the advantage of viewing transport as a network is to combine it with other conditions such as the environment and security. Networks also allow transport structure and behavior to be related to the economy and Newman (2010, p.32) traces this to the early work of Kansky (1963).

The applicability of network concepts and theories to transportation systems goes back many decades at least to the mid-twentieth century. Gorman (2005, p.31) reviews historical studies on land use and transportation relationships from a network perspective. Lynch (1960) writing on the principles of places, uses transportation networks as a major underpinning for alternative views of a city: links appear in the form of paths and edges and nodes appear in the form of districts, nodes and landmarks.

Under ordinary circumstances system transfers are a key part of transportation networks. Hadas and Ceder (2010, p.2) formulate three types of transfer points: those that are nonadjacent, adjacent or shared. These can occur in multiple dimensions or layers (Hadas and Ceder 2010, p.4).

The Sen et al. (2003) study of rail transit in India introduced by Newman (2010, pp.32–3) makes a distinction between those links that provide through traffic between two nodes and those that allow stops at nodes along the links. Newman (2010, p.33) suggests a way of representing such a network in terms of a "bipartite network" in which the two kinds of nodes can be distinguished.

According to Ceder and Teh (2010), connectivity improves public transport (PT) systems. Ceder and Teh (2010) identify and compare PT connectivity in central business districts of three New Zealand cities using measures based on factors influencing individual choice of PT as a travel mode. They conclude that more paths between origin and destination are best. Moreover, centrally locating a PT terminal helps to improve connectivity (by increasing the number of paths). Such a solution may not be optimal for security unless extreme precautions are used to protect the single terminal or node.

In disasters, networks are routinely broken and reconstructed. When passageways are needed to reconnect washed out roads and collapsed bridges, engineers have relied on unique approaches. Some noteworthy examples are bridges that can be floated in very quickly to replace a disabled unit. Rapid bridge replacement has been described by Bai and Kim (2007). Floating bridges described by Zoli and Englot (2008) temporarily route traffic to safer locations.

The ability of traffic flows to be redirected in emergencies has gained momentum (Cho et al. 2001). Contraflow enables road traffic to be redirected away from hazardous conditions toward temporary shelters (Urbina and Wolshon 2003). For example, according to the Disaster Center web page, during Hurricane Rita traffic was directed north and west along many major roadways. Trains can reverse direction also, rerouted for the same reason as roads, and this ability saved major exposure to disaster.

Transportation networks have been commonly used to analyse node disruption either by natural hazards, accidents or terrorism. Cho et al. (2001) use transport networks to calculate the economic effects of a disruption of transportation systems in an earthquake.

Concentration

Concentration is one aspect of transportation networks particularly critical for both environmental compatibility and security. There is no single measure to describe it and definitions vary according to context.

For transport, concentration is necessary for users to access many different areas efficiently and with fewer environmental impacts, for economic viability (economies of scale), or to tap concentrated resources. Perrow (2007) has presented examples of drawbacks of concentration. Parfomak (2008) raises the issue of concentration in the context of critical infrastructures. Simonoff et al. (2011) analyse the impact of infrastructure concentration on resource allocation. Concentration becomes particularly critical where infrastructures are interdependent either spatially or functionally (Rinaldi et al. 2001; Zimmerman 2006; Zimmerman and Restrepo 2006).

The "upstream" resources for transport, or those used as inputs for transport services, are particularly noted for their concentration. A few examples illustrate how the vulnerability of supplies for transport is affected by concentration. For example, the convergence point of nine interstate pipelines and four intrastate lines is called the Henry Hub, located near Erath, Louisiana (Budzik c2000). The area is in the major striking zone of hurricanes; however, it has not sustained much damage from hurricanes (DisasterCenter.com web page). On September 13, 2008, the owner of the Henry Hub shut it down due to the threat from Hurricane Ike (Reuters 2008). Another example of a threat to concentrated transport-related resources is an account by Coker (2010) of a Japanese tanker traveling through the Strait of Hormuz that was damaged and allegedly attacked, and an estimated 20 percent of global oil shipments travel that route daily. Thus, the potential of a similar attack on oil supplies could be significant. In the wake of threats by Iran to affect transport through the Strait of Hormuz (Sanger and Lowrey 2011), alternative routes have been put forth to convey oil, for example, the construction of a pipeline by Abu Dhabi (Hamdan 2012).

Concentration as a network attribute is highly compatible with environment and security objectives. Concentration of critical infrastructure and population can occur within urban settlements in ways that support environmental needs as well as focusing resources for security, though the threat might be greater in concentrated areas. Savitch (2008, pp.148–53) argues against the "dystopia" or arguments for "defensive dispersal" following the September 11, 2001 attacks indicating that such views ignore the resilience of cities. For environmental compatibility, renewable resources, for example, can be dispersed within dense urban settlements as solar cells on rooftops. Transportation systems adopting matrix structures with numerous intersections and transfer points promote both dispersion and flexibility within dense urban areas. Thus, if concentration increases vulnerability, it is countered by the resilience that concentration and its unique features create.

CONNECTING

The Land Use, Population and Transportation Connection: One More Time

Land use and population characteristics have a fundamental and historically prominent role in defining transportation (Ewing and Cervero 2010) and the relationship between transportation and other goals such as the environment and security. Three areas are discussed as they shape these relationships – the amount of land consumed by transportation, land use and GHG relationships, and characteristics of rapidly growing urban areas.

Land consumption by transportation

In connecting people with places, transport consumes a significant amount of land. Although there is little systematic information on land consumption and measures that do exist are not consistent, that is, measure different kinds of spaces, some estimates exist. Forman (2000, p.31) estimates that 1 percent of the US area is covered by roads and roadsides, and the ecological effects of roads extend over 22 percent of the continental US, which enlarges the actual area that roads impact (Forman 2000, p.34). Evink (2002, p.16) cites a similar figure of 1 percent but does not include parking areas. Cambridge Systematics, Inc. (2005, p.5 citing Lawrence Berkeley National Laboratories) showed that in four large urban areas,

Sacramento, Chicago, Salt Lake City, and Houston, 33–59 percent of the pavement area was devoted to streets, and very little, 16 percent or less, was devoted to sidewalks (Cambridge Systematics, Inc. 2005, p.6 citing other studies). Rodrigue et al. (2009) give an estimate of 155,000 square kilometers as the land devoted to car use in the US. Estimates per car, per roadway section, and per household or per capita also exist. Brown (2001) provides some unit figures per car – that in the US 0.07 hectares or 0.18 acres is required per car in the form of roads and parking areas. In total, he indicates 6.3 million kilometers (3.9 million miles) or 16 million hectares (61,000 square miles). He argues that food shortages could result from the competition for land between growing food and transportation. An earlier estimate of the rate of land consumption by roadways is 80 acres of land for an intersection and 24 acres of land per mile for a freeway (Detwyler 1971, p.419). Litman (2011, p.38) estimates about 3,600 square feet of paved road per household based on assumed average dimensions of residential lots and roads. The US Department of Transportation (October 2010) compares road density and road extent per capita for eight countries, and the US with about 21 kilometers per 1,000 persons ranks second behind Canada in per capita road mileage. These estimates point to significant transport-related paved areas with their potential for adverse environmental impacts without suitable design or material changes.

Land use patterns, transport, and GHG emissions
One of the more intense debates about transportation and land use connections centers around the contribution of land uses to GHG emissions. Automobile usage is often the focus of the transportation and GHG relationship in terms of vehicle miles of travel (VMT), fuel efficiency, and type of fuel addressed in Chapter 3 in connection with transportation and climate change. In particular, the argument focuses on whether density in the form of compact development holds the answer to GHG emission reduction by reducing automobile usage. Burchell et al. (2005) have shown that suburbanization is more costly in terms of the amount of energy consumed, GHG emissions, and oil dependency created by increased automobile dependency. A National Research Council (NRC), TRB (2009) study addresses compactness and vehicle miles of travel (VMT) created by automobile dependency (NRC, TRB 2009 p.1), though other aspects of compactness are presented also.

Specifically, the NRC TRB (2009) study cites literature that indicates compact development can reduce VMT by 5 to 12 percent and possibly by 25 percent, but only if accompanied by mass transit improvements and proximity to employment (NRC, TRB 2009 p.4). According to the NRC, compactness in turn can also reduce direct and indirect energy use and CO_2 emissions but these reductions are modest at first increasing over time (NRC, TRB 2009 pp.5–6) (cited by Zimmerman 2011, Lecture 1).

Calthorpe Associates (2010), however, critiques the NRC TRB findings, arguing that more detailed modeling shows that land use is of greater importance in reducing VMT and CO_2 emissions. They also argue that (cited by Zimmerman 2011, Lecture 1) VMT reductions reported by NRC TRB are even low based on existing literature, assumptions about the VMT of non-compact development against which their scenarios are compared are too low, and the study underestimates the behavioral and demographic changes that will occur on the part of travelers toward favoring compact growth, biking and walking (Calthorpe Associates 2010, pp.2–3). Cervero and Murakami (2010) found an inverse relationship between urban density and VMT tempered somewhat by road density characteristics but the relationship still held.

Population size, rate of growth and density are seen as a foundation for shaping land use patterns and trends. The Brookings Institution (2010, p.40) review of metropolitan area growth trends finds that the Far West and Southeast have the higher growth rates in the 1990–2009 time period overall, and during that period, a couple of Texas cities emerge in the higher group (cited by Zimmerman 2011, Lecture 2). In that group, Las Vegas leads with the highest growth rate of 84 percent from 1990–2000. The Northeast or Midwest is where cities with slowest or declining rates of growth are located, though New Orleans has the highest declining growth rate in the latter part of the two decade period (Brookings 2010, p.40 and cited in Zimmerman 2011, Lecture 2). The American Association of State Highway and Transportation Officials (AASHTO) (2010) reports similar findings with Far West and Southeast cities leading the growth rate.

Beatley (2000) argues that density produces transportation savings and economic benefits (Beatley 2000, p.31). Transportation by car versus transit is influenced by the density of cities, and a higher transit usage occurs in the denser European cities than in American cities (Beatley 2000, p.30). Beatley further argues that compact cities are supported by spatial forms that promote green spaces, emphasize city center activity and mixed use, infill, reuse of land, pedestrian access, connectivity, and other sustainability strategies.

Burchell et al. (2005, pp.59–60) point to the strong relationship between population density and road mileage density, arguing that one is a surrogate for the other, and use this as a basis for modeling the impact of development scenarios on road expansion, construction and hence cost.

Rapidly growing urban areas

An in-depth look at the US Census Bureau's 2010 results sheds light on what Brookings (2010), AASHTO (2010), Beatley (2000), Burchell et al. (2005) and others have emphasized. A key outcome of the overall trends significant for the transportation, environment and security linkage is that the fastest growing areas are not the most populous areas. Romero-Lankao and Dodman (2011, p.114) identify as one of the key processes of change worldwide for urban areas that the small urban areas are undergoing rapid growth as well as changes in their form with half of the urban population in areas under a half million people.

The US Census Bureau (2011, p.6) identified ten areas as the fastest growing metropolitan statistical areas (MSAs). A number of insights about the relationship between rate of growth and transportation-related characteristics are apparent in these fast-growing areas and some computations using the data are presented below.

- As Romero-Lankao and Dodman (2011) indicate, the fastest growing areas are not the most populous MSAs. In fact, there is no overlap between the Census' fastest growing urban area list and the Census' top ten most populous MSAs, and this MSA pattern is also true of the Census' listing of populous and fast-growing counties and incorporated places (US Census Bureau 2011, p.9; 11).
- These fastest growing MSAs are growing faster than the states in which they are located. The ratio of the rate of change in the MSA compared to the state it is in is always above one.
  - Palm Coast, Florida has 5.2 times the growth rate of Florida, followed by Bend, Oregon which is growing at 3.1 times the rate of Oregon.
  - Half of the top ten fastest growing are growing about twice the rate of the states they are in. These are St. George, Utah; Raleigh–Cary, North Carolina; Cape Coral–Fort Myers, Florida; Greeley, Colorado; and Myrtle Beach, South Carolina.
  - Three areas, Las Vegas–Paradise, Nevada, Provo–Orem, Utah and Austin–Round Rock–San Marcos, Texas are growing between about 1–2 times the states they are in.
- Four of the top ten fastest growing MSAs are in states that rank high in terms of VMT based on US Department of Transportation (DOT) Federal Highway Administration (FHWA) VMT data (2011, Table VM-2 dated January 2012): the two Florida MSAs, Palm Coast and Cape Coral–Fort Myers; the Austin area in Texas, and the Raleigh area in North Carolina. The other MSAs rank low, which may imply a radical change in how they accommodate

vehicular traffic. A closer but still broad estimate of transportation sufficiency is VMT per lane mile based on US DOT, FHWA (2011, Tables HM-20 dated December 2011 and VM-2 dated January 2012) data. According to the FHWA data, the states in the US ranged from 95,000 to over 2 million VMT per lane mile in 2010. Two of the fast growing MSAs are located in states towards the high end of that range – Palm Coast and Cape Coral–Fort Myers, both in Florida. The other MSAs are in states with lower VMT.

INRIX, Inc. (2011) identified roadway bottlenecks within some of these areas. Finally, transit availability is sparse in these fast growing areas. Heavy rail systems tend to be more common in the highly populous cities rather than those that are growing fast. None serve these faster growing MSAs but heavy rail exists in other parts of the states in which they are located, such as in Portland, Oregon, Pompano Beach, Florida, and Dallas–Fort Worth, Texas. This is also the case for light rail, where light rail exists in the state in which a fast growing MSA is located: Portland, Oregon, Dallas and Houston, Texas, Charlotte, North Carolina, and Tampa, Florida, but not in the fast growing MSAs themselves. Commuter rail is not located in the rapidly growing MSAs but in other cities in their states: Dallas–Fort Worth, Texas, Portland, Oregon, and Pompano Beach, Florida. Thus, growth in newer areas tends to be in areas that are auto dependent, which increases the potential for GHG emissions and other environmental effects.

DISCONNECTING

The reach of transportation often follows, as well as shapes, human settlements. It disconnects as well as connects. A few forces of disconnection are described briefly below: equity issues, sprawl, disasters, and the deconstruction of roads.

Equity and Transport Networks

Social injustice arises as a force disconnecting areas within cities, with transportation playing a major role. In its broadest construction, environment encompasses social justice, and in fact the environmental justice movement historically combined those two issues with transportation often at the center. The creation of nodes in a transport system is often driven by some social need. The need for station access in disadvantaged areas has achieved in many places the status of a social movement in and

Table 1.1   Poverty and mode of travel to work, US, 2010

	Total*	Drove alone**	Car-pooled**	Public transportation***
		(%)		
Below 100% of the poverty level	6.9	5.8	10.0	11.2
100–149% of the poverty level	6.7	6.0	9.6	9.4
At or > 150% of the poverty level	86.3	88.3	80.5	79.3

Notes:
*   Based on 135,861,000 workers 16 years and over for whom poverty status was known.
**   In cars, trucks or vans.
***   Excludes taxis.

Source: Compiled from the US Census Bureau, *American Community Survey 2010*, Table B08122.

of itself. The US EPA (2010), for example, used access to light rail transit to combine the need for social equity and environmental compatibility. In 2010, the US EPA awarded St. Paul, Minnesota an achievement award for the partnership it created to build three light rail stations to provide access to communities that depend on transit to connect them to their livelihoods. The US EPA announcement noted that "Construction of the three light rail transit stations will directly benefit the 8,331 people who live within a quarter mile of the stations (81% minority; average median household income for homes near the three stations is $32,000)", and will connect downtown St. Paul with downtown Minneapolis (US EPA 2010).

The 2010 American Community Survey data (US Census Bureau 2010) reveals differences in how workers in various levels of poverty travel to work, as shown in Table 1.1 (for example, based on a one-year estimate, of those who take public transportation to commute to work 11.2 percent were below 100 percent of the poverty level, whereas only half of that, or 5.8 percent, of those who drove alone were in that poverty category).

Nationwide, the American Community Survey (ACS) shows that 4.4 percent of all commuters had no vehicle available, but for those using public transportation, 36.5 percent had no vehicle available (US Census Bureau 2010, Table B08141).

Bullard (2007) links land use to equity in terms of the lack of access to public transit and private vehicles and funding for transportation (Bullard

2007, pp.36–7). He notes the absence of rail transit in Detroit, considered heavily racially segregated (Bullard 2007, p.40).

Wachs (2010) argues persuasively that mobility is key to reducing poverty throughout the world, and the manner in which this connectivity occurs and can promote sustainability differs depending on the nature of each place.

A number of different aspects of social justice pertain to transport. One is environmental justice, which initially arose in the context of protecting people from the environmental effects of waste processing and disposal, and later expanded to transportation. The initial US federal action was Executive Order 12898 and subsequent guidance and plans to implement US EPA policy (US EPA 2011).

Another is access to transport services in outlying areas. Some unique case studies identify the disconnectedness of outlying areas usually housing lower income residents from urban centers, and transportation plays a key part in this (Shannon and Wells 2007). The coverage of transport networks has often been the target of claims regarding equity, where lines may pass through low income areas but have no access points there.

Nine cities were reported by Kneebone (2011; also cited by Tavernise 2011) similar to earlier work (Kneebone and Garr 2010a, 2010b) with more than 50 percent of their poor populations in suburbs in 2010. When the ratio of the share of poor populations living in metropolitan areas is computed from the Kneebone data (2011) for 2010 versus 2000, the results show 33 cities with ratios exceeding 1.0, that is, the percentage of their populations that were poor increased between 2000 and 2010. Table 1.2 shows an illustrative group of 11 whose ratios exceed 1.20. Only two to four of these areas are served by rail systems and those that are account for a relatively low share of nationwide rail trips. The Chicago–Naperville–Joliet is the one exception which has 6 percent of US heavy rail passenger trips and 15.5 percent of US commuter rail system trips (computed from the National Transit Database). This suggests that the suburban poor tend to be disconnected from public transportation in these cases though further research is needed to evaluate specific access.

Sprawl as Disconnecting Core and Region

The spatial demands of sprawl illustrate unconnected development. Though in a sense sprawl developments are connected to urban cores and the infrastructure to support them is inevitably connected to some centralized area, they are unconnected in the sense that they produce discontinuities at least in the way transportation is provided to connect them to urban centers. It is analogous to habitat fragmentation in ecology.

Table 1.2   *Comparisons between changes in shares of poor populations in*
            suburbs from 2000 and 2010 and prevalence of rail transit in
            2009 for selected US cities

Metropolitan area	Ratio of 2010 versus 2000 share of poor populations (>1.20)*	Prevalence of rail transit % share of trips**		
		HR (w NY)	CR	LR
Provo, UT	1.38			
Milwaukee, WI	1.34			
Jacksonville, FL	1.31			
Chicago–Naperville–Joliet IL–IN–WI	1.30	5.8	15.5	
Detroit–Warren, MI	1.29			
Austin–Round Rock, TX	1.26			
Cleveland, OH	1.24	0.1		0.5
Houston, TX	1.23			
Minneapolis–St. Paul, MN–WI	1.22		0.0	2.1
New Orleans, LA	1.21			1.2
Dallas–Fort Worth–Arlington, TX	1.21		0.2–0.3	4.1

Note: HR=heavy rail, CR=commuter rail, and LR=light rail.
These urban areas are those that had a change in the percent share of their population that
was poor in suburbs of greater than 1.20 from 2000 to 2010, computed from Kneebone
(2011) data. Tavernise (2011) using Kneebone work has discussed the movement of the
poor to some suburbs.

Sources:
*   Computed from Kneebone (2011). Data provided courtesy of E. Kneebone.
       Metropolitan areas are arranged in descending order of the ratio of the percentages in
       2000 versus 2010. For earlier work see Kneebone and Garr (2010b).
**   Computations from the US DOT, National Transit database 2009.

Burchell et al. (2005, p.3) refer to this as "leapfrog" developments where
land uses become separated spatially, requiring longer utility lines and
increased automobile dependency (Burchell et al. 2005, p.14). Now the
imperative of climate change and energy resource needs are proposing to
reshape the way transportation is done to achieve greater connectivity.

AASHTO has made a similar point about discontinuities between urban
and rural areas from a different perspective. AASHTO (2010) argues that
the decline in or lack of connectivity between rural and urban areas is
associated with the lack of roadway capacity. Their argument is that while
population and roadway dependent users have increased in relatively
distant areas of the country, reflected in increasing VMT, roadway mileage

has not increased and access to the interstate is limited. Yet another consideration is that the widening of roadways (reflected in lane miles) has occurred to accommodate some increased capacity. Firestine (February 2011) attributes the decline in connectivity of rural areas to intercity public transportation from 2005 to 2010. Similar arguments have been made for inner city and intercity connectivity in terms of rail transportation, and some attention to increasing rural transit is given in the AASHTO report.

The disconnecting effects of sprawl and some of the constraints on transportation systems it produces can lead to serious gaps in the ability of emergency services to respond in disasters. Characteristics of street connectivity in sprawl areas also affect transportation for emergency services. Trowbridge et al. (2009) focus on the response time of emergency medical services (EMS) and in a nationwide study, correlated the occurrence of motor vehicle crashes, vehicle response time to those crashes, and the degree of sprawl defined at the county level. They found significantly higher delayed response times in counties with a high degree of sprawl, which they explain in terms of the relatively low connectivity of streets and longer driving distances in sprawl areas. Not only was response time correlated with degree of sprawl, but they found that the delay in arrival of ambulances in sprawling counties was double that in non-sprawling areas (Trowbridge et al. 2009, p.430). In addition, streets in sprawl areas were originally designed to be narrower with fewer lanes. As development increased, congestion also increased, especially in and around the small town centers that dominate these sprawled areas. Traffic management in such instances is also a factor, but cannot fully compensate for the street patterns of sprawl communities. Finally, they indicate that the availability of emergency vehicles may be lower in more spread out areas.

Natural Hazards, Terrorism, Accidents and Other Disasters

Transport systems are routinely disrupted due to extreme weather, earthquakes or severe accidents and intentional terrorist attacks, which disrupt how people travel and disconnect communities. Communities are often isolated for long periods of time, and in extreme cases relocated where the transportation infrastructure cannot be restored. The experience of Vermont communities following Hurricane Irene is a case in point. Chapters 6 and 7 go into this in some detail.

Road Deconstruction

Road length has been increasing slightly during the century following the introduction of the automobile, while lane mileage has been increasing much faster due to roadway widening. In the US there has been a general movement toward not only introducing non-structural approaches but also eliminating structural approaches for the provision of public transportation services, such as eliminating or deconstructing structures to allow for the return of natural processes and promote new transport modes. The deconstruction of roads, addressed in Chapter 4, represents a disconnecting force in transportation networks, though it does not appear to be widespread. Within the US, roads in urban areas have come down in Seattle, Buffalo, Toronto, New Haven, and Milwaukee (Peirce 2008). In New York City, communities have called for the removal of the Sheridan Expressway due to safety and other concerns.

RECONNECTING

Whether disasters or incomplete transport networks disconnect the way people want to travel, innovative ways of reconnecting seem to find their way into the traveler's portfolio. A revolution has occurred in the ways people travel and are willing and able to travel.

Avoiding Conflicts with Security and Environment While Reconnecting

Sometimes transport modes are consistent with environmental and security needs and other times they are disruptive of those needs, requiring regulatory action to rectify the adverse impacts.

Overland passage where roads and rails do not exist or are not used has generated its own set of vehicles. Here is where the environment and security intersect with transport.

The means of transport that do not involve roads or rail or do not involve them exclusively are either motorized or non-motorized. Non-motorized forms, which are fairly benign relative to motorized transport in non-road areas, include various forms of walking, running and hiking and the use of animals such as horses, camels and alpaca for transport. The attention here is on the motorized forms.

In order to overcome distances where few roads exist or roadway capacity is limited, a number of different forms of motorized transport have arisen for different types of trips. Many of them originated as recreational vehicles but their purposes have expanded. They are distinguished by the fact that they do not use public roads but rather paths, trails or even no defined routes moving freely over land. The names that typically are used are all-terrain vehicles, all purpose vehicles, and off-road vehicles.

The history of one such vehicle – snowmobiles – exemplifies the struggles between transport and the environment as well as issues of equity and social class, and is described in detail in Chapter 5. The snowmobile, invented at about the same time as the automobile, paralleled the history of the automobile in non-road-based environments. To some it connected people with the recreational opportunities of wilderness areas and to others it disconnected people from the natural environment in those areas.

Unusual Connections and Reuse: Pedestrian and Multi-use Paths

Cities have an advantage in designing vertically, given their density. Old elevated transport networks that have fallen into disuse often find new uses. Shevory (2011) identified a number of the initiatives to convert rails into pedestrian routes:

- Paris, France: Promenade Plantée;
- Atlanta: BeltLine;
- Chicago: Bloomingdale Trail;
- New York: The High Line;
- Philadelphia: The Reading Viaduct;
- Seattle: Waterfront Seattle; and
- St. Louis: The Iron Horse Trestle.

Although old rail stations have commonly been reused as public buildings, the conversion of rail networks is not as common and is far more extensive when it occurs.

The High Line in New York City is an example of parkland and walkways which have been combined with new commercial and residential uses on and around an abandoned rail line. With the completion of the second section in 2011, the High Line is 1 mile long and 30 feet above the street, and according to NYC its 29 projects (some completed and some underway) represent an investment of $2 billion (NYC Office of the Mayor 2011). The positive economic impacts of the High Line have been underscored by many (NYC Office of the Mayor 2011), but questioned by others who have businesses beneath the line (Feeney 2011; NYC Office of the Mayor 2011). Planning for a third section began in 2011. Similar initiatives are emerging in other inner city areas (Giles 2010). "Walkway Over the Hudson Historic State Park" uses a former old rail bridge, the Poughkeepsie–Highland Railroad Bridge, which stopped operating in 1974, as a walkway extending 1.28 miles and used by about 600,000 visitors per year (Applebome 2011).

Bridges commonly provide pedestrian walkways, but one unusual example is the suggestion of using an old bridge to be replaced with a new one as a pedestrian walkway – the 3 mile long Tappan Zee Bridge in New York State (Applebome 2011).

Alternative Transport Modes

Non-motorized and motorized transport modes that reduce emissions are environmentally compatible and promote security given their degree of decentralization yet supporting urban density. A few examples provide an introduction to these alternatives, which are revisited in Chapter 4.

Biking

Biking is considered compatible with environmental quality due to the reduced need for energy and its associated emissions, yet the full life cycle and hence environmental costs of biking will need to consider all of its production components. The growth in biking as a means of transport is reconnecting areas within and around cities as well as many other places. Biking overcomes many obstacles of urban transport such as congestion. The growth in bicycle commuting continues to increase in some of the larger US cities. Based on the work of Pucher et al. (2011, p.459; Bruni 2011) rates of commuting in six US cities have increased dramatically between 1990 and 2009, at least doubling and often tripling or more. Pucher et al. (2011, p.459) estimated that in 2009, the rates of commuting using biking for each of the six US cities were: Portland, Oregon 5.8 percent, Minneapolis, Minnesota 3.9 percent, San Francisco, California 3.0 percent, Washington, DC 2.2 percent, Chicago, Illinois 1.2 percent, and New York, NY 0.6 percent.

The percentages probably reflect in part the relative extent of rail and bus transit in these cities. New York, Chicago and Washington, DC, for example, rank lower in the percentage of people commuting by bike yet rank among the highest in rail passenger trips. This growth does not include the many biking trips taken for non-work related purposes. The increasing trend is no doubt supported by bike share facilities and such facilities have in turn probably grown in response to the demand.

Electric vehicles

Electric vehicles have grown in popularity, given that they reduce emissions. Efforts to take into account the full life cycle costing have been underway, in particular, focusing on the origins of the electric power. As cited earlier in this chapter, electric vehicles unexpectedly showed up for disaster recovery following the catastrophic earthquake and tsunami in Japan on March 11, 2011 (Belson 2011). Chapter 4 addresses electric vehicles and other alternative vehicles, focusing on the importance of infrastructure charging stations and their location, access to rare earths for batteries, and the use of a life cycle approach to assessing the environmental effects that are key to their viability.

Adaptable Street Networks

Street networks that have become transformed to accommodate multiple uses – the "complete streets" – are increasing the connectivity between transport and the environment. Chapter 4 explores the many functions streets have assumed and many of their new functions to achieve environment and security goals as well as transport. Streets provide often overlooked environmental management functions of drainage, waste clearance, and sanitation. They are also the front line for security. In supporting transport, streets need to meet existing and new competing demands made by multiple modes of travel that are motorized and non-motorized, operate at different speeds and purposes, and have different storage needs. New innovations are now transforming streets to begin to meet transport and environmental needs, and the next challenge is to meet security requirements.

The adaptability of streets for biking has not only occurred along existing street networks but also along other kinds of conduits. Pucher et al. (2011, p.464) mention three distinct types as bike routes that are on and off streets and are lanes or paths. Thus, biking is partially breaking away from street networks. They argue that more bike networks encourage more biking. For the six US cities they studied, in decreasing order of the percent of the commuting population using biking, the extent (in kilometers) of bike lanes and paths per 100,000 people in 2010 was Portland, Oregon 73, Minneapolis, Minnesota 70, Washington, DC 27, San Francisco, California 15, Chicago, Illinois 9, and New York, NY 8 (Pucher et al. 2011, p.464).

Bringing in the Outliers

Transit systems are unique in their ability to change routes and direction and connect many thousands of people through common transfer points.

In that sense they are highly connected and interconnected networks. On the other hand, transport systems inevitably end somewhere. At the end of the line serious disconnects can occur – some are intentional and others not. Some make connections to new forms of transport or to limited access environmental corridors. Newman (2008) painted a very colorful picture of the last stop about places frozen in time, and identified 24 stops in the NYC system where the rail service terminated. In fact, as he points out, the end points are always listed on the train. Some end in cemeteries, neighborhoods that mark a stopping point, or some physical barrier such as one of NYC's many waterfronts or recreation areas: the parks, stadiums, and play areas. Others exist to serve large concentrations of people such as schools. Shannon and Wells (2007) painted a less poetic picture of the connectivity of outlying areas in New York City. They argue that many of the commutes are longer in the outer parts of the city where neighborhoods are not well-connected to rail transit and bus connections may not always be that reliable. Other forms of transportation, such as vans and automobiles, may provide such connectivity, but at higher cost. End points are analysed in Chapter 2 for heavy rail transit across the US to illustrate how they occur in transit networks.

Connectedness is in part reflected structurally in transit systems in terms of transfer points (Hadas and Ceder 2010). The connectivity of rail systems displays a high degree of variability in terms of travel activity and physical infrastructure. The next chapter begins with an analysis of the structure of transport.

GOING FORWARD

The phenomena of connecting, disconnecting and reconnecting of networks provide a powerful foundation to integrate transport, environment and security. The chapters that follow identify where the vulnerabilities are occurring in transport networks and how these connections can be strengthened.

REFERENCES

Aderinlewo, O. and N. Attoh-Okine (2009), 'Effect of transportation infrastructure network size on its performance during disruptions', *International Journal of Critical Infrastructures*, **5** (3), 285–98.

American Association of State Highway and Transportation Officials (AASHTO) (August 2010), *Transportation Reboot: Connecting Rural and Urban America. Report 3*, available at http://expandingcapacity.transportation.org/connecting_communities/images/Connecting_Communities_0810.pdf (accessed November 21, 2011).

Applebome, P. (October 2011), 'Long-shot alternative to demolition: Tappan Zee as a walkers' haven', *The New York Times*, available at http://www.nytimes.com/2011/10/17/nyregion/future-for-tappan-zee-bridge-styled-after-the-high-line-is-proposed.html?scp=1&sq=Tappan%20Zee%20Bridge&st=cse (accessed November 21, 2011).

ApSimon, H., M. Amann, S. Åström and T. Oxley (2009), 'Synergies in addressing air quality and climate change', *Climate Policy*, **9**, 669–80.

Bai, Y. and S.H. Kim (2007), 'Processes and techniques for rapid bridge replacement after extreme events', *Journal of the Transportation Research Board*, **1991**, 54–61.

Barabasi, A.-L. (2002), *Linked: The New Science of Networks*, Cambridge, MA, USA: Perseus Publishing.

Beatley, T. (2000), 'Land use and urban form: planning compact cities', in *Green Urbanism*, Washington, DC, USA: Island Press, pp.29–75.

Belson, K. (May 2011), 'After disaster hit Japan, electric cars stepped up', *The New York Times*, available at http://www.nytimes.com/2011/05/08/automobiles/08JAPAN.html?hpw (accessed November 21, 2011).

Bohannon, J. (July 2009), 'Counterterrorism's new tool: "Metanetwork" analysis', *Science*, **325**, 409–11.

Bollen, J.C., C.J. Brink, H.C. Eerens and A.J.G. Manders (2009), 'Co-benefits of climate policy', Bilthoven, The Netherlands: Netherlands Environmental Assessment Agency, available at http://www.rivm.nl/bibliotheek/rapporten/500116005.pdf (accessed November 21, 2011).

The Brookings Institution (2010), *The State of Metropolitan America*, Washington, DC, USA: The Brookings Institution.

Brown, L.R. (February 2001), *Paving the Planet: Cars and Crops Competing for Land*, Washington, DC, USA: Earth Policy Institute, available at http://www.earth-policy.org/Alerts/Alert12.htm (accessed November 21, 2011).

Bruni, F. (September 2011), 'Bicycle visionary', *The New York Times*, available at http://www.nytimes.com/2011/09/11/opinion/sunday/bruni-janette-sadik-khan-bicycle-visionary.html?scp=1&sq=Biking%20September%2011%202011&st=cse (accessed November 21, 2011).

Budzik, P. (c2000), 'US natural gas markets: relationship between Henry Hub spot prices and US wellhead prices', Washington, DC: US EIA, available at http://www.eia.gov/oiaf/analysispaper/henryhub/pdf/henryhub.pdf.

Bullard, R.D. (ed.) (2007), *Growing Smarter*, Cambridge, MA, USA: MIT Press.

Bunkley, N. (December 21, 2011), 'Tsunami Reveals Durability of Nissan's Leaf', *The New York Times*, available at http://www.nytimes.com/2011/12/22/business/tsunami-reveals-durability-of-nissans-leaf.html?scp=1&sq=Nisson%20Leaf&st=cse.

Burchell, R.W., A. Downs, B. McCann and S. Mukherji (2005), *Sprawl Costs. Economic Impacts of Unchecked Development*, Washington, DC, USA: Island Press.

Calthorpe Associates (August 2010), 'The role of land use in reducing VMT and GHG Emissions: critique of TRB special report 298', available at http://www.calthorpe.com/files/TRB-NAS%20Report%20298%20Critique_0.pdf (accessed November 21, 2011).

Cambridge Systematics, Inc. (2005), *Cool Pavement Report*, Cambridge, MA, USA: Cambridge Systematics.

Ceder, A. and C.S. Teh (2010), 'Comparing public transport connectivity measures of major New Zealand cities', *Journal of the Transportation Research Record*, **2143**, 24–33.

Cervero, R. and J. Murakami (2010), 'Effects of built environments on vehicle miles traveled: evidence from 370 US urbanized areas', *Environment and Planning A*, **42**, 400–418.

CH2MHill (April 2009), *Solar America Cities, Integration of Solar Energy in Emergency Planning*, Final Report, Prepared for New York City Office of Emergency Management, available at http://www.nycedc.com/News Publications/Studies/Documents/SolarNYCReport.pdf (accessed November 21, 2011).

Cho, S., P. Gordon, J.E. Moore, H.W. Richardson, M. Shinozuka and S. Chang (February 2001), 'Integrating transportation network and regional economic models to estimate the costs of a large urban earthquake', *Journal of Regional Science*, **41** (1), 39–65.

Coker, M. (August 2010), 'U.A.E. says terrorist in motorboat attacked oil tanker', *The Wall Street Journal*, available at http://online.wsj.com/article/SB10 00142405274870398830457541264059271941 2.html?mod=WSJ_hps_MIDDLE FifthNews (accessed November 21, 2011).

Detwyler, T.R. (1971), 'Environmental effects of highways', in *Man's Impact on Environment*, New York, NY, USA: McGraw-Hill.

Deutsch, K.W. (1966), *The Nerves of Government: Models of Political Communication and Control*, New York, NY, USA: The Free Press.

DisasterCenter.com, 'The Disaster Center's tropical storm – Hurricane Rita's page', available at http://www.disastercenter.com/Tropical%20Storm%20-%20 Hurricane%20-%20Rita.html (accessed October 7, 2011).

Elbakidze, L. and B.A. McCarl (2004), 'Should we consider the co-benefits of agricultural GHG offsets', *Choices*, **19** (3), 25–6.

Elbakidze, L. and B.A. McCarl (2007), 'Sequestration offsets versus direct emission reductions: consideration of environmental co-effects', *Ecological Economics*, **60**, 564–71.

Evink, G.L. (2002), *Interaction Between Roadways and Wildlife Ecology: A Synthesis of Highway Practice*, National Cooperative Highway Program Synthesis 305, Washington, DC, USA: Transportation Research Board of the National Research Council, available at http://onlinepubs.trb.org/onlinepubs/ nchrp/nchrp_syn_305.pdf (accessed November 21, 2011).

Ewing, R. and R. Cervero (2010), 'Travel and the built environment: A meta-analysis', *Journal of the American Planning Association*, **76** (3), 265–94.

Feeney, S.A. (September 2011), 'Hard times near the High Line', *amNY*, available at http://www.amny.com/urbanite-1.812039/hard-times-under-the-high-line-for-small-businesses-1.3208587 (accessed September 29, 2011).

Firestine, T. (February 2011), 'The U.S. Rural Population and Scheduled Intercity Transportation in 2010: A Five-Year Decline in Transportation Access', Washington, DC, USA: US Department of Transportation, Research and Innovation Technology Administration, Bureau of Transportation Statistics.

Forman, R.T.T. (2000), 'Estimate of the area affected ecologically by the road system in the United States', *Conservation Biology*, **14** (1), 31–5.

Giles, D. (July 2010), 'A high-line for Harlem', New York, NY, USA: Center for an Urban Future, available at http://www.nycfuture.org/images_pdfs/pdfs/ HighLineforHarlem.pdf (accessed November 21, 2011).

Gorman, S.P. (2005), *Networks, Security and Complexity: The Role of Public Policy in Critical Infrastructure Protection*, Cheltenham, UK and Northampton, MA, USA: Edward Elgar.

Grubesic, T.H. and A.T. Murray (2006), 'Vital nodes, interconnected infrastructures, and the geographies of network survivability', *Annals of the Association of American Geographers*, **96** (1), 64–83.

Hadas, Y. and A. Ceder (2010), 'Public transit network connectivity spatial-based performance indicators', *Transportation Research Record: Journal of the Transportation Research Board*, Transportation Research Board of the National Academies, Washington, DC, USA, **2143**, 1–8.

Hamdan, S. (January 2012), 'Pipeline Avoids Strait of Hormuz', *The New York Times*, available at http://www.nytimes.com/2012/01/12/world/middleeast/pipeline-avoids-strait-of-hormuz.html?pagewanted=all.

Holland, M.R. (2008), *The Co-benefits to Health of a Strong EU Climate Change Policy*, Ecometrics Research and Consulting, The Health and Environment Alliance (HEAL), Climate Action Network (CAN) and WWF Europe, available at http://www.env-health.org/IMG/pdf/10-_The_co-benefits_to_health_of_a_strong_EU_climate_change_policy.pdf (accessed November 21, 2011).

Holme, P., B.J. Kim, C.N. Yoon and S.K. Han (2002), 'Attack vulnerability of complex networks', *Physical Review E*, **65**, 056109.

Huizenga, C. and M. Ajero (2005), *Co-benefits Approach to Urban Air Quality Management and GHG Reduction in Asian Cities*, the 15th Asia-Pacific Seminar on Climate Change, September 11–15, Yokohama, Japan, Clean Air Initiative for Asian Cities.

Inrix, Inc. (March 2011), *INRIX National Traffic Scorecard 2010 Annual Report*, available at http://scorecard.inrix.com/scorecard/ (accessed November 21, 2011).

Kansky, K.J. (1963), *Structure of Transportation Networks: Relationships between Network Geometry and Regional Characteristics*, Chicago, IL, USA: University of Chicago Press.

Kneebone, E. (2011), Brookings Institution analysis of decennial census and American Community Survey data, '2010 SuburbanPoverty 9-26-11; suburban tip'. Data provided courtesy of E. Kneebone.

Kneebone, E. and E. Garr (January 2010a), *The Suburbanization of Poverty: Trends in Metropolitan America, 2000 to 2008*, Washington, DC, USA: The Brookings Institution.

Kneebone, E. and E. Garr (January 2010b), 'Metropolitan area profiles', available at http://www.brookings.edu/~/media/Files/rc/papers/2010/0120_poverty_knee bone/0120_poverty_profiles.pdf (accessed November 21, 2011).

Krebs, V.E. (2001), 'Mapping networks of terrorist cells', *Connections*, **24** (3), 43–52.

Levinson, D.M. and K.J. Krizek (2008), *Planning for Place and Plexus. Metropolitan Land Use and Transport*, New York, NY, USA and London, UK: Routledge.

Litman, T. (March 2011), 'Why and how to reduce the amount of land paved for roads and parking facilities', *Environmental Practice*, **13**, 38–46.

Lynch, K. (1960), *The Image of the City*, Cambridge, MA, USA: MIT Press.

Motter, A.E. and Y-C. Lai (2002), 'Cascade-based attacks on complex networks', *Physical Review E*, **66**, 65–8.

Murray-Tuite, P.M. (2008), 'Transportation network risk profile for an origin–destination pair: security measures, terrorism, and target and attack method substitution', *Journal of the Transportation Research Board*, **2041**, 19–28.

Murray-Tuite, P.M. and X. Fei (2010), 'A methodology for assessing transportation network terrorism risk with attacker and defender interactions', *Computer-Aided Civil and Infrastructure Engineering*, **25**, 396–410.

Nagurney, A. and Q. Qiang (2009), *Fragile Networks. Identifying Vulnerabilities and Synergies in an Uncertain World*, Hoboken, NJ, USA: Wiley.

National Research Council, Transportation Research Board (August 2009), *TRB Special Report 298 Driving and the Built Environment*, Washington, DC, USA: National Academy Press, available at http://onlinepubs.trb.org/Onlinepubs/sr/sr298.pdf (accessed November 21, 2011).

New York City Office of the Mayor (June 2011), 'Press release PR-194-11 Mayor Bloomberg, Speaker Quinn and Friends of the High Line open section two of the High Line', New York City, Office of the Mayor, available at http://www.nyc.gov/portal/site/nycgov/menuitem.c0935b9a57bb4ef3daf2f1c701c789a0/index.jsp?pageID=mayor_press_release&catID=1194&doc_name=http%3A%2F%2Fwww.nyc.gov%2Fhtml%2Fom%2Fhtml%2F2011a%2Fpr194-11.html&cc=unused1978&rc=1194&ndi=1 (accessed November 21, 2011).

Newman, A. (August 2008), 'The curious world of the last stop', *The New York Times*, available at http://www.nytimes.com/2008/08/24/nyregion/24laststop.html?_r=1&scp=3&sq=Going%20to%20the%20End%20of%20the%20Line&st=cse (accessed November 21, 2011).

Newman, M.E.J. (2010), *Networks: An Introduction*, New York, NY, USA: Oxford University Press.

Parfomak, P.W. (2008), Congressional Research Service (CRS), U.S. Congress Report RL33206, *Vulnerability of Concentrated Critical Infrastructure: Background and Policy Options*, available at http://www.fas.org/sgp/crs/homesec/RL33206.pdf (accessed November 21, 2011).

Pattanayak, S.K., B.A. McCarl, A.J. Sommer, B.C. Murray, T. Bondelid, D. Gillig and B. de Angelo (2005), 'Water quality co-effects of greenhouse gas mitigation in US agriculture', *Climatic Change*, **71**, 341–72.

Peirce, N. (August 2008), 'City curbs on cars: now accelerating', available at http://citiwire.net/post/144/ (accessed November 21, 2011).

Perrow, C. (2007), *The Next Catastrophe*, Princeton, NJ, USA: Princeton University Press.

Pucher, J., R. Buehler and M. Seinen (2011), 'Bicycling renaissance in North America? An update and re-appraisal of cycling trends and policies', *Transportation Research Part A*, **45**, 451–75.

Reuters (September 2008), 'Henry Hub shut, NYMEX declares force majeure', available at http://www.reuters.com/article/2008/09/13/us-storm-ike-nymex-forcemajeure-idUSN1339082820080913 (accessed November 21, 2011).

Rinaldi, S.M., J.P. Peerenboom and T.K. Kelly (December 2001), 'Identifying, understanding and analyzing critical infrastructure interdependencies', *IEEE Control Systems Magazine*, 11–25.

Rodrigue, J-P., C. Comtois and B. Slack (2006), *The Geography of Transport Systems*, London, UK and New York, NY, USA: Routledge.

Rodrigue, J-P., C. Comtois and B. Slack (2009), 'Land area consumed by the car in selected countries, 1999', in *The Geography of Transport Systems*, 2nd edition, London, UK and New York, NY, USA: Routledge, available at http://people.hofstra.edu/geotrans/eng/ch6en/conc6en/carlandarea.html (accessed November 3, 2011).

Romero-Lankao, P. and D. Dodman (2011), 'Cities in transition: transforming urban centers from hotbeds of GHG emissions and vulnerability to seedbeds of sustainability and resilience', *Current Opinion in Environmental Sustainability*, **3**, 113–20.

Sanger, D.E. and A. Lowrey (December 2011), 'Iran threatens to block oil shipments, as U.S. prepares sanctions', *The New York Times*, available at http://www.nytimes.com/2011/12/28/world/middleeast/iran-threatens-to-block-oil-route-if-embargo-is-imposed.html?_r=1&hp.

Savitch, H.V. (2008), *Cities in a Time of Terror – Space, Territory, and Local Resilience*, Armonk, NY, USA and London, UK: M.E. Sharpe.

Sen, P., S. Dasgupta, A. Chatterjee, P.A. Sreeram, G. Mukherjee and S.S. Manna (2003), 'Small-world properties of the Indian railway network', *Physical Review E*, **67**, 036106.

Shannon, E. and J. Wells (October 2007), *A Long Day's Journey into Work. An Analysis of Public Transportation Options into Manhattan from Selected Neighborhoods*, New York, NY, USA: Permanent Citizens Advisory Committee to the MTA, available at http://www.pcac.org/wp-content/reports/2007_Long_Commutes.pdf (accessed November 21, 2011).

Shevory, K. (August 2011), 'Cities see the other side of the tracks', *The New York Times*, available at http://www.nytimes.com/2011/08/03/realestate/commercial/cities-see-another-side-to-old-tracks.html?hp (accessed November 21, 2011).

Simon, H.A. (1966), *The Science of the Artificial*, Cambridge, MA, USA: MIT Press.

Simonoff, J.S., C.E. Restrepo, R. Zimmerman, Z.S. Naphtali and H.H. Willis (2011), 'Resource allocation, emergency response capability and infrastructure concentration around vulnerable sites', *Journal of Risk Research*, **14** (5), 597–613.

Stefanini, A. and M. Masera (2008), 'The security of power systems and the role of information and communication technologies: lessons from the recent blackouts', *International Journal of Critical Infrastructure Systems*, **4** (1–2), 32.

Tavernise, S. (October 2011), 'Outside Cleveland, snapshots of poverty's surge in the suburbs', *The New York Times*, available at http://www.nytimes.com/2011/10/25/us/suburban-poverty-surge-challenges-communities.html?_r=1&scp=2&sq=suburbs&st=cse (accessed November 21, 2011).

Taylor, M.A.P. and G.M. D'Este (2007), 'Transport network vulnerability: a method for diagnosis of critical locations in transport', in A.T. Murray and T.H. Grubesic (eds), *Critical Infrastructure Systems: Reliability and Vulnerability*, Berlin and Heidelberg, Germany: Springer, pp.10–30.

Trowbridge, M.J., M.J. Gurka and R.E. O'Connor (2009), 'Urban sprawl and delayed ambulance arrival in the U.S.', *American Journal of Preventive Medicine*, **37** (5), 428–32.

Urbina, E. and B. Wolshon (2003), 'National review of hurricane evacuation plans and policies: a comparison and contrast of state practices', *Transportation Research Part A*, **37**, 257–75.

US Census Bureau (2010), *American Community Survey 2010*, available at http://www.census.gov/acs/www/ (accessed November 21, 2011).

US Census Bureau (March 2011), *Population Distribution and Change: 2000 to 2010*, Washington, DC, US Department of Commerce, Economics and Statistics Administration, US Census Bureau, available at http://www.census.gov/prod/cen2010/briefs/c2010br-01.pdf (accessed November 21, 2011).

US Department of Transportation, Federal Highway Administration (FHWA) (October 2010), *Highway Statistics 2009 Road System Measures for Selected*

Countries (Metrics), Table IN-3 available at http://www.fhwa.dot.gov/policy information/statistics/2009/in3.cfm (accessed November 21, 2011).

US Department of Transportation, Federal Highway Administration (2011), *Highway Statistics 2010*, available at http://www.fhwa.dot.gov/policyinformation/statistics/2010/ (accessed March 13, 2012).

US Environmental Protection Agency (EPA) (June 2009), *Integrated Environmental Strategies*, available at www.epa.gov/ies/ (accessed November 21, 2011).

US Environmental Protection Agency (December 2010), *2010 National Achievements in Environmental Justice Awards*, available at http://www.epa.gov/environmentaljustice/awards/index.html; http://www.epa.gov/environmental justice/resources/publications/awards/2010/trans-equity.pdf (accessed November 21, 2011).

US Environmental Protection Agency, Office of Environmental Justice (September 2011), *Plan EJ 2014*, available at http://www.epa.gov/compliance/ej/resources/policy/plan-ej-2014/plan-ej-2011-09.pdf (accessed November 21, 2011).

Wachs, M. (2010), 'Transportation policy, poverty, and sustainability: history and future', *Transportation Research Record: Journal of the Transportation Research Board*, **2163**, 5–12.

Wasserman, D. and K. Faust (2009), *Social Network Analysis: Methods and Applications*, New York, NY, USA: Cambridge University Press.

Zimmerman, R. (2006), 'Critical infrastructure and interdependency', in D.G. Kamien (ed.), *The McGraw-Hill Homeland Security Handbook*, New York, NY, USA: McGraw-Hill, p.523.

Zimmerman, R. (2011), Lecture presentations for the course 'Adapting the Physical City', New York University, Wagner Graduate School of Public Service.

Zimmerman, R. and C.E. Restrepo (2006), 'The next step: quantifying infrastructure interdependencies to improve security', *International Journal of Critical Infrastructures*, **2** (2/3), 215–30.

Zoli, T. and J. Englot (2008), 'Floating bridge concepts for emergency preparedness and temporary traffic routing', in J.G. Khinda (ed.), *Proceedings of New York City Infrastructure's Critical Needs*, ASCE Metropolitan Chapter, pp.25–6.

2. Rail and road networks

INTRODUCTION

Transportation activity includes two familiar networks: roads and rail. Public services for transport are supported by a vast infrastructure of nodes, links and transport activity. There are many miles of distribution lines, access points, and users. The extent of transport networks in the US can be summarized as follows (US DOT, RITA 2011, Table 1-1; US DOT, FHWA 2011a, Table HM-20; US DOT, FTA, National Transit Database (NTD) for 2009):

- Roadways:
  - Highways: 4,050,717 miles (4,067,077 for 2010 (US DOT, FHWA 2012))
- Rail:
  - Class I rail (owned): 93,921 miles
  - Amtrak (operated): 21,178 miles
- Transit (data for 2009 from NTD are in parenthesis along with the size of the NTD combined service areas of all US systems within each rail category):
  - Commuter Rail 7,561 (7,740) miles with service areas of 43,563 square miles
  - Heavy Rail 1,623 (2,272) miles with service areas of 10,892 square miles
  - Light Rail 1,477 (1,632) miles with service areas of 31,178 square miles.

The National Research Council (NRC) (2002, p.212) underscores the extensiveness of rail networks, indicating there are more than 300,000 miles of freight rail lines in addition to the passenger lines given above.

These systems have evolved over more than a century. Although they are distinctly different systems, road and rail networks often follow the same routes, are usually in close proximity to one another, and have formal interconnections between them. Where they do follow one another, rail corridors may be found along median highway divides, along the side of roadways, or intersecting them. In heavily urbanized areas underground rail often follows street systems below ground. In some places, such as New York City, the streets actually form the top of subway tunnels. The interconnectedness of these networks inevitably increases the complexity of incorporating the multiple goals of environment and security into transport activities.

Roadways dominate the volume of passenger traffic, yet rail transit systems provide critical links within and among cities that are environmentally compatible. Rail transit serves a large portion of the US population, particularly people residing in urban areas as well as the workers who commute to and within those areas and the tourists who visit them.

The growth in the usage of the nation's roads and rail systems has occurred in spite of what has been estimated as a serious deterioration in condition. The American Society for Civil Engineers (ASCE) produced its latest infrastructure condition ratings in 2005 and 2009. The overall rating for over 15 different major categories of infrastructure was D in both years. Rail stayed at C− for both years, and roads went from D in 2005 to D− in 2009 (ASCE 2005, 2009). According to the US DOT (2010, pp. ES-4 and ES-5), levels of and changes in condition ratings for road and rail facilities vary by type of roadway and type of transit facility, respectively.

After a relatively brief coverage of roadway connectivity, this chapter is devoted primarily to public transportation via rail given the nature of its connectivity to urban populations. The year 2009 is primarily used for both road and rail data as well as earlier years to establish trends.

TRANSPORTATION CONNECTIVITY: ROADWAYS

Extent of Roadway Connectivity in the United States

Roadways are one component of the network of travel that is fundamental to how travel intersects with the environment and security. The length and width of roadways reflect both capacity and reach and data are provided on an annual basis by the US Department of Transportation Federal Highway Administration (US DOT FHWA). When roadway extent is combined with many other characteristics of roads and their usage patterns, broader questions of overall access, equity, environmental quality, and security can be addressed. Road characteristics include the distribution of roads relative to population and work centers, the distribution relative to population sectors for example by income and race, the use of support services such as energy and environmental resources, and other aspects of performance, including the quality of the travel experience, such as the extent of congestion.

The many purposes that roads serve complicate the network structure. For example, roadways were always key to national security reflected by the designation of the Strategic Highway Network (STRAHNET) for defense purposes, connecting military establishments to highways (US DOT, FHWA 2011b; US DOT, FHWA 2010). That function was underscored after the September 11, 2001 attacks on the World Trade Center in NYC (US DOT, FHWA 2002). A National Academy of Sciences committee included transportation systems and their major characteristics as components of the key critical infrastructures (National Research Council 2002) and transportation systems including roads are a major sector in the US Department of Homeland Security (DHS) sector-specific reports.

The National Highway System (NHS) encompasses roadways of many different types, and is defined by FHWA: "It is approximately 160,000 miles (256,000 kilometers) of roadway that is important to the nation's economy, defense, and mobility. The National Highway System (NHS) includes the following subsystems of roadways: Interstate, . . . Other Principal Arterials, . . . STRAHNET, . . . Major Strategic Highway Network Connectors, . . . and intermodal connectors" (US DOT, FHWA 2011b).

The extent of US roadways has not increased dramatically when measured in terms of linear miles or "statute miles" (US DOT, RITA 2011, Table 1-1). Between 1998 and 2009 linear mileage increased by 3.7 percent, or 144,427 miles. Between 1960 and 2009, mileage increased by 14.2 percent (without correcting for the withdrawal of about 43,000 miles of US Bureau of Land Management (BLM) roads that occurred from 1998 onwards).

Lane miles are commonly used to reflect roadway expansions, and are computed by "multiplying the centerline length by the number of through lanes" (US DOT, RITA, BTS 2011, Appendix E, p.465). Lane miles are available annually from 1980. From 1980 to 2009 while linear miles increased by 5.0 percent (computed from US DOT, FHWA 2011a, Table HM-220), lane miles increased by 8.3 percent (computed from US DOT, FHWA 2011a, Table HM-260). Between 1998 and 2009 linear miles increased by 3.7 percent (US DOT, FHWA 2011a, Table HM-220), while lane miles increased by 5.1 percent (computed from US DOT, FHWA 2011a, Table HM-260). Thus, the increase in lane mileage between 1980 and 2009 was 1.7 times the rate for linear miles, reflecting increased capacity through the widening of roadways rather than increasing in length.

Between 1998 and 2009, the percent change in lane miles was higher again, 1.4 times the rate for linear mileage, but the difference was decreasing. On an annual basis, the rate of change of the ratio (percent change of lane miles and linear miles) was lower in the later 1998–2009 time period than in the earlier 1980–2009 period.

Included in the total US roadway mileage of 4,050,717 miles in 2009 is the interstate system, which is a small share of the total roadway miles in the US (1.2 percent) (US DOT, FHWA 2011a, Table HM-220), but these roads accounted for about 25 percent of the total vehicle miles of travel (VMT) (US DOT, FHWA 2011a, Table VM-202).

What is not as apparent is the dominance of non-interstate system roads in the total road mileage picture. According to US DOT, FHWA data, individually these roads constitute small amounts of road mileage but in the aggregate they can far exceed the mileage of the roadways included in the National Highway System. A wide variety of these smaller roads exist. They are the access roads to new developments and circulation roads within them built as extensions of major arteries. They are also small side streets in dense urban areas.

Urban areas contain about a quarter of the total roadway mileage in the US – 1,081,371 miles in 2009 compared with about 4,050,717 in total for 2009 (US DOT, FHWA 2011a, Table HM-220). Yet, as in the case of the interstates, urban areas account for far more of the VMT (about two-thirds of total VMT) than their share of roadway mileage (computed from US DOT, FHWA 2011a, Table VM-202).

As shown in Table 2.1, *within urbanized areas* only, by 2009, local roads constituted the majority of roadway mileage (70.8 percent) (US DOT, FHWA 2011a, Table HM-260). But the disparity between mileage and VMT was apparent again, with local roads accounting for only 14 percent of the VMT in urbanized areas; however, other non-interstate roadways constituted a significant share of the VMT (US DOT, FHWA 2011a, Table VM-202).

State agencies play a smaller role in the ownership of local roads relative to other kinds of roads, with local roads accounting for about 20 percent of state-owned roads in 2009 (US DOT, FHWA 2011a, Table HM-80). This percentage is about the same for both rural and urban roads separately. In 2009, rural local roads owned by state highway agencies constituted 130,368 out of a total of 631,245 miles of rural roads (20.1 percent), and urban local roads owned by state highway agencies constituted about the same percentage – 28,288 out of 148,535 miles of urban state-owned roads (19.1 percent) (US DOT, FHWA 2011a, Table HM-80).

Table 2.1 Public road mileage and vehicle miles of travel (VMT) by
roadway type for urban areas, US, 2009

	Urban areas only			
	Road mileage* (2009)		VMT** in millions (2009)	
	Number	Percent	Number	Percent
Total	1,081,371	100.0	1,973,274	100.0
Interstate	16,578	1.5	474,963	24.1
Other freeways and expressways	11,399	1.1	220,434	11.2
Other principal arterials	64,524	6.0	455,918	23.1
Minor arterials	108,958	10.1	375,719	19.0
Collector (major and minor)	114,687	10.6	179,176	9.1
Local	765,224	70.8	267,064	13.5

Sources:
* US DOT, FHWA (2011a), 'Highway Statistics 2009', Table HM-220: Public Road and Street Length, 1980–2009, Miles by Functional System, available at http://www.fhwa.dot.gov/policyinformation/statistics/2009/; http://www.fhwa.dot.gov/policyinformation/statistics/2009/hm220.cfm.
** US DOT, FHWA (2011a), 'Highway Statistics 2009', Table VM-202: Annual Vehicle Miles of Travel, 1980–2009 by Functional System, National Summary, available at http://www.fhwa.dot.gov/policyinformation/statistics/2009/vm202.cfm.

Roadway Concentration

One key indicator of the concentration of roadways is congestion. INRIX, Inc. (2011) provides this data annually for major metropolitan areas and selected intersections within them. The Texas Transportation Institute's annual mobility report provides relationships between congestion, delay time, cost and other factors.

As one might expect, the INRIX report (INRIX, Inc. 2011) and the Texas Transportation Institute report (Schrank et al. 2011) show that the most congested metropolitan areas and intersections are in areas where population is generally highest.

What is interesting about the set of urban regions that rank in the top ten regions for congestion in 2010 (INRIX, Inc. 2011, p.ES-5) is that only half of them are also on the list of top 25 as having the most congested corridors (INRIX, Inc. 2011, p.ES-7). The areas where regional and corridor congestion overlap are Los Angeles, New York, Chicago, Washington and Boston. The other five are not on the top 25 congested corridors list.

Table 2.2   *Metropolitan Statistical Areas (MSAs) with high roadway*
               congestion and transit use (annual trips) compared, selected
               cities, US

City (only major city is listed, but data pertains to MSA)*	HR % share**	CR % share**	LR % share**
Boston	4.3	8.7	15.2
Dallas	–	–	4.1
Chicago	5.8	15.5	–
Houston	–	–	2.5
Los Angeles	1.3	2.6	9.9
New York***	67.6	56.1	4.8
Philadelphia	2.7	7.7	6.4
San Francisco	–	–	10.9
Seattle	–	0.5	0.1
Washington	8.5	–	–

Note: Dashes (–) indicate the absence of a particular system in a given urban area.
Abbreviations: HR = Heavy rail; CR = Commuter rail; LR = Light rail.
Cities listed are those indicated as being the top ten congested cities by INRIX, Inc.

Sources:
*   Cities listed as being in the top ten with respect to congestion in 2010 by INRIX, Inc.
        (March 2011), *INRIX National Traffic Scorecard 2010 Annual Report*, available at
        http://scorecard.inrix.com/scorecard/, p. ES-5.
**   Percentages computed for annual passenger trips from the US Department of
        Transportation (2009), National Transit Database (NTD) (Zimmerman 2011). They
        represent the percentage the transit systems in each of the cities are of the total in
        2009.
***   For light rail, New York represents Newark. For commuter rail, New York
        represents NYC (MTA) Jamaica, NY (LIRR), and Newark (NJ Transit). For heavy
        rail, New York represents NYC (NYCT); with regional HR the percent would be 70
        percent.

Similarly, four areas that are in the top 25 congested corridors list do not
make the top ten congested regions list. These four are Austin, Baton
Rouge, Portland, and Pittsburgh. This suggests that the patterns of congestion differ between corridor-specific and urban region-specific areas.

What is also interesting, however, is the prevalence of transit use in
these very congested cities. The top ranking metropolitan areas by congestion according to INRIX, Inc. (2011, p.ES-5) are listed in Table 2.2.
Next, for comparison, the percentage share of heavy rail, commuter rail
and light rail trips each city has of the US total is added, computed from
the National Transit database (Zimmerman 2011; US DOT, FTA 2010)
analysed in a lot of detail in the following sections.

Glancing across the table it is apparent that very congested areas may also have a large number of trips taken by transit. This is clear for New York City. For the other cities, even though the share of transit may be small relative to other areas, there are still substantial numbers of transit trips for one type of rail system or another for all of the other cities in the top ten list for road congestion. This implies that transit may be relieving some roadway congestion but not all.

System Use Trends

Measures of system usage show an increase in the use of transportation systems worldwide and the consumption of resources to maintain them for many modes. Usage patterns are in large part shaped by development patterns, some of which increase transportation while others decrease overall transportation or otherwise alter the way in which transportation occurs.

Road-based transportation activity is traditionally measured in terms of number of vehicles (registrations) and passenger volume or VMT. VMT, a key indicator of road-based travel activity, continue to rise steadily in general for both passenger travel (US DOT, FHWA 2011a, Table VM-2) and freight movement (US DOT, FHWA 2011c, Figure 3-1).

Vehicular use in the US varies considerably from place to place. According to the US DOE Energy Information Administration (EIA) (2011) at the level of states, the higher the population density in a state the lower the VMT are. Using VMT per licensed driver, the US DOE EIA finds that VMT per driver are lower where alternative modes of travel exist, such as transit, whereas the less dense areas with more rural and suburban living have higher VMT per driver.

In contrast to trends in roadway mileage, VMT have been increasing almost steadily (US DOT, FHWA 2011a). The contrast between the rates of change of VMT and roadway mileage is often used to support the claim that more investment in highways is needed to reduce congestion; however, other theories maintain that increasing roads will attract more traffic. According to US DOT, FHWA (2011b) data, between 1980 and 2009, VMT increased overall by 93 percent though the trend flattened and became uneven between 2007 and 2009. A slight initial drop in VMT occurred at around 2007–2009 but quickly rebounded according to Young (2010). During the period of slight decline, some experts readily attributed the decline to oil prices and other fuel supply factors (Puentes and Tomer 2008) and the economy in general. According to US DOT FHWA data, this growth was not evenly distributed. Between 1980–2009 VMT in rural areas increased 46 percent while in urban areas the increase was dramatically higher at 131 percent. This was also reflected in the rural/urban share of VMT. In 1980 the urban share of VMT was 56 percent and by 2009 it was 67 percent. Variations similarly arise among state and metropolitan areas and these patterns and trends have been well-studied. This happened while road mileage did not increase very much and lane mileage did not increase as fast as VMT.

The upward trend in VMT is expected to continue. The US DOE, EIA (2010, p.32) estimates that between 2008 and 2035 the transportation sector will grow 1.7 percent per year in terms of VMT for both light duty vehicles and freight trucks. Their figures indicate that the growth rate in VMT is more than double the estimated growth in rail-ton miles of 0.8 percent per year over that same time period. The US DOE, EIA notes that the transportation growth rate exceeds the growth rate for population, households, commercial floor space, the real value of non-manufacturing shipments, and growth in energy-intensive manufacturing, but is below the growth of real Gross Domestic Product (GDP). The US DOE, EIA explains this as follows (2010 p.32): "Because the growth rate for real GDP is higher than any of the other growth rates, energy consumption in each sector would be expected to grow more slowly than real GDP, and energy intensity would be expected to decline, even in the absence of efficiency gains." The US DOE, EIA (2010 p.32, Table 4) suggests a number of factors positively associated with VMT such as real GDP, population, and the presence of economic activity.

Within states, the distribution of VMT, in urban and non-urban areas, and its changes over time show important differences geographically. As indicated above, VMT in urban areas are about two-thirds (66.8 percent) of the US total VMT (calculated from US DOT, FHWA 2011, Table VM-202), whereas urban areas account for only about a quarter (26.7 percent) of total road mileage (calculated from US DOT, FHWA 2011a, Table HM-220) and 28.2 percent of total lane miles (calculated from US DOT, FHWA 2011a, Table HM-260). This is a potential explanation for the greater congestion in urban areas; however, other factors contribute to congestion in more rural areas.

Filling in Uses for Road Networks

Of particular interest is the increasing use of "infill" transport, that is, means of transport that are relatively more dispersed than rail transit and automobile or other light duty vehicle transportation that uses roadways. These tend to connect to rail transit and vehicular travel and often parallel it as well. Two types of modes in particular provide important infill functions – bus transit and vehicles tailored to individual needs, and though these are beyond the scope of this book, how they provide these functions is important to note briefly.

Bus transit not only parallels rail transit networks, but also provides more frequent stops or stations than rail transit along the same routes, extends beyond rail transit areas providing service where rail service does not exist, and provides connectivity to rail transit points (Niles and Callaghan 2010).

Vehicles tailored to individual needs are often called "demand response" vehicles as well as "vanpools". The fleets are comprised of a wide variety of different kinds of vehicles depending on the need and availability.

The NTD (US DOT, FTA 2010 p.6) defines demand response services as:

> Service (passenger cars, vans or small buses) provided upon request to pick up and transport passengers to and from their destinations. Typically, a vehicle may be dispatched to pick up several passengers at different pick-up points before taking them to their respective destinations and may be interrupted en route to these destinations to pick up other passengers.

Vanpools are defined by NTD (US DOT, FTA 2010 p.6) as:

> Service operating under a ride sharing arrangement providing transportation to individuals traveling directly between their homes and a regular destination. The vehicles (vans, small buses, and other vehicles) must have a minimum seating capacity of seven. Vanpool(s) must also be in compliance with mass transit rules including Americans with Disabilities Act (ADA) provisions, be open to the public, availability must be advertised and the service must be operated by a public entity or a public entity must own, purchase or lease the vehicle(s).

As funding for transit is threatened in major cities, various kinds of paratransit to restore or create links are filling in the gap. Ironically, in addition to their own role in meeting certain kinds of demand, vans also fill in when bus services or other forms of transit are infrequent or are terminated (White 2010; Santos 2010). In some areas, automobile services are also filling in, such as taxicabs and livery cabs, depending on local regulations.

TRANSPORTATION CONNECTIVITY: URBAN RAIL SYSTEMS

Introduction

As Chapter 1 summarized, transportation systems are networks, and the network concept is commonly used to describe them (Levinson and Krizek 2008; Rodrigue et al. 2006, 2009; Nagurney and Qiang 2009). Networks simply defined are structures with nodes or points connected with links and the activity or flows that occur among nodes through the links. These simple components are the basis for defining many more complex characteristics of network behavior (Wasserman and Faust 2009; Newman 2010).

The network concept provides a foundation for understanding transportation characteristics and the behavior of its users, since transportation systems reflect many of the intrinsic characteristics of networks. In particular, the transportation, environment and security connections – their conflicts and synergies – are best understood through network concepts in order to characterize the interconnectedness of these areas. As addressed in Chapter 1, there is a strong tradition for applying network concepts to transportation for the purpose of analysing impacts ranging from ordinary travel behavior to changes in transportation capacity in extreme events.

This chapter sets the framework for transportation networks to link them to environment and security by focusing on transit. The emphasis is on intracity rail transit systems, though many of the principles that govern intracity travel also provide insights into the broader networks for both intracity and intercity travel by many different modes. The network concepts emphasized are importance (centrality) in terms of concentration and density of transit links and nodes.

The key theme is the connectivity that rail transit provides. Other forms of transportation extend that connectivity through intermodal connections. Connections or transfers between rail transit and bus, automobiles, bikes and walking require close connections between road and rail networks. That interconnectivity is an important factor in the interplay between the urban fabric and transportation networks that support and create that fabric and how transportation is connected to specific societal needs such as environmental protection and security. The configuration of transit networks is reflected in its physical attributes and travel activity and the interrelationships between these two sets of attributes.

Network Concepts for Rail Systems

A number of network concepts and their applications to transportation systems were introduced in Chapter 1. For reference, some of those that are applied here to US rail transit systems and the characteristics to which they apply are briefly summarized below. In this application, nodes are stations and links are tracks. Summarizing from Newman (2010), some of these concepts related to centrality or importance and examples from transit are:

- Degree centrality: number of links connected to a node (control over activities), exemplified by transfer points;
- Betweenness centrality: extent to which a node lies between other nodes along a path (influence), such as the number or frequency of stations per track mile; and
- Closeness centrality: closeness of nodes to other nodes (accessibility of nodes to one another), such as station density.

Other related network concepts are:

- Concentration: the extent to which rail physical infrastructure and travel activity are concentrated among the US rail systems;
- Remoteness: existence of outliers or nodes to a single node or link. The extent to which systems have stations that are connected in only one direction, that is, they are at "the end of the line", and
- Flexibility/Adaptability: the ability of travelers to move from one system to another such as the ability to reroute trains.

The remoteness concept illustrates the importance of one of the network properties for transport. One aspect of connectivity related to the remoteness concept is the prevalence of unconnected end points and heavily connected intersection points. To explore this, for the ten largest heavy rail systems, the number of intersections or transfer points among rail lines and end points was computed from system maps. Excluded from the intersection count were parallel rail lines or loops where tracks join at some point but essentially represent the same line. Examples are the joining of local and express train services.

The data for the ten systems is shown in Table 2.3. New York City, as one would expect given the size of the system, leads other heavy rail systems in the country in the number of lines, intersection points and end points. Chicago is second but has half the lines and end points and about a quarter of the intersections that New York has. The other systems have more end points than intersections.

Correlation coefficients in Table 2.4 are just for heavy rail system characteristics to illustrate relationships among network characteristics. This set of correlations emphasizes an unusual aspect of the structure of rail systems. End points (indicative of remoteness) and intersections (indicative of concentration) are highly correlated ($r=0.9$) and each of those two characteristics are correlated with some of the basic transit characteristics (Table 2.4).

The relationships between rail line intersection or transfer points and the basic transit characteristics suggest that such transfer points support a

Table 2.3   *Rail system end points, transfer points and transit characteristics, heavy rail, US, 2009*

Location	Stations*	Track miles*	Trips*	Lines**	End points**	Intersections**
			(in thousands)			
New York	468	829.9	2,358,313	22	24	35
Chicago	143	287.8	202,569	10	13	9
Boston	53	108.0	148,684	4	12	5
Washington	86	269.8	296,857	5	10	8
Oakland	43	267.6	114,655	5	10	4
Atlanta	38	103.7	83,347	4	8	3
Philadelphia	75	99.8	95,110	2	4	1
Baltimore	14	34.0	13,523	1	2	0
Miami	22	55.9	18,245	1	2	0
Los Angeles	16	34.1	46,891	1	2	1

Sources:
*   US DOT, FTA (undated website) National Transit Database 2009.
**   Lines, end points and intersections were measured from heavy rail transit maps.

Table 2.4   *Associations for rail system end points, transfer points and transit characteristics, heavy rail, US, 2009*

	Correlation coefficient
Correlation of *Number of End Points* with:	
Number of stations	0.88
Number of lines	0.94
Correlation of *Number of Intersection or Transfer Points* with transit infrastructure characteristics:	
Number of track miles	0.98
Number of stations	0.99
Number of lines	0.98
Correlation of *Number of Intersection or Transfer Points* with population and travel characteristics:	
Number of trips	0.98
Population (MSA)	0.80
Population density (MSA)	0.59
Area (MSA)	0.38

greater amount of physical infrastructure (stations, tracks, and lines) and a larger user population (number of trips, population), which one would expect. Area (the land area of the Metropolitan Statistical Area (MSA) in which the transit system is located) is not correlated well with the number of intersection points and the correlation with population density is moderate.

Rail Transit Systems: Definitions and Trends

Before proceeding with other network characteristics, some of the fundamental characteristics of transit are presented. The definition of Public Transportation used by the NTD is "as defined in the Federal Transit Act, 'transportation by a conveyance that provides regular and continuing general or special transportation to the public, but does not include school bus, charter, or intercity bus transportation or intercity passenger rail transportation provided by the entity described in chapter 243 (or a successor to such entity)'"; the term transit is considered by the NTD as a "synonymous term with public transportation" (US DOT, FTA 2011).

Transit is generally a mode of travel that has a fixed and published schedule and set of rates and is available to the general public, not just for specific subpopulations or individuals (Grava 2003, p.810).

The Federal Transit Administration's National Transit Database (NTD) (http://www.ntdprogram.gov/ntdprogram/) was used as the basis for analysing transit characteristics and networks and their relationship to transit use. The NTD is one of the major databases. Other sources are the American Public Transportation Association (APTA 2011), in part based on the NTD, and the US DOT Bureau of Transportation Statistics. The characteristics used here are based on average annual characteristics primarily in the NTD 2009 database (http://www.ntdprogram.gov/ntd-program/data.htm) defined for transit systems covering the US. Trend data provided by the FTA, NTD Annual National Transit Summary and Trends (NTST) (2009) for the years 2000 and 2009 is also used. Additional characteristics were constructed using US Bureau of the Census data as presented in the *State and Metropolitan Area Data Book* (US Census Bureau 2010) and the *County and City Data Book* (US Census Bureau 2007).

Rail transit is categorized by the NTD as heavy rail, commuter rail, and light rail. Detailed definitions of these three categories are available from the NTD glossary (US DOT, FTA 2011). Briefly, according to the glossary and NTD's annual reports, the three types of systems tend to differ in terms of their physical infrastructure, geographic extent, and passenger volumes. Heavy rail systems usually use at-grade electric rails for electric power, typically have high traffic volume, and tend to operate at higher speeds (US DOT, FTA, NTD 2010, p.6). Commuter rail draws from a mix of power sources and covers shorter distances within and between urbanized areas (NTD 2010, p.5); however, the distances are usually longer than distances traveled by heavy rail or light rail, since commuter rail connects local areas with their regions. Light rail draws its power primarily from overhead electrical lines, has relatively lower traffic, and covers more limited distances (NTD 2010, p.6).

Introduction to Transit Infrastructure and Travel Trends

The NTD includes physical characteristics and characteristics of travel for 2000 and 2009. The changes over these two time periods are shown in Table 2.5.

Light rail infrastructure has expanded dramatically over the time period, with stations increasing by a third and track mileage by two-thirds. This is in part due to the increase in the number of light rail systems which was an increase of 42.9 percent over the time period, a larger increase than either heavy rail or commuter rail experienced. Increases in light rail transit are occurring in many parts of the US. The rate of increase for light rail infrastructure is greater than the rates for the other two systems though it started from a smaller base than the others for stations and track mileage. The increase in passenger trips between 2000 and 2009 was larger for light rail relative to other systems though heavy rail trips also showed a large increase.

In 2009, passengers took about 4.4 billion trips via urban rail-based public transportation that amounted to 30.1 billion miles of travel (based on the 2009 US DOT, NTD). This accounts for a third (34.4 percent) of all public transportation trips, with bus transit accounting for the largest proportion of the rest – about a half (52.9 percent) or with adjustments 30.2 percent and 57.8 percent (US DOT, FTA, NTD 2010, p.51). (According to the US DOT, the adjustments were made by the NTD based on a single heavy rail provider resulting in these percentages becoming 30.2 and 57.8 percent for rail and bus respectively (US DOT, FTA. NTD 2010, p.51).) Although buses account for the largest share of transit ridership, trips by bus have been increasing the least – by 6.3 percent between 2000 and 2009. Other modes include vanpool, "demand response" (such as paratransit), and other systems. These transit modes other than buses and the three rail systems account for only 3.5 percent of the ridership (calculated from US DOT, FTA, NTD 2010, p.50).

An analysis of the NTD data sheds more light on these systems. In 2009 in the US, the three rail transit systems combined accounted for 11,645

Table 2.5   Selected rail system and travel characteristics, US, 2000 and 2009

Characteristic and year	Heavy rail	Commuter rail	Light rail	Total
Stations				
2000	1,009	1,151	615	2,775
2009	1,041	1,214	836	3,091
% change	3.2%	5.5%	35.9%	11.4%
Track miles				
2000	2,177.8	7,364.6	1,000.9	10,543.3
2009	2,272.2	7,740.0	1,632.9	11,645.1
% change	4.3%	5.1%	63.1%	10.5%
Systems				
2000	14	19	21	54
2009	15	25	30	70
% change	7.1%	31.6%	42.9%	29.6%
Trips				
2000	2,632,000,000	412,770,100	316,237,100	3,361,007,200
2009	3,489,503,588	463,965,963	464,234,762	4,417,704,313
% change	32.6%	12.4%	46.8%	31.4%

Sources: 2000 data from US DOT, Federal Transit Administration, National Transit Database (NTD) (2000), *2000 National Transit Summaries and Trends*, Washington, DC, USA: Federal Transit Administration. (HR pp.90–91; CR pp.92–3; LR pp.88–9). 2009 data from US Department of Transportation, Federal Transit Administration (undated website), National Transit Database, available at http://www.ntdprogram.gov/ntdprogram/; http://www.ntdprogram.gov/ntdprogram/data.htm.

miles of track and 4.4 billion passenger trips. These were distributed by each of the three systems as follows (summarized from Table 2.5):

- The 15 heavy rail systems accounted for about 3.5 billion passenger trips over 2,272 miles of track.
- The 25 commuter rail systems accounted for 464 million passenger trips over 7,740 track miles.
- The 30 light rail systems accounted for 464 million passenger trips over 1,633 track miles.

Rail transit trips grew about 30 percent nationwide between 2000 and 2009 (calculated from US DOT, FTA, NTD 2000 and 2009 NTD data). Though system changes in the rail infrastructure occurred over this ten-year period to accommodate increased ridership, the rate of increase in station and track infrastructure was not as rapid as ridership. Across all rail systems, though the number of rail systems increased by about 30 percent, the number of stations and miles of track increased by about 11 percent between 2000 and 2009, which was about a third of the increase in ridership. APTA (2011, p.10) has emphasized the high levels of travel noting that ridership during the 2006 to 2009 period has exceeded 1956 ridership levels. Moreover, APTA (2011, p.11) also notes that public transportation ridership rates have exceeded the rate of population growth in the US (34 percent versus 15 percent between 1995 and 2009) as well as the rate of VMT growth (23 percent).

To explore these broad patterns and trends further, physical character-istics of transit systems are presented and compared with population and travel activity. Since NYC's heavy rail transit system is so large compared to the others, results are given both with and without New York City.

Population and Physical Characteristics of Areas in which Transit Systems Are Located

The characteristics of rail transit services vary considerably by type of system (heavy, commuter and light rail) and location. Details for how each transit system ranks with respect to population, area, physical characteris-tics and ridership are summarized below.

Size characteristics
Rail transit systems vary enormously from one another in size both by type of transit system and for systems within each type. Comparing all of the systems in the US, size is not always related to the degree of activity on the system reflected in activity measures such as passenger trips. System

size is described in different ways. First, it is defined physically in terms of measures in the NTD such as service area, the number of stations and number of miles of track. Second, the metropolitan statistical area (MSA) from the US Census Bureau can serve as a proxy for the size of the area from which users are drawn. Third, is the number of people served, again using the MSA as a proxy, as the population of the MSA within which the system is located. Although it might be argued that employment is related to transit usage to a greater extent than population, the US Census Bureau (2011, p.4) employment to population ratios for MSAs in which many transit systems are located are relatively similar.

Population served and land area characteristics

The population potentially served by a transit system is an important indication of the size and magnitude of its user base. The task of identifying and defining populations at the system level and making comparisons among systems is a difficult one. First, defining a catchment area for a transit system ideally requires knowledge of the origins and destinations of its users, which is often unstable over time, and the availability of that data is uneven across systems. Second, transit systems not only serve resident populations but also employment and visitors that may or may not correspond to the population defined as being served. Third, the same transit agency may own and/or operate multiple systems, and the same population and area may be assigned to the same agency for different systems. Descriptive and other statistics for population, service area and population density, therefore, have to be used cautiously.

MSA population was primarily used as a measure of size for each of the transit systems; however, there were some notable exceptions given the nature of some specific systems. The population for a heavy rail system, the Staten Island Rapid Transit Operating Authority (SIRTOA), on Staten Island, New York City was defined as the population of Staten Island since that system primarily draws from and is fully contained within that borough. The population for the Port Authority Transit Corporation (PATCO), connecting New Jersey and Pennsylvania was defined as the population of the two counties it connects.

The mean population and area of the MSA by type of system is presented in Table 2.6. Many of the heavily populated urban areas in the New York area influence the overall characteristics of both heavy rail and commuter rail. Thus, both of these systems have the largest average populations due to the dominance of New York area systems. Light rail is more commonly located in relatively smaller urban areas so the mean population is smaller.

The NTD defines the population of a transit service area. The population of the NTD service area and the MSA population, however, are

Table 2.6 Characteristics of Population, Land Area, and Population Density, Rail Transit, US, 2009

Mean MSA Population	Observations or Cases	Mean	Std. Dev.	Min	Max
HR (w NYC)	15	5,649,627	4,943,820	487,400	1.90E+07
HR (wo NYC)	14	4,695,544	3,408,373	487,400	1.29E+07
CR	25	5,916,479	5,835,024	514,065	1.90E+07
LR	30	4,611,005	4,650,895	1,115,692	1.90E+07
Mean MSA land area (in sq. mi.)	**Observations or Cases**	**Mean**	**Std. Dev.**	**Min**	**Max**
HR (w NYC)	15	4,155.8	2,226.7	58.5	8,376.5
HR (wo NYC)	14	3,972.2	2,189.8	58.5	8,376.5
CR	25	5,415.2	2,508.4	1,399.3	9,538.8
LR	30	5,553.4	2,824.7	1,567.2	14,572.7
MSA population density (per sq. mi.)	**Observations or Cases**	**Mean**	**Std. Dev.**	**Min**	**Max**
HR (w NYC)	15	1,770.7	1,946.7	1022.2	8,331.8
HR (wo NYC)	14	1,695.4	1,997.3	1022.2	8,331.8
CR	25	1,078.5	867.8	91.1	2,825.9
LR	30	895.5	735.1	117.0	2,825.9

Note: Abbreviations: HR = Heavy rail; CR = Commuter rail; LR = Light rail; MSA = Metropolitan Statistical Area; w = with; wo = without.

Source: Computed from the US DOT, FTA (undated website), National Transit Database 2009.

highly correlated: for heavy rail with NY (r=0.86), heavy rail without NY (r=0.80), commuter rail (r=0.80), and light rail (r=0.91). Thus, using the population of the MSA reflects the population of the NTD defined service area as well.

As indicated earlier, many ways of describing area exist. Three delineations that describe the area of transit systems are the MSA Total Area and Land Area (not including water), the City Area, and the Service Area as defined by the NTD. All of these measures define area in terms of square miles.

Land area accounts for a very large portion of total MSA area in practically all metropolitan areas containing transit systems. In fact, the MSA land area and total area were highly correlated. For example, for heavy rail it was r=0.94. Thus, land area was primarily used in this analysis to characterize the MSA area for a given transit system. Some of the exceptions are noteworthy of areas that have large water areas within their borders and both rail and roadways may require more track, roads or bridges to span them. The city area was generally not used, since it usually did not correspond to and underestimates the regional extent of most transit system service areas. The service area for rail is defined by the NTD glossary (US DOT, FTA, NTD, 2011, p.62) as contained in the Americans with Disabilities Act of 1990 (ADA): "Rail. (i) For rail systems, the service area shall consist of a circle with a radius of 3/4 of a mile around each station. (ii) At end stations and other stations in outlying areas, the entity may designate circles with radii of up to 1 1/2 miles as part of its service area, based on local circumstances." This definition is taken from the US Department of Transportation (2011).

Unlike MSA population and service area population, the MSA land area and the NTD defined service area are unrelated across the various systems as indicated by the correlation coefficients. The correlations are close to zero regardless of the system, being slightly negative (r=−0.04 and r=−0.03 for heavy and commuter rail respectively) or very slightly positive (r=0.05 for light rail).

Commuter rail and light rail cover a larger average MSA land area than heavy rail as indicated by the average land areas. This is consistent with the more compact nature of heavy rail and the areas they serve. Only small differences in the mean area exist between commuter and light rail systems; however, the variability is dramatic, with light rail having a much larger range in area than commuter rail.

The "reach" or coverage of public transportation can be measured on a citywide or metropolitan area-wide basis in terms of the ratio of the service area to the particular jurisdiction it serves. Table 2.7 presents the reach for 11 of the 15 heavy rail systems in the US from the NTD as the ratios of

*Table 2.7   Comparison of heavy rail transit NTD service areas to city and
         MSA areas, US, 2009*

	Service area ratio to:	
	City area	MSA area
	(Land area)	
Massachusetts Bay Transportation Authority (MBTA) Boston, MA	67.0	0.9
MTA New York City Transit (NYCT) New York, NY	1.1	0.1
Staten Island Rapid Transit Operating Authority (SIRTOA) Staten Island, NY	1.0	N/A
Southeastern Pennsylvania Transportation Authority (SEPTA) Philadelphia, PA	6.4	0.2
Washington Metropolitan Area Transit Authority (WMATA) Washington, DC	11.3	0.1
Maryland Transit Administration (MTA) Baltimore, MD	22.2	0.7
Metropolitan Atlanta Rapid Transit Authority (MARTA) Atlanta, GA	3.8	0.6
Miami–Dade Transit (MDT) Miami, FL	8.6	0.6
The Greater Cleveland Regional Transit Authority (GCRTA) Cleveland, OH	5.9	0.2
Chicago Transit Authority (CTA) Chicago, IL	1.4	0.5
San Francisco Bay Area Rapid Transit District (BART)	1.7	0.6
Oakland, CA (Oakland and San Francisco, CA)*	(0.9)	0.0
Los Angeles County Metropolitan Transportation Authority (LACMTA) Los Angeles, LA	3.2	0.3

Notes:
The other three heavy rail systems do not have equivalent city or MSA designations and are
not listed.
* Although BART is designated as Oakland, CA on the NTD database it serves the San
Francisco MSA also. Therefore, the figure used for the city is for San Francisco and
Oakland combined and the figure used for the MSA is for the San Francisco MSA of which
the Oakland MSA is a part.
Areas were obtained from the US Census Bureau (2007 and 2010).
Transit data was obtained from the US DOT, FTA (undated website), National Transit
Database 2009.

the NTD service area and the city and MSA areas. The larger the number,
the larger the service area is relative to the area of the geographic area
defined for the urban area in which the transit system is located. In all
cases shown, the reach is much larger for cities than for MSAs, as one
might expect. For MSAs the NTD area is always much smaller than the
MSA area.

Concentration of transit services by population and land area
Concentration is a key factor in linking transportation to environment and security. Many infrastructure services are concentrated in just a few urban areas (Zimmerman 2006). Such concentration has environmental benefits analogous to the environmental benefits of compact development. Whether or not these concentrations make certain areas have a greater security risk depends on the configuration of the systems within the urban areas.

Only a small percentage of the individual rail systems account for most of the MSA population and land area served. In any given rail category, typically between three and eight systems account for about half of the MSA population within the rail category and between five and ten systems account for about half of the MSA land area. The specific cities that were in the 50th percentile with respect to transit characteristics for both physical attributes and travel activity are presented in the next section.

The following details are presented for the 50th percentile for each of the rail systems.

Half of the *MSA population* defined for each type of rail system was accounted for by:

- A fifth (three) of the 15 heavy rail systems including New York City;
- About a quarter (28.6 percent or four) of the 14 heavy rail systems without New York City;
- A fifth (five) of the 25 commuter rail systems; and
- Either 16.7 percent (five) or 26.7 percent (eight) of the 30 light rail systems (depending on whether Newark is counted twice or not).

This suggests a degree of concentration of population within each of the different rail systems.

Half of the *MSA area* defined for each type of rail system was accounted for by:

- A third (five) of the 15 heavy rail systems including New York City;
- About a quarter (28.6 percent or four) of the 14 heavy rail systems without New York City;
- About a third (36 percent or nine) of the 25 commuter rail systems; and
- A third (ten) of the 30 light rail systems.

This suggests a degree of concentration of transit system area within each of the different rail systems.

Heavy rail (HR) At the MSA level, the concentration of population in HR systems occurred in New York, Los Angeles and Chicago, followed by Philadelphia, Miami, Atlanta and Washington in that order. The very smallest systems in MSA population, each with less than 5 percent of the total population, are in Baltimore, Jersey City, Cleveland and Staten Island.

The MSAs with the highest concentration of area for HR systems were led by Atlanta and Chicago with New York, Washington and Miami following in that order. Baltimore, Oakland, Jersey City, Cleveland and Staten Island each have less than 5 percent of the total area.

Commuter rail (CR) About half of the MSA population was accounted for by about a fifth of the CR systems in the three New York area systems – Jamaica, NY (LIRR), Newark (NJ Transit), NY (MTA Metro North), and Los Angeles and Chicago (Metra) in that order (though Chicago was tied with Chesterton (the Northern Indiana Commuter Transportation District or NICTD)). In contrast, about half of the area was accounted for by a third of the CR systems – nine systems in Salt Lake City, Albuquerque, Dallas, Fort Worth, Chicago, Chesterton (Indiana), Newark and New York (MTA Metro North) in that order (and the MTA Long Island Railroad (LIRR) was tied with Metro North). The first four systems account for over a quarter (27.1 percent) of commuter rail land area alone. There are numerous small CR systems in terms of both population and area. The smallest in population, each under 2 percent, were in Baltimore, Portland (Oregon), Nashville, Newington (Connecticut), Salt Lake City, Albuquerque, Stockton, Harrisburg, and Portland (Maine). The smallest systems that each account for under 2 percent of the total CR area are, in descending order, in Baltimore, San Carlos, Portland (Maine), Harrisburg, Newington, and Stockton. Thus, the CR transit systems are more dispersed with respect to area than population.

Light rail (LR) Almost half of the MSA population is accounted for by 16.7 percent or five of the 30 LR systems located in Newark (two NJ Transit systems), Los Angeles, Kenosha (Wisconsin) which connects to the Chicago area and Dallas, Philadelphia, Houston, Boston, Phoenix and San Francisco rank next in that order. More than half of the MSA area is accounted for by about a third of the 30 LR systems (but they are different from those listed above for population), which are Phoenix, Salt Lake City, Dallas, Houston, St. Louis, Denver, Kenosha, Newark (two NJ Transit systems), and Portland (Oregon), in that order. The smallest light rail systems in MSA area (fewer than 2 percent) are in San Francisco, Cleveland and Buffalo and in MSA population the smallest (fewer than 2 percent) are San Jose, Charlotte, Memphis, New Orleans, Buffalo, and Salt Lake City. Thus, the dispersion of LR transit systems is less for population than area.

Of the three systems, heavy rail has the highest *population density* whether NYC is included or not, followed by commuter rail, and then light rail. As one might expect within each of the systems, the very largest systems also serve the most people and have the highest density. For heavy rail, the New York area systems rank highest in density.

In conclusion, within each of the three rail types a few rail systems account for the most of the MSA area, population served, and population density served by rail transit systems.

Measures of area, population and population density are not generally correlated, with the following exceptions: for heavy rail, land area and population are somewhat correlated ($r=0.63$) and land area and population density are somewhat negatively correlated ($r=-0.50$); for commuter rail systems population and density are highly correlated ($r=0.93$); and for light rail area and population density are somewhat correlated ($r=0.41$).

The Physical Transit Infrastructure: Tracks and Stations

Transit system characteristics
Transit systems consist of extensive infrastructure not only for the direct transport of passengers but also for the overall maintenance and operation of the systems. Stations and tracks are the mainstay of passenger travel, representing very spatially extended infrastructure, and are the focus of this work. Table 2.8 summarizes station and track mileage characteristics.

Heavy rail systems have on average the largest number of stations; however, when NYC is removed, commuter rail systems have the largest average number of stations. Commuter rail exceeds others by far in average track mileage per system. The number of stations and track mileage for systems within each of the three types are generally highly correlated regardless of the rail system: for HR it is 0.97, for HR without NYC it is 0.82, for CR it is 0.95, and for LR it is 0.67.

The lower correlation for light rail systems again reflects the broader variability in those systems. As shown in Table 2.9, the ratio of the mean number of stations per track mile reflects these patterns. Light rail has a relatively higher ratio of stations per track mile than the other systems. The relatively lower ratio of stations per track mile in commuter rail systems reflects the far flung nature of those systems.

Table 2.8   Stations and miles of track, rail transit, US, 2009

Stations	Obs	Mean	Std. Dev.	Min	Max	Total
HR (w NYC)	15	69	116	13	468	1041
HR (wo NYC)	14	41	38	13	143	573
CR	25	49	65	5	240	1,214
LR	30	28	18	2	74	836

Miles of track	Obs	Mean	Std. Dev.	Min	Max	Total
HR (w NYC)	15	151.5	209.8	25.5	829.9	2,272.2
HR (wo NYC)	14	103.0	97.4	25.5	287.8	1,442.3
CR	25	309.6	333.5	19.2	1,206.1	7,740.0
LR	30	54.4	47.9	1.9	218.6	1,632.9

Note: Abbreviations: Obs = Observations; HR = Heavy rail; CR = Commuter rail;
LR = Light rail.

Source: Computed from the US DOT, FTA (undated website), National Transit
Database 2009.

*Table 2.9   Selected comparisons for characteristics of rail transit systems,
US, 2009*

	N	Mean no. of stations	Mean no. track miles	Ratio of mean stations/track mile
HR (with NY)	15	69	152	0.45
HR (wo NY)	14	41	103	0.40
CR	25	49	310	0.16
LR	30	28	54	0.52

Note: Abbreviations: HR = Heavy rail; CR = Commuter rail; LR = Light rail.

Source: Computed from the FTA (undated website), National Transit Database 2009.

Concentration of physical infrastructure
There are dramatic differences among the systems in terms of where the
physical infrastructure tends to cluster reflected in the share of infrastructure that each of the different systems has within the three rail categories.
This is similar to the concentration of MSA population and area for the
systems described earlier. Stations and track mileage are used to illustrate
the concentration of physical infrastructure. Below is a summary for all of
the rail systems giving the number of systems with respect to stations and
track miles.

About half of the *number of stations* defined for each type of rail system was accounted for by:

- Seven percent (one) of the 15 heavy rail systems including New York City;
- About a fifth (21.4 percent or three) of the 14 heavy rail systems without New York City;
- Twelve percent (three) of the 25 commuter rail systems; and
- About a quarter (26.7 percent or eight) of the 30 light rail systems.

Half of the *track mileage* defined for each type of rail system was accounted for by:

- About 13 percent (two) of the 15 heavy rail systems including New York City;
- About a fifth (21.4 percent or three) of the 14 heavy rail systems without New York City;
- Sixteen percent (four) of the 25 commuter rail systems; and
- About a quarter (23.3 percent or seven) of the 30 light rail systems.

This suggests some degree of concentration of both stations and track mileage within the different rail systems.

Heavy rail The ranks of specific systems with respect to their share of 1,041 US heavy rail stations along 2,272 miles of track are as follows. Almost half the stations are accounted for by New York alone. Those with relatively larger shares of stations are New York (45 percent), Chicago (14 percent), Washington, DC (8 percent), and Philadelphia (7 percent). The share of stations is lowest in Baltimore, Port Authority TransHudson (PATH) in Jersey City and PATCO in Lindenwold (1 percent each) followed by Cleveland, Los Angeles, Miami, San Juan, and Staten Island each with a share of 2 percent. When New York City is removed, the Chicago Transit Authority (CTA) ranks highest in the share of stations (25 percent) followed by Washington Metropolitan Area Transit Authority (WMATA) (15 percent) and the Southeastern Pennsylvania Transportation Authority (SEPTA) in Philadelphia (13 percent).

The distribution of the heavy rail systems with respect to miles of track is similar to that for the share of stations. New York and Chicago account for half of the total mileage. The systems with the highest share of the total track mileage of 2,272 miles are New York (37 percent), Chicago (13 percent, Washington, DC (12 percent), and San Francisco/Oakland (12 percent). Boston and Atlanta follow with 5 percent. Systems with the lowest track mileage share are in Puerto Rico, Staten Island, and Baltimore each with a share of 1 percent then Los Angeles (LA), the systems in Jersey City and Lindenwold, Miami and Cleveland, each with a share of about 2 percent. When New York City is removed, Chicago (CTA), Washington, DC (WMATA), and San Francisco together account for 60 percent of heavy rail miles of track (each with about an equal share of 20 percent).

Commuter rail   The total number of commuter rail stations is 1,214 along 7,740 miles of track. Chicago has the largest number with 240 (19.8 percent) stations which far exceeds other systems. In the highest category, Chicago is followed by commuter rail systems in Newark (13.5 percent), Philadelphia (12.7 percent), Boston (11 percent), and New York (10.2 percent and 9.1 percent). The systems with the smallest number of stations, each with 0.5 percent shares or less, are Minneapolis, Nashville, Dallas, Fort Worth and Portland (Oregon).

The number of miles of commuter rail track totals 7,740. Chicago with 1,206 miles (15.6 percent) far exceeds other systems in track mileage. Newark's NJ Transit and New York's Metro North rank as the second and third largest systems after Chicago respectively. Chicago and Newark alone account for a quarter of the track mileage. Almost half of the mileage (46.6 percent) is accounted for by adding in just New York's Metro North and the LIRR. Portland (Oregon) and then Fort Worth have the smallest track mileage.

Light rail   The number of light rail stations totals 836 along 1,633 miles of track. After Boston (8.9 percent) California has light rail systems with the largest number of stations with the highest in San Jose (7.8 percent) closely followed by San Diego (6.3 percent), LA (5.9 percent), and Sacramento (5.7 percent). At the low end is the Kenosha Transit system in Wisconsin with just two stations.

The specific systems are distributed differently with respect to miles of track. The system with the largest track mileage is Philadelphia with 219 miles (13.4 percent). After Philadelphia a number of cities follow with similar shares: Los Angeles (7.1 percent), San Diego (6.3 percent), Dallas (6.1 percent), St. Louis (5.9 percent), Portland (Oregon) (5.9 percent), and San Francisco (5.8 percent). The systems with the least track mileage, each with a share of 0.2 percent or lower, are in Seattle, Washington; Tampa, Florida; and Kenosha, Wisconsin.

Physical System Density

Physical system density characteristics
Physical density of rail systems provides important measures of the dispersion of the components and the availability and access to its users as well

as for the ability of the system to accommodate environmental needs. As in the case of area, the physical density of the transit systems was measured in a number of different ways. First, densities for number of stations and miles of track were computed relative to areas: the MSA and the special service area as defined in the NTD. Four density measures were generated for stations and track mileage. For stations these were number of stations per square mile of MSA area and number of stations per square mile of NTD service area. For track mileage these were number of miles of track per square mile of MSA area and number of miles of track per square mile of NTD service area. Second, station density was measured as density of stations along tracks, that is, as number of stations per track mile. Third, the overall service area was computed as a proportion of the MSA land area. Another possibility for a fourth measure, not used here, is to compute population density in terms of population in the MSA land area and population in the service area and then use this as the basis for another measure of station and track density. To summarize, the following density measures were generated for physical facilities:

- number of stations per square mile of MSA area;
- number of stations per square mile of NTD service area;
- number of miles of track per square mile of MSA area;
- number of miles of track per square mile of NTD service area;
- number of stations per track mile; and
- square miles of service area per square mile of MSA land area.

The stations per square mile of MSA area is, as one would expect, much smaller than stations per square mile of NTD service area regardless of the type of system, given the way the two densities are measured.

Table 2.10 contains summaries for the averages for two density measures by type of rail transit system:

- number of stations per square mile of MSA area;
- number of miles of track per square mile of MSA area.

Heavy rail is consistently the most dense regardless of density measure. Heavy rail is used in the examples below to illustrate where specific transit systems were along the distribution of two density measures:

- For the MSA station density, density was highest for SIRTOA on Staten Island NYC (0.4 stations per square mile).
- For the NTD defined service area (not shown), station density ranged from 1.5 stations per square mile for NYC's MTA to the

Table 2.10   Average density characteristics of rail systems, US, 2009

Station density	Obs	Mean	Std. Dev.	Min	Max
HR (w NYC)	15	0.039	0.099	0.003	0.393
HR (wo NYC)	14	0.037	0.103	0.003	0.393
CR	25	0.010	0.012	0.001	0.038
LR	30	0.006	0.006	0.000	0.024
Track density	Obs	Mean	Std. Dev.	Min	Max
HR (w NYC)	15	0.069	0.140	0.007	0.559
HR (wo NYC)	14	0.065	0.145	0.007	0.559
CR	25	0.067	0.061	0.003	0.190
LR	30	0.012	0.012	0.000	0.047

Notes:
Abbreviations: Obs = Observations; HR = Heavy rail; CR = Commuter rail; LR = Light rail.
Density for stations and track miles is calculated per square mile of MSA area.

Source: Computed from the US DOT, FTA (undated website), National Transit
Database 2009.

Metropolitan Transportation Administration in Baltimore, MD
where the number was less than a hundredth per square mile.
Ranking after NYC were San Francisco, Chicago and Staten Island
(in NYC) in that order.

Physical system characteristics and population density combined
Relationships between population density and the density of selected
infrastructure characteristics (stations and track miles) and infrastructure
density (stations per square mile and track mileage per square mile of area)
are shown in Table 2.11. With the exception of commuter rail, population
density is unrelated to stations and track mileage. However, for heavy rail
(with or without NYC) and commuter rail, population density is highly
correlated with the station and track density measures.

Travel Activity

Extent and density of travel
Travel activity is measured in terms of both the extent of travel and the
density of travel. Extent of travel is measured here in terms of trips, miles
of travel, and miles per trip. Density is measured in terms of trips per
station, and trips per square mile in the service area.
    Table 2.12 provides a comparison of the three rail systems with respect
to the total and mean number of trips, miles of travel, and miles per trip.

Table 2.11   *Correlations for population density (with respect to MSA land area) and physical system characteristics, US, 2009*

	Stations	Tracks	Stations per square mile	Tracks per square mile
HR w NYC	0.106	0.062	0.955***	0.952***
HR wo NYC	−0.119	−0.164	0.957***	0.952***
CR	0.627***	0.740***	0.545***	0.580***
LR	0.150	0.230	0.144	0.297

Notes:
Abbreviations: HR=Heavy rail; CR=Commuter rail; LR=Light rail.
Density is defined with respect to the MSA land area. "Tracks" signify miles of track.
*** p=0.00–0.01; ** p=0.01–0.05; * p=0.05–0.10; p=>0.10.

Source: Computed from the US DOT, FTA (undated website), National Transit Database 2009.

Heavy rail dominated the two other systems in terms of the mean total number of trips taken and the annual miles traveled (2009). Commuter rail, as one might expect, exceeded both heavy and light rail in the mean number of miles per trip given the typical size of those systems.

Travel activity measures are heavily interrelated. Though the correlations are not shown here, two measures of travel activity, trips and miles traveled, are very highly correlated with one another (at least r=0.8 for each of the rail systems).

Concentration of travel activity: trips and miles of travel
The degree of concentration of travel activity relative to the physical infrastructure is a critical factor in understanding system connectivity at an aggregated level. The picture for travel activity is in many cases very different from physical characteristics.

Heavy rail   Heavy rail systems in the US are still dominated by New York City which accounted in 2009 for 68 percent of trips and 59 percent of miles traveled in the US. While its share of basic facilities is still larger than other systems, the share of physical facilities accounting for 45 percent of stations and 37 percent of miles of track is relatively less than its share of measures of trip activity. When New York City is removed from the heavy rail group, Washington, DC (WMATA) dominates the trips, accounting for 26 percent of trips and 24 percent of miles traveled.

Commuter rail   Commuter rail is again dominated by the New York area. Three commuter rail systems account for about 60 percent of both

Table 2.12 *Average values for trips and miles traveled, rail transit, US, 2009*

Trips	Obs	Mean	Std. Dev.	Min	Max	Total
HR (w NYC)	15	232,633,600	593,997,200	4,491,100	2,358,314,000	3,489,503,500
HR (wo NYC)	14	80,799,290	86,997,370	4,491,100	296,857,200	1,131,190,100
CR	25	18,600,000	30,700,000	78,782	97,400,000	463,965,983
LR	30	15,500,000	17,400,000	56,149	70,700,000	464,234,762

Annual miles traveled	Obs	Mean	Std. Dev.	Min	Max	Total
HR (w NYC)	15	1,120,341,000	250,600,000	31,419,600	9,972,779,000	16,805,109,900
HR (wo NYC)	14	488,023,600	551,730,300	31,419,600	1,667,900,000	6,832,330,700
CR	25	445,000,000	743,000,000	1,066,771	2,340,000,000	11,129,418,953
LR	30	73,200,000	80,900,000	62,426	327,000,000	2,195,933,767

Miles per trip	Obs	Mean	Std. Dev.	Min	Max
HR (w NYC)	15	6.188527	2.239399	3.826742	12.57799
HR (wo NYC)	14	6.328509	2.254803	3.826742	12.57799
CR	25	29.12514	16.6857	8.62846	78.43972
LR	30	4.478265	2.426408	0.843976	8.916471

Note: Abbreviations: Obs = Observations; HR = Heavy rail; CR = Commuter rail; LR = Light rail; w NYC = including NYC; wo NYC = excluding NYC.

Source: Computed from the US DOT, FTA (undated website), National Transit Database 2009.

trips and miles traveled in the US. These are Metro North, the Long Island Railroad and NJ Transit. Chicago follows with 15.5 percent of trips and 14.9 percent of miles traveled. Boston ranks next in terms of trips (8.7 percent) and miles traveled (7.4 percent) followed by Philadelphia with 7.7 percent of trips and 4.5 percent of miles traveled. The other commuter rail systems account for well under 5 percent of trips or miles traveled, with the least amount of travel in terms of trips and miles traveled in Portland, Nashville and Minneapolis.

Light rail Light rail is dominated by five systems in terms of trips together accounting for about half (52.4 percent) of trips: Boston (15.2 percent), San Francisco (10.9 percent), Los Angeles (9.9 percent), Portland (Oregon) (8.5 percent), and San Diego (8.0 percent). Those that dominate in terms of miles of travel, accounting for 50 percent of the miles traveled are: Los Angeles (14.9 percent), San Diego (10 percent), Portland (Oregon) (9.4), Boston (8.4), and St. Louis (7.1 percent).

For specific systems, concentration patterns appear for trips and miles of travel as they do for population, area and physical characteristics.

About half of the *trips* defined for each type of rail system were accounted for by:

- About seven percent (one) of the 15 heavy rail systems including New York City;
- About a fifth (21.4 percent or three) of the 14 heavy rail systems without New York City;
- Twelve percent (three) of the 25 commuter rail systems; and
- Almost a fifth (16.7 percent or five) of the 30 light rail systems.

Half of the *miles traveled* defined for each type of rail system were accounted for by:

- About seven percent (one) of the 15 heavy rail systems including New York City;
- About fourteen percent (14.3 percent or two) of the 14 heavy rail systems without New York City;
- Twelve percent (three) of the 25 commuter rail systems; and
- About a fifth (16.7 percent or five) of the 30 light rail systems.

Thus in the aggregate, half of the trips and miles traveled are accounted for by fewer than half of the number of systems, indicating a high degree of concentration within each type of system.

*Table 2.13   Average values for trip density as trips per station, rail transit,
US, 2009*

Trips per station	Obs	Mean	Std. Dev.	Min	Max
HR (w NYC)	15	2,110,280	1,756,000	249,507	6,158,092
HR (wo NYC)	14	1,901,078	1,614,000	249,507	6,158,092
CR	25	233,161	197,273	13,130	785,085
LR	30	590,914	1,000,770	28,075	5,638,318

Note: Abbreviations: Obs = Observations; HR=Heavy rail; CR=Commuter rail;
LR=Light rail.

Source: Computed from the US DOT, FTA (undated website), National Transit
Database 2009.

Density of travel

Travel density was defined in terms of four measures:

- Trips per station as the number of passenger trips at each station averaged over the system;
- Trips per square mile of MSA area;
- Trips per square mile of service area; and
- Trips per track mile.

The average values for the first measure are shown in Table 2.13.

Travel Activity and Physical Characteristics of the Systems Combined: Correlations

Do people take trips more often where stations are available or tracks are available? That is, does the presence of infrastructure encourage its use? This is the central question, and is addressed from a number of perspectives that expand the general findings above.

First, travel activity is compared with the extent of the physical facilities – number of stations and track mileage, and second with the density of those physical facilities. These relationships are initially described using correlations shown in Table 2.14, and then expanded in a regression analysis that follows.

Travel activity and the extent of physical infrastructure

Positive correlations between trips or miles of travel and stations or miles of track reflect in part the ability of travelers to move more freely in systems. In other words, trips and miles of travel would be expected

Table 2.14 Associations for travel activity and alternative measures of transportation density

Trips	LR	CR	HR w NY	HR wo NY
	N=30	N=25	N=15	N=14
Number of stations	0.616***	0.869***	0.976***	0.802***
Miles of track	0.656***	0.873***	0.940***	0.856***
Stations per track mile	−0.280	0.371*	0.156	−0.229
Trips per track mile	0.507***	0.881***	0.767***	0.471*
Station density (stations per MSA area)	0.424**	0.725***	0.056	−0.201
Track density (track miles per MSA area)	0.657***	0.631***	0.086	−0.150
Population per MSA area	0.294	0.794***	0.118	−0.216
Trips per station	0.849***	0.593***	0.516**	0.472*

Miles of travel	LR	CR	HR w NY	HR wo NY
Number of stations	0.643***	0.829***	0.976***	0.721***
Miles of track	0.661***	0.867***	0.966***	0.968***
Stations per track mile	−0.325*	0.310	0.096	−0.434
Trips per track mile	0.335*	0.844***	0.749***	0.255
Stations per MSA area	0.334*	0.667***	0.043	−0.189
Tracks per MSA area	0.513***	0.615***	0.087	0.087
Population per MSA area	0.262	0.818***	0.108	−0.183
Trips per station	0.849***	0.365**	0.527**	0.404

Trip density (MSA)	LR	CR	HR w NY	HR wo NY
Stations	0.445**	0.885***	0.338	−0.109
Miles of track	0.497***	0.874***	0.318	−0.072
Stations per mile of track	−0.246	0.437*	0.360	0.316
Trips per mile of track	0.614***	0.891***	0.120	−0.259
Stations per MSA area	0.461***	0.844***	0.928***	0.975***
Tracks per MSA area	0.695***	0.737***	0.952***	0.994***
Population per MSA area	0.319***	0.788***	0.917***	0.943***

Table 2.14   (continued)

Trips per station	LR	CR	HR w NY	HR wo NY
Miles of track	0.308***	0.649***	0.505*	0.233
Stations per mile of track	−0.183	0.206	−0.327	−0.477*
Trips per mile of track	0.888***	0.914***	0.874***	0.885***
Stations per MSA area	−0.035	0.465**	−0.206	−0.277
Tracks per MSA area	0.508***	0.415**	−0.160	−0.237
Population per MSA area	−0.012	0.836***	−0.122	−0.218

Notes:
*** $p=0.00$–0.01; **$p=0.01$–0.05; *$p=0.05$–0.10; $p=>0.10$.
Abbreviations: HR=Heavy rail; CR=Commuter rail; LR=Light rail.
"Tracks" is an abbreviation for miles of track; Population per MSA is population density for the MSA.

Source: Computed from the US DOT, FTA (undated website), National Transit Database 2009.

to be larger in systems with a greater number of stations and miles of track. This in fact occurred generally in all three systems as shown in Table 2.14. Number of trips (unlinked passenger trips) is highly correlated with number of stations for light rail ($r=0.62$; $p=0.00$), commuter rail ($r=0.0.87$; $p=0.00$), and heavy rail (without NYC) ($r=0.80$; $p=0.00$).

These findings can be interpreted in a couple of ways. Either the demand is responding to a large supply of transit service or the supply is meeting the demand for larger systems.

Travel activity and infrastructure density
The number of transit trips people take is highly correlated with track and station density (measured per unit area for the MSA) for commuter rail and light rail but not at all for heavy rail (whether NYC is included or not), as Table 2.14 indicates. The heavy rail pattern may be due to the influence of outlying areas and other factors including how population and area were defined. For all systems, correlations are very weak or non-existent between trips and another density measure, stations per mile of track.

Travel Activity and Physical Characteristics of the Systems Combined: Regression Analysis

The rail-based transit systems in the United States identified in the National Transit Database (NTD) were analysed with respect to system characteristics affecting trip-related travel activity. This was designed as a cross-sectional analysis for the year 2009 for each of the three rail systems separately.

The purpose of the analysis was to analyse and corroborate earlier findings about whether or not trips and/or trip density (trips per station) for rail travel were associated with or predicted by system characteristics such as the number and density of stations, track mileage, and the length of the trip. The potential influence of population size and population density of the service area was also taken into account. As indicated earlier, employment potentially influences transit ridership; however, the ratio of employment to population did not vary much for different MSAs at least for the MSA geographic level (US Census Bureau 2011, p.4), therefore, this supports using population as a surrogate for employment (as well as in its own right) in the type of analysis presented here.

Variable definition and selection
The measures of trip taking and system characteristics were defined by the NTD and in some cases were combined and transformed into indicators. These measures along with their definitions as given in the NTD glossary are listed below and are a subset of those used for the correlation analysis. All variables are annual totals or averages for 2009.

- Dependent variables used for travel activity:
  - Trips (for commuter rail and light rail): Unlinked passenger trips.
  - Trips per station (for heavy rail only): Average number of trips per station.
- Independent variables used primarily for physical characteristics and one travel activity measure for transit systems:
  - Stations: Number of stations.
  - Station density: Stations per square mile of MSA land area.
  - Stations per track mile: Stations per mile of track.
  - Average trip length: Number of miles traveled per trip.

Equations were constructed that included another set of independent variables pertaining to population (run separately for each of these variables):

- Population served (NTD service area)
- Population density (MSA).

Tests for robustness, heteroskedasticity, and multicollinearity were undertaken. A Variance Inflation Factor (VIF) score above 5 indicates a concern about the existence of multicollinearity. Standard guidelines were followed for interpreting the t values for the regression results.

Rationale for the selection of variables

For the dependent variables:

- Number of trips was used for commuter and light rail since it showed the strongest relationships in numerous preliminary regression runs.
- Trips per station was used for heavy rail, since in previous regression runs findings for number of trips were never significant regardless of the structure of the equation. Trips per station was not significant for commuter or light rail.

For the independent variables:

- Number of stations was used instead of miles of track since the two characteristics are highly correlated within all of the systems.
- Trips and miles traveled are also heavily correlated so number of trips was used as the major measure for travel activity.
- Average trip length, which is actually a travel activity measure, was incorporated into the regression equations as an independent variable given its significance and potential influence on the dependent variables.

Results

The results of the regression analyses for each of the three systems are shown in Table 2.15. The overall finding from the regression analyses across all of the systems is a positive association between travel activity (trips or trips per station) and stations, consistent with the correlation analyses. The greater the number of stations, the greater the travel activity. This is significant across all three systems, controlling for stations per track mile, station density, average trip length, and either population served or population density.

Although this finding seems very obvious, that is, people travel more in systems with more infrastructure (stations), the significance is that the direction of the association is clear: the existence of more stations may in fact influence the extent of trip taking in transit systems. People are drawn to stations within the network. Stations are significant nodes in the transit system and afford riders greater access to the system and thus make it easier to use.

One anomaly appeared for heavy rail systems. The number of trips per station was significantly negatively correlated with the number of stations per track mile. This implies that the lower the clustering or concentration

Table 2.15   Regression analysis results

System: Heavy Rail	Dependent variables	
Independent variables	Trips per station	Trips per station
Stations	5.48***	6.361***
	(7.19)	(4.99)
Stations per mile of track	−10,607.8**	−10,659.1**
	(−2.38)	(−2.54)
Station density (per sq. mi.)	3,694.06	−4,456.48
	(1.33)	(−0.81)
Average trip length	−535.95	−615.10**
	(−1.65)	(−2.25)
Population served (NTD)	0.00012	
	(1.29)	
Population density		0.395*
(per sq. mi. MSA)		(1.86)
N	15	15
R-squared	74.0%	74.1%

System: Commuter Rail	Dependent variables	
Independent variables	Trips	Trips
Stations	387,448**	452,397***
	(2.57)	(4.02)
Stations per mile of track	5,172,103	18,500,000
	(0.20)	(0.64)
Station density (per sq. mi.)	0.000	0.00*
	(−1.28)	(−2.05)
Average trip length	−64,083.73	92,782.85
	(−0.89)	(1.62)
Population served (NTD)	2.913**	
	(2.28)	
Population density (MSA)		14,243.56**
		(2.18)
N	25	25
R-squared	85.6%	88.0%

System: Light Rail	Dependent variables	
Independent variables	Trips	Trips
Stations	847,930**	806,360**
	(2.57)	(2.72)
Stations per mile of track	−46,347.15	−63,325.09
	(−0.65)	(−1.00)

Table 2.15   (continued)

System: Light Rail	Dependent variables	
Independent variables	Trips	Trips
Station density	0.00	0.00
	(−1.15)	(−1.29)
Average trip length	−1,907,820	−1,719,861
	(−1.75)	(−1.59)
Population served (NTD)	0.1194265	
	(0.18)	
Population density		5,571.85
(per sq. mi. MSA)		(1.11)
N	30	30
R-squared	45.1%	49.9%

Notes:
*** p <0.01, ** p <0.05, * p <0.10
This table reflects the results of two sets of equations, one using population served and the other using population density. The first column of numbers represent equations run with population served as one of the independent variables and the second column represents population density as one of the independent variables.
Entries in the table represent coefficients and t-scores in parentheses.
All regressions run with robust standard errors.
Technically, dependent variables are outcome variables and independent variables are predictive variables.

Source: Computed from the US DOT, FTA (undated website), National Transit Database 2009.

of stations along a system's track mileage, the greater the number of trips per station. Thus as stations become spread out, travelers will be forced to concentrate their trips between fewer stations. This appears in earlier findings for correlations and descriptive statistics.

One possible explanation is the relationship between trip length and stations per track mile. Length of the trip and the density of stations in terms of number of stations per track mile are negatively or not associated for heavy rail. This suggests that the longer the trip the fewer the stations per track mile and vice versa. This is what would be expected for the very large heavy rail systems which cover long distances and have sparse station coverage in the outer areas. Another factor as indicated earlier may be related to how the population of the MSA is defined in this analysis.

CONCLUSIONS

Several approaches were taken to examine the transportation systems as networks. Concentration indicators, correlations, and regression analysis are used to analyse how travel activity relates to physical infrastructure. All of these analyses primarily focus on concentration as the fundamental network property.

Both road and rail transit systems exhibit levels of concentration both across networks in terms of fewer areas accounting for larger shares of travel and within the networks in terms of intersection points in systems where high levels of travel activity occur.

For road systems, traffic nationwide is concentrated in a few metropolitan areas that also generally have the highest populations. Within metropolitan areas, there are a few intersections that appear routinely as congestion points.

Rail transit is highly concentrated nationwide with just a few systems accounting for most of the infrastructure and travel activity. Heavy rail tends to be more concentrated than commuter rail or light rail. Travel activity is very much a function of the number of stations. Stations provide important nodes that generate travel activity for travelers, or alternatively, system providers may respond to demand at certain locations by providing more stations for access. These transit characteristics have substantial implications for security and environmental goals supported by transit.

First, across the three systems, some differences occur with respect to the concentration of area, physical system, and travel attributes. The comparisons below are for the 50 percent level.

- For all three systems, area and population tend to show less concentration than physical infrastructure or travel activity.
- Heavy rail is the most concentrated with respect to all of the characteristics (area, infrastructure and travel activity) largely due to the dominance of the New York City system. Removing NYC reduces the concentration somewhat, but heavy rail still remains more concentrated than the other two systems for all three types of characteristics. This is confirmed looking at both the concentration of systems in the top 25 percent and top 50 percent of systems and the means.
- For commuter rail, concentration of travel activity and infrastructure usually lies between that of heavy rail and light rail.
- Light rail is less concentrated than commuter rail for both physical infrastructure and travel activity but about equal to commuter rail for MSA land area and population.

Second, within each of the three types of systems, the concentration of travel activity compares with physical characteristics as follows:

- For heavy rail, both travel activity and infrastructure are highly concentrated but in similar ways, whether NYC is included or not.
- For commuter rail, travel activity (in terms of trips and miles traveled) is about equal in concentration to the infrastructure that supports that travel (stations and track mileage).
- For light rail, travel activity (in terms of trips and miles traveled) is more concentrated (located in fewer rail systems) than the infrastructure that supports that travel (stations and track mileage).

Finally, the larger the system, the more complex the network in terms of how many points there are where two or more different transit lines come together.

These characteristics provide an important framework for the chapters that follow as to how transport network characteristics can relate to the needs of environment and security and be resilient or vulnerable in the face of hazards and accidents.

REFERENCES

American Public Transportation Association (APTA) (April 2011), *2011 Public Transportation Fact Book*, Washington, DC, USA: American Public Transportation Association, available at http://apta.com/resources/statistics/Documents/FactBook/APTA_2011_Fact_Book.pdf.

American Society for Civil Engineers (ASCE) (2005), *2005 Report Card for America's Infrastructure*, available at http://www.asce.org/reportcard/2005/index.cfm (accessed November 7, 2005).

American Society for Civil Engineers (ASCE) (2009), *2009 Report Card for America's Infrastructure*, available at www.asce.org/reportcard.

Grava, S. (2003), *Urban Transportation Systems*, New York, NY, USA: McGraw-Hill.

INRIX, Inc. (March 2011), *INRIX National Traffic Scorecard 2010 Annual Report*, available at http://scorecard.inrix.com/scorecard/.

Levinson, D.M. and K.J. Krizek (2008), *Planning for Place and Plexus: Metropolitan Land Use and Transport*, New York, NY, USA and London, UK: Routledge.

Nagurney, A. and Q. Qiang (2009), *Fragile Networks: Identifying Vulnerabilities and Synergies in an Uncertain World*, Hoboken, NJ, USA: Wiley.

National Research Council (2002), *Making the Nation Safer*, Washington, DC, USA: National Academies Press.

Newman, M.E.J. (2010), *Networks: An Introduction*, New York, NY, USA: Oxford University Press.

Niles, J. and L. Callaghan (June 2010), *From Buses to BRT: Case Studies of Incremental BRT Projects in North America*, San Jose, CA, USA: San Jose State University, Mineta Transportation Institute.

Puentes, R. and A. Tomer (December 2008), *The Road . . . Less Traveled: An Analysis of Vehicle Miles Traveled Trends in the US*, Washington, DC, USA: The

Brookings Institution, available at http://www.brookings.edu/~/media/Files/rc/ reports/2008/1216_transportation_tomer_puentes/vehicle_miles_traveled_report .pdf.

Rodrigue, J-P., C. Comtois and B. Slack (2006), *The Geography of Transport Systems*, London, UK and New York, NY, USA: Routledge.

Rodrigue, J-P., C. Comtois and B. Slack (2009), *The Geography of Transport Systems*, 2nd edition, London, UK and New York, NY, USA: Routledge.

Santos, F. (June 2010), 'Yearlong effort will add vans to transit options', *The New York Times*, available at http://www.nytimes.com/2010/06/23/nyregion/23vans. html.

Schrank, D., T. Lomax and B. Eisele (2011), *2011 Urban Mobility Report*, College Station, TX, USA: The Texas A&M University System, Texas Transportation Institute, available at http://tti.tamu.edu/documents/mobility-report-2011-wappx.pdf.

US Census Bureau (2007), *County and City Data Book: 2007*, Washington, DC, USA: The US Census Bureau.

US Census Bureau (2010), *State and Metropolitan Area Data Book: 2010*, 7th edition, Washington, DC, USA: The US Census Bureau.

US Census Bureau (2011), *Employment/Population Ratios for the 50 Largest Metropolitan Statistical Areas: 2008, 2009, and 2010*, Washington, DC, USA: The US Census Bureau, available at http://www.census.gov/prod/2011pubs/ acsbr10-09.pdf.

US Department of Energy, Energy Information Administration (April 2010), *Annual Energy Outlook 2010*, Washington, DC, USA: US Department of Energy, Energy Information Administration, available at http://www.eia.doe. gov/oiaf/aeo/pdf/0383%282010%29.pdf.

US Department of Energy, Energy Information Administration (April 2011), 'Today in energy: vehicle use varies across US regions', US Energy Information Administration based on US Department of Transportation, Highway Statistics 2008, Table PS-1, available at http://205.254.135.24/todayinenergy/detail. cfm?id=1050.

US Department of Transportation (September 2011), 'Rules and regulations, Americans with Disabilities Act of 1990 (ADA)', *Federal Register*, **56** (173), B-10, RU-10.

US Department of Transportation, Federal Highway Administration (2002), 'Status of the Nation's Highways, Bridges, and Transit: 2002 Conditions and Performance Report', Chapter 12 'National Security', available at http://www. fhwa.dot.gov/policy/2002cpr/ch12.htm.

US Department of Transportation, Federal Highway Administration (2010), Glossary, available at http://www.fhwa.dot.gov/policyinformation/statis tics/2010/16_glossary.cfm.

US Department of Transportation, Federal Highway Administration (2011a), 'Highway statistics 2009', available at http://www.fhwa.dot.gov/ policyinformation/statistics/2009/.

US Department of Transportation, Federal Highway Administration (April 2011b), 'Planning, national highway system', available at http://www.fhwa.dot. gov/planning/nhs/.

US Department of Transportation, Federal Highway Administration (2011c) 'Freight facts and figures', available at http://ops.fhwa.dot.gov/freight/freight_ analysis/nat_freight_stats/docs/11factsfigures/index.htm.

US Department of Transportation, Federal Highway Administration (2012), 'Highway statistics 2010', available at http://www.fhwa.dot.gov/policyinformation/statistics/2010/.

US Department of Transportation, Federal Highway Administration, Federal Transit Administration (2010), 'Status of the Nation's Highways, Bridges, and Transit: Conditions and Performance Report to Congress', Washington, DC: US Department of Transportation, Federal Highway Administration and Federal Transit Administration.

US Department of Transportation, Federal Transit Administration (undated website), National Transit Database 2009, available at http://www.ntdprogram.gov/ntdprogram/; http://www.ntdprogram.gov/ntdprogram/data.htm.

US Department of Transportation, Federal Transit Administration, National Transit Database (NTD) (2000), *2000 National Transit Summaries and Trends*, Washington, DC, USA: Federal Transit Administration, available at http://www.ntdprogram.gov/ntdprogram/pubs.htm.

US Department of Transportation, Federal Transit Administration, National Transit Database (NTD) (2010), *2009 National Transit Summaries and Trends*, Washington, DC, USA: Federal Transit Administration, available at http://www.ntdprogram.gov/ntdprogram/pubs.htm.

US Department of Transportation, Federal Transit Administration, National Transit Database (NTD) (2011), *NTD Glossary*, available at http://www.ntdprogram.gov/ntdprogram/Glossary.htm.

US Department of Transportation, Research and Innovative Technology Administration (RITA), Bureau of Transportation Statistics (2011), *National Transportation Statistics 2011*, available at http://www.bts.gov/publications/national_transportation_statistics/pdf/entire.pdf.

Wasserman, D. and K. Faust (2009), *Social Network Analysis: Methods and Applications*, New York, NY, USA: Cambridge University Press.

White, R. (September 2010), 'Where buses once ran, van services start filling gaps', *The New York Times*, available at http://www.nytimes.com/2010/09/14/nyregion/14vans.html?_r=1&scp=1&sq=van%20services&st=cse.

Young, P. (April 2010), *Upward Trend in VMT Resumed: Transportation Trends in Focus*, Washington, DC, USA: Federal Highway Administration, available at http://www.bts.gov/publications/bts_transportation_trends_in_focus/2010_04_01/pdf/entire.pdf.

Zimmerman, R. (2006), 'Critical infrastructure and interdependency,' Chapter 35 in D.G. Kamien (ed.), *The McGraw-Hill Homeland Security Handbook*, New York, NY, USA: McGraw-Hill, pp.523–45.

Zimmerman, R. (2011), ongoing research on the National Transit database, New York, NY, USA: New York University.

3. The climate connection

INTRODUCTION

Transportation networks evolve over time as new public concerns and preferences emerge. They both shape and are shaped by social, political, economic and environmental issues. Public health, land use, air and water quality and other environmental conditions have dominated and continue to dominate transportation debates.

Beginning in the latter part of the 20th century, global climate change and resource use, particularly energy use, that affects climate change, became one of the most critical environmental issues. It shaped what, where, when and how transportation is used. The triangulation of transportation, energy, and climate is a common basic framework for understanding the problem. Approaches based on that framework are presented here for the US including selected international comparisons.

First, the interrelationships among transportation, energy, and climate change underscore the influence of the transportation sector on energy consumption and climate change (for example, Transportation Research Board 2008; Sperling and Cannon 2009; Gilbert and Perl 2008; Kahn Ribeiro et al. 2007; US Department of Energy (DOE), Energy Information Administration (EIA) 2010; US Environmental Protection Agency (EPA) 2010; Davis et al. 2010, 2011; and Mehrotra et al. 2011). One can envision energy use at the top of the pyramid with climate change and transportation at its base. That is, energy is a major factor in the relationship between transportation and climate change, with greenhouse gas (GHG) as an intermediary.

Note that transportation affects climate change in ways other than by its contributions to GHG emissions. For example, the vast network of roadways use surfacing material that can change the reflectivity of the earth's surface or albedo value, which in turn affects heat entrapment in the atmosphere (US EPA c2008) and paved areas, identified for roadways in Chapter 1, can contribute to the release of water and chemicals into natural waterways from land areas (American Rivers undated).

Second, global climate change affects transportation primarily through changes that include the movement of water and heat (Karl et al. 2009). Thus, transportation has not only shaped climate, but has also been shaped by these conditions (Schmidt and Meyer 2009, p.66), though transportation as a cause and consequence has usually been analysed and managed separately. Thus, this opposite and reciprocal relationship, how elements of climate change shape transportation, is evaluated for major climate change impacts – heat and the movement of water. As a context, climate elements most likely to influence transportation are presented along with the science behind how those elements are considered a consequence of climate change. Then their potential impacts on transportation in terms of materials, operational performance, and passenger disruption are presented.

Third, interconnections among energy, transportation, and environment can affect distributional or social equity issues. Differences can arise in transportation access, cost and affordability, suitability, and quality across different sectors of the population locally and globally where shifts in transportation networks occur as an outcome of the effects of climate change and the means to adapt to it. These create the potential for disproportionate social, economic and environmental impacts that are both positive and negative across population groups.

Finally, institutional mechanisms are currently emerging to manage GHGs and their impacts in general, and the extent to which transportation is emphasized is mixed. Institutional mechanisms consist of planning and implementation addressed in Chapter 4 and build upon technology, development and behavior that are a foundation for mitigation and adaptation which are addressed in this chapter. Technological and developmental foundations of mitigation and adaptation include innovations in mode of travel, fuel technology, and travel behavior to mitigate many of the problems the transportation, energy and climate connections create (Randolph and Masters 2008). Key programs are introduced and whether or not these efforts are incorporating transport and at what level of planning. In this chapter, the need for quantification and numeracy underlies the popularity of "footprint" calculators, which can be used as a metric to understand the influence of the transportation component in light of other influences on climate and how to begin to frame mitigation measures. The assumptions and underlying logic of these methods and their results are presented in this chapter along with their potential effect on policy and decision-making.

A more formal institutional mechanism is energy and climate action planning. These plans and planning processes are emerging worldwide, and are aimed at altering how human actions, including the transportation sector, contribute to climate change. The plans are often accompanied by detailed practices that begin to identify and implement planning goals from local to multi-national contexts and integrate technologies to meet those goals. Other mechanisms are the innovations that shape the transport network that require institutional support. One set of innovations is energy conservation measures in the form of fuel efficiency, decreasing carbon content of fuel via low carbon fuel standards, and new fuels (Sperling and Cannon 2009, pp.4–8). Another set consists of entirely new forms of transportation depending on where they draw their energy from such as electric vehicles (Sperling and Cannon 2009, pp.8–10). Still others emphasize behavior, such as decreasing travel and land use changes in the form of compact development. All of these alter transportation networks and the way people use and shape those networks and hence global climate change. Technological and developmental aspects are addressed here and institutional mechanisms are addressed in Chapter 4.

The linkages among these areas and transportation connectivity or the shape of transportation networks are only beginning to be understood or at most are at a conceptual level. Such network alterations if they are occurring may directly or indirectly affect the environment, climate, and resource use as well as the ability to protect transport systems and their users against these hazards. Complicating the picture even further is the fact that the science is changing very rapidly. Transportation is an important lens through which global climate change phenomena and their impacts can be understood.

TRANSPORTATION, ENERGY AND CLIMATE CHANGE

Introduction

Transportation, energy and climate interconnections are key factors in the linkages between transportation and the environment. The Transportation Research Board (TRB) (2008, 2011) in its reports on transportation data needs, cited energy and climate as two areas in which transportation has an important impact and which also impact transportation. Other earlier, more traditional connections between transportation and the environment, such as air and water quality, are addressed in Chapter 5.

The components of the transportation, energy and climate change triangle are first presented in terms of their respective components of emissions, energy consumption, climate changes, and their physical manifestations. Then, the backlash of these climate changes are presented in terms of how they occur as specific impacts on transportation.

According to US EPA and US DOE GHG inventories, GHG emissions have been on the rise in the US as they have been worldwide. In 2009, the US contribution to GHG emissions was 6633.2 teragrams (Tg), expressed as "million metric tons carbon dioxide (CO_2) equivalents", which represented an increase of 7.3 percent over the entire period from 1990 through 2009 or 0.4 percent on average annually (US EPA, April 2011, p.ES-3). In the US these increases in GHG emissions have been occurring while changes in other air pollutants have shown a somewhat different trend, addressed in Chapter 5.

Energy use has been increasing in the US for decades and with the exception of some relatively slight declines in the mid-1970s and 1980s, the trend shows a steady rise since the 1950s until about 2008 (US DOE, Energy Information Administration (EIA) August 2010, p.xix). The transportation component of energy consumption is substantial and has been increasing as well. In 2009, transportation accounted for 27 percent of the total primary energy flow (94.6 quadrillion Btu) of the United States, according to the US Department of Energy (US DOE, EIA August 2010, p.37). As one might expect, energy consumption by transportation has been largely driven by and paralleling increases in fossil fuel consumption with the exception of slight declines in the mid-1970s and mid-1980s, like energy use overall (US DOE, EIA August 2010, p.xix). Fossil fuel consumption is the largest energy consumption sector in the US (US DOE, EIA August 2010, p.xix) and petroleum accounts for the largest portion of fossil fuels (US DOE, EIA August 2010, p.xx). How energy is used shapes the contribution of transportation to GHGs.

The implications of this situation for vehicular and fuel technologies as well as travel behavior is potentially substantial, and has already produced dramatic changes in vehicle mix and fuel usage. The question here is whether or not these relationships and dependencies are likely to shape the way travel occurs in ways that will change transportation networks and alter environmental and security circumstances influenced by these networks.

Transportation and Climate Change

GHG and CO_2 emissions
The impact of transportation on climate change is primarily discussed here in terms of GHG emissions. CO_2 equivalents are often used to represent GHG emissions and to identify trends and patterns in transportation emissions, since CO_2 accounts for a large portion of GHGs. In 2009, CO_2

accounted for 98 percent of net GHG emissions, adjusted for sources and sinks, and 83 percent of total emissions without the adjustment (in terms of Tg CO_2 Eq.) (US EPA, April 2011, pp.ES-4,ES-5, calculated from Table ES-2).

The relationship of transportation and CO_2 emissions (and other GHGs) occurs at several levels. First, is the contribution of transportation-related energy use to CO_2 emissions, then the contribution of one type of transportation energy source – fossil fuels – to CO_2 emissions, and third, the contribution of a major component of fossil fuels – petroleum – to CO_2. Each of these levels is addressed below as the direct contributions of transportation to GHG emissions. In addition to these direct contributions, transportation contributes indirectly to GHG emissions over the course of the life cycle of producing and ultimately disposing of transportation vehicles and their infrastructure including fuel. The US EPA has provided estimates of these additional emissions just for fuel: "for every 100 lb of CO_2 emitted from the burning of conventionally derived gasoline, another 20 to 25 lb of CO_2-equivalent gases is emitted during fuel production and distribution" (TRB 2011, p.32; Partial text, p.32, reproduced with permission of the Transportation Research Board, Copyright, National Academy of Sciences). Dave (2010, p.11) provides estimates for many of the life cycle stages for fuel, infrastructure, and manufacture, maintenance and operation. The category, operating vehicles, ranges from 230 to 420 kg of GHG emissions per passenger mile of travel (PMT) for sedans, SUVs and pickup trucks and 64 to 123 kg of GHG/PMT for selected rail transit systems.

Transportation and GHG emissions
Transportation's share of total GHG emissions (CO_2, CH_4, N_2O and HFCs) expressed in terms of CO_2 equivalents continues to increase, though slowly. Using EPA's estimates of GHGs (both direct emissions and electricity-related emissions), the following patterns and trends are apparent:

- The absolute value of GHG emissions increased through about 2007, but declined in 2008 (to 1895.5 Tg CO_2 Eq.) and again in 2009 (to 1816.9 Tg CO_2 Eq.) with a slight depression in 2006 over 2007 levels (US EPA, April 2011 Table 2-14, pp.2–21).
- Transportation's share of total direct and electricity-related GHG emissions (in CO_2 equivalents) from all US sectors was 27.4 percent in 2009, ranking second to the industry sector (US EPA, April 2011 Table 2-14, pp.2–20). The 2009 share was slightly higher than its share of 26.8 percent in 2008 and higher still than its share of 25 percent in 1990 (US EPA, April 2011 Table 2-14, pp.2–20). It should be noted

that the electricity-related share of total emissions constitutes only a very small portion of transportation emissions. Electricity-related emissions were only 0.1 percent of the total transportation emissions in 1990 (US EPA, April 2011 Table 2-14, pp.2–20).

- US DOE EIA shows similar patterns and trends, since the frame of reference is energy-related CO_2 emissions. According to EIA, although the total absolute amount of energy-related CO_2 declined in all of the major sectors between 2008 and 2009, the share accounted for by the transportation sector went up between those two years. In 2009, transportation accounted for 34.1 percent of CO_2 emissions in the US (US DOE, EIA 2011, p.2). This was a slight increase over the share of 33.1 percent reported for 2008 (US DOE, EIA December 2009, p.2). According to US DOT, BTS data, transportation accounted for 33 percent of the GHG emissions emitted by all US sectors in 2008 (US DOT, BTS Table 4-49).

The origins of CO_2 emissions in the transportation sector are best understood by first addressing fossil fuel combustion in transportation and then focusing on the petroleum component of fossil fuels.

In summary, the transportation sector contributes over a quarter of GHG emissions to about a third of CO_2 emissions according to US EPA and US DOE data, respectively.

Transportation, fossil fuel and petroleum emissions

Fossil fuel combustion-based CO_2 emissions in the transportation sector   The following patterns and trends reinforce the prominence of transportation as a user of fossil fuel and the CO_2 emissions from fossil fuel combustion (US EPA, April 2011, pp.ES-4, ES-5, calculated from Table ES-2 unless indicated otherwise). The patterns and trends below are for CO_2 emissions only. The term "CO_2 emissions" in this section signifies GHG emissions as CO_2 equivalents.

- According to the US EPA, the transportation sector accounted for 33 percent of total CO_2 emissions (not other gases) from fossil fuel combustion only in 2009 up slightly from the 31.4 percent share in 1990 (US EPA, April 2011, p.ES-4, calculated from Table ES-2).
- Transportation CO_2 emissions from fossil fuel combustion in the transportation sector have been increasing at a faster rate than all of the sectors combined. Between 1990 and 2009, CO_2 in all sectors increased by 8 percent, CO_2 emissions from fuel combustion from all sectors using fossil fuel combustion increased by 9.9 percent, but CO_2 emissions from transportation related fossil fuel combustion

increased by much more, that is, by 15.7 percent. (US EPA, April 2011, p.ES-4, calculated from Table ES-2). EPA affirms this noting that "The primary driver of transportation-related emissions was CO_2 from fossil fuel combustion, which increased by 16 percent from 1990 to 2009. This rise in CO_2 emissions, combined with an increase in hydrofluorocarbons from close to zero emissions in 1990 to 60.2 Tg CO_2 Eq. in 2009, led to an increase in overall emissions from transportation activities of 17 percent" (US EPA, April 2011, pp.2–21).

- Between 2008 and 2009, the trends in CO_2 emissions appeared to slow down in part due to the economy and at least in the transportation sector from gains in fuel economy. However, between 2008 and 2009, the rate of decline in CO_2 emissions attributed to fossil fuel combustion in the transportation sector was lower than it was in other sectors. While total US CO_2 emissions declined by 7.0 percent between 2008 and 2009 in all sectors and sources, fossil fuel combustion related CO_2 emissions from all sources declined by 6.4 percent, and transportation CO_2 attributed to fossil fuel combustion declined by only 4.0 percent (US EPA, April 2011, p.ES-4, calculated from Table ES-2).

Note that all figures are calculated from US EPA, April 2011, Table ES-2, unless indicated otherwise. Thus, all of these figures account for a slightly increasing trend in the share of CO_2 emissions accounted for by transportation, implying that transportation is not keeping pace with other sectors in reducing CO_2 emissions.

Petroleum use in transportation The contribution of transportation-related energy use to GHG emissions is dominated by the use of petroleum by road-based vehicles. Petroleum is one sub-sector of fossil fuels. This section addresses the petroleum portion of fossil fuels.

The distribution of fuels within the transportation sector reflects petroleum's dominance. US transportation systems primarily use petroleum, out of a mix of possible fossil and other fuels. According to the US DOE (August 2010, p.37), in 2009, the percentage distribution of fuels in the transportation sector was 94 percent petroleum, 3 percent natural gas, and 3 percent renewable fuel (which includes "conventional hydroelectric power, geothermal, solar/PV, wind, and biomass").

The percentage of the usage of each type of fossil fuel that is accounted for by transportation also reflects transportation's dominance in the petroleum sector and vice versa (US DOE, EIA August 2010, p.37, Tables 1.3, 2.1b–2.1f, 10.3, 10.4):

- Petroleum
  - 72% transportation
  - 22% industry
  - 5% residential and commercial
  - 1% electric power
- Natural gas
  - 3% transportation
  - 32% industry
  - 35% residential and commercial
  - 30% electric power
- Renewable energy
  - 12% transportation
  - 26% industry
  - 9% residential and commercial
  - 53% electric power.

Finally, the consumption of petroleum by transportation has been increasing in absolute terms at least until 2007 and continuously as a share of total petroleum consumption in the US since 1973. US consumption of petroleum by transportation was 9.05 million barrels per day (52.3 percent of the total consumption) in 1973 and in 2007 it was 14.00 million barrels per day or 68.7 percent of the petroleum sector (Davis et al. 2010, pp.1–19). In 2008 and 2009 the consumption dropped to 13.36 million barrels per day and 12.91 million barrels per day respectively; however, the transportation share still increased from 69.8 percent to 71.4 percent respectively (Davis et al. 2010, pp.1–19).

Petroleum and CO_2 emissions　　Petroleum dominates the CO_2 emission picture within the fossil fuel sector. Within a narrower set of fuels that includes coal, natural gas and electricity (but not including renewables), petroleum accounts for 98 percent of the CO_2 emissions within that group (calculated from US DOE, EIA March 2011, p.27).

Given the large amount of petroleum used by transportation and the fact that petroleum dominates the CO_2 picture within the fossil fuel sector, it is not surprising that transportation-related petroleum use accounts for a large portion of CO_2 emissions. According to the US Department of Energy, petroleum use in the US has accounted for most of the energy consumption related CO_2 emissions in the transportation sector, and this has not changed much since 1990 even though the absolute amount of emissions changed.

The CO_2 contribution of the transportation sector by virtue of petroleum use is very high. In 2008, for example, within the transportation sector, the share of CO_2 accounted for by petroleum was 98 percent, that is, 1,889.4 million metric tons of CO_2 out of a total of 1,930.1 million metric tons of CO_2 for all fuel sources in the transportation sector (US DOE, EIA December 2009, p.23).

In 2009, petroleum again accounted for 98 percent of the CO_2 within transportation energy consumption, but the absolute amount from transportation dropped to 1,815.7 million metric tons of CO_2 and the total also dropped to 1,854.5 (US DOE, EIA 2011, p.27).

The US DOE, EIA (April 2010, p.82) does not anticipate the distribution of CO_2 emissions from energy consumption within the transportation sector to vary by type of fossil fuel used through 2035. Overall, EIA (April 2010, p.82) indicates that petroleum accounted for about 40 percent of all CO_2 emissions from all sources and this is not expected to change: "Petroleum, used mainly in the transportation sector, remains the largest source of CO_2 emissions, accounting for 42 percent of the total in 2008 and 41 percent in 2035."

The petroleum sector consists of a number of different types of fuel, for example motor gasoline and distillate fuel. Within the petroleum sector, motor gasoline ranks first in the contribution to CO_2 emissions, accounting for about two-thirds (62.7 percent) of the petroleum CO_2 emissions followed by distillate fuel accounting for about one-third (35.6 percent) (US DOE, EIA March 2011, Table 11, p.27).

Geographic variations in transportation GHG emissions
The share that transportation emissions are of total emissions varies geographically, by state and sub-state areas within the US and from country to country. As Zimmerman and Faris (2011) observe, New York City and King County, Washington reflect a contrast in how transportation contributes to GHG emissions and hence the focus on emission reduction. Some examples follow for New York City.

New York City illustrates how transportation policy and GHG emission information are interrelated. New York City's 2011 GHG emissions inventory for 2010 underscores the fact that buildings, not transportation, account for the majority of the energy use and emissions – 75 percent of the total (New York City 2011, p.11). They use that information as the basis for prioritizing changes in building codes as a means of reducing GHG emissions.

- According to the 2011 inventory, the transportation sector accounts for 21 percent of NYC's emissions of CO_2 equivalents for 2010 (New York City 2011, p.10), which was a slight increase over what was reported in its 2010 inventory of 20 percent for 2009 (New York City 2010, p.6).

- The City indicates a per capita level of emissions of CO_2 equivalents of 6.5 metric tons citing the US EPA 2010 inventory of GHGs (New York City 2011, p.3), which is about a third of the US average of 19.0.
- Over three-quarters of New York City's commuters (76.7 percent) use non-automobile forms of sustainable transportation (New York City 2011, p.3).
- The previous inventory reported that in 2009, 54.5 percent do not have cars, and 9.9 percent walk to work (New York City 2010, p.7).
- However, automobile usage is still prominent in the transportation sector. Of the transportation total for 2010, road-based vehicles accounted for 92 percent (with passenger cars accounting for 69 percent of that) and rail and subways accounted for the remaining 8 percent (New York City 2011, p.10).
- The City's 2011 priority is buildings, though other actions are in place to promote non-motorized forms of travel. However, its 2010 inventory (for 2009) indicated several transportation-related factors contributed to the City's footprint decline of 4.2 percent between 2008 and 2009: a reduction in the use of transit fuel, fuel economies, and reduced usage of vehicles as well as efficiency in street lighting and signaling (New York City 2010, pp.12–13), though these figures tend to vary slightly from year to year.
- Transportation seemed to fare slightly less well in 2010 than in 2009 (see Table 3.1). While citywide emissions increased by 10 percent, transportation emissions increased by 14 percent even though the percent change in transportation as a share of total emissions was only 5 percent.

Where different types of fuel are used by mode over time reveals important patterns and trends in New York City's transportation energy use as shown in Table 3.2.

Other information on characteristics of transportation in New York City, reported from the 2010 American Community Survey, indicates strong use of transit, biking and walking in New York City, all of which reduce emissions; however, there is a high degree of variability from neighborhood to neighborhood. Bernstein (2011) summarizes some of the findings for commuting to work in New York City:

- Transit and walking are common throughout the City, except in the boroughs of Staten Island and the eastern part of Queens.
- The area with the highest proportion of walkers is Lower Manhattan (about one-third of the residents there).

Table 3.1   Transportation emissions (GHGs), New York City, 2009 and 2010

	2009*	2010**	% change
Transportation share of total emissions	20%	21%	5.0%
Transportation emissions	10 MMT	11.4 MMT	14.0%
Total emissions	49.3 MMT	54.3 MMT	10.1%

Note: MMT = million metric tons.

Sources:
*   New York City (September 2010), *PlaNYC Inventory of New York City Greenhouse Gas Emissions*, pp.23, 25, available at http://nytelecom.vo.llnwd.net/o15/agencies/planyc2030/pdf/greenhousegas_2010.pdf. [for 2009].
**   New York City (September 2011), *PlaNYC Inventory of New York City Greenhouse Gas Emissions*, pp.9, 10, available at http://nytelecom.vo.llnwd.net/o15/agencies/planyc2030/pdf/greenhousegas_2011.pdf. [for 2010].
The City's emissions inventory provided more detailed emissions and changes over time (New York City (September 2011), *PlaNYC Inventory of New York City Greenhouse Gas Emissions*, pp.34–5).

Table 3.2   Changes in energy consumed for transport, New York City (citywide), 2005 through 2010

| | % change in amount consumed ||
	2009–2010	2005–2010
Gasoline (passenger cars)	0.36	2.37
Electricity (street lights and traffic signals)	−12.47	−25.46
Electricity (subway and commuter rail)	−6.87	3.00

Source: Adapted from New York City (September 2011), *PlaNYC Inventory of New York City Greenhouse Gas Emissions*, p.33.

- Citywide, the use of transit has slightly and statistically significantly increased. In 2006 it was 54.2 percent and in 2010, 55.7 percent.
- Similarly, the use of cars fell from its 2006 level of 23.6 to 22.7 percent in 2010 and carpooling fell from 5.7 to 5.0 percent over the same time period.

Seattle, in contrast, has placed a heavy emphasis upon reducing transportation emissions at least from government vehicles. The City notes that the transportation facilities used by the City are a substantial user of energy compared to its other operations. Fifty-three percent of the energy used by King County's government is used by the King County Transit

Division of which 43 percent is accounted for by diesel (King County, WA 2010, p.4).

Challenges in emission measurement

The US DOT, FHWA (2008, pp.35–6) identified challenges to adapting analytical methods for estimating GHG from transport. Although they recognize that it is easier to estimate CO_2 emissions than the criteria air pollutants regulated under the Clean Air Act that have dominated air quality management since the mid-twentieth century, there are still complexities that have to be overcome, such as adapting GHG inventories from one scale to another and adapting emission models to assess transportation.

The latency effect of emission controls

Even if inputs of GHGs into the atmosphere completely cease immediately, there are a number of estimates of how long it will take to stabilize GHG concentrations and temperatures. This will have a profound effect on how transportation networks are planned and adapted. If in fact, as Matthews and Caldeira (2008, p.1) and others indicate, the effects on climate change are irreversible beyond a certain stabilization point (which is influenced by CO_2 emissions), a course of action before and after climate stabilization that emphasizes adaptation will be critical. The estimates for the stability point range from 30 years for the removal of half of the CO_2 in the atmosphere in the IPCC 2007 report (Denman et al. 2007, p.501; Eby et al. 2009, p.2501) to many centuries or even many thousands of years usually for complete removal (Denman et al. 2007, p.501; Matthews and Caldeira 2008, p.1; Eby et al. 2009, pp.2501–2; Solomon et al. 2009, p.1704). Ewing et al. (2007, p.13) underscored the need to reduce 1990 CO_2 levels 15–30 percent by 2020 and by 2050 to reduce it by 60–80 percent to stabilize CO_2 in the US.

Transportation and Energy: Factors Associated with Transportation Energy Use and GHG Emissions at the Vehicle Level

The previous section focused on transportation emissions and their relationship to emissions produced by the fuels traditionally used in transportation. What follows is another part of the triangle – the relationship between transportation and energy focusing on factors that contribute to that relationship which at the vehicle level provides a foundation for the emissions picture discussed previously. The transportation and energy connection is a function of a number of factors. These include the mode and vehicular mix of travel, fuel usage or fuel economy, the fuel mix, characteristics of vehicle operation (speed) and many other factors. These have been combined in different ways for different strategies, but remain as among the key components. For example, Cambridge Systematics, Inc. (2009, p.11) has aggregated a number of individual factors into a three pronged set of transportation strategies to address climate change.

Travel indicators show increasing trends for fossil fuel powered, road-based travel by automobiles and trucks as reflected in the number of vehicles in use as measured by vehicle registrations, Vehicle Miles of Travel (VMT) and Trips (US DOT, FTA 2010). To the extent that transportation is linked to energy use and climate change, one would expect the patterns and trends in these indicators to parallel those for energy use and GHG emissions taking into account fuel economies.

Vehicle use
Passenger cars account for the largest share of the number of vehicles in use (Davis et al. 2011, p.3-5). Davis et al. (2011, p.3-9) reported that in the US 828.04 cars per thousand people were in use in 2009. This represents a 3.5 percent increase since 2000 (though the increase has not been steady with declines and increases occurring periodically since about the mid-2000s) and many thousandfold since 1900 at the outset of the motor revolution. The US still exceeded many other areas in terms of vehicles per thousand people with Canada, Western Europe, and the Pacific following the US in that order (Davis et al. 2011, p.3-8). In 2009, US car registrations accounted for 19.4 percent of car registrations in fourteen selected countries including the US (Davis et al. 2011, p.3-2) and US truck and bus registrations accounted for 40.8 percent in those same countries (Davis et al. 2011, p.3-3).

Extent of travel: vehicle miles of travel (VMT) by type of vehicle
In the US in 2009, vehicle miles traveled (VMT) equaled 2.954 trillion miles (Davis et al. 2011, p.3-10). Passenger cars accounted for 52.7 percent of VMT and two-axle, four-tire trucks accounted for 36.4 percent (Davis et al. 2011, p.3-10). As indicated in Chapter 2, VMT have been increasing steadily for many decades, though since 2006, the trend has been somewhat unstable, attributed primarily to economic conditions. What contributes to VMT has been a constant source of debate. Population density for example, has commonly been put forth as a factor in reducing VMT though the relationships are complicated by other factors. Cervero and Murakami (2010) found, for example, that VMT per capita was negatively related to population density for 370 metropolitan areas, suggesting that compact areas will have lower VMT; however, the degree to which the relationship held was reduced (but still negative) by the existence of dense urban road networks that enable people in those areas to access retail and commercial activity by car.

Vehicular petroleum consumption
The passenger vehicle and other light duty vehicles are large consumers of energy in the form of petroleum-based fossil fuels, and the transportation network in large part reflects the network of sources of supplies and the network of distribution centers. According to Davis et al. (2011 p.1-15), in 2010 the use of petroleum by transportation accounted for 172.5 percent of the production of petroleum domestically reflecting reliance on imported petroleum, though this represents a slight decline since the mid-2000s consistent with the trends in number of vehicles and VMT. Davis et al. (2011, p.1-15) indicate that the overall dependence on imported petroleum was 50 percent of total US consumption of petroleum in 2010.

GHG emissions by vehicle type
According to the US EPA (April 2011, p.2-22), in 2009, within the transportation sector, passenger cars accounted for 34.5 percent and light duty trucks accounted for 30.3 percent of all GHG emissions expressed in CO_2 equivalents or together, these two sectors account for almost two-thirds of the transportation emissions nationwide. Medium and heavy duty trucks accounted for about another fifth of the emissions. These percentages for 2009 represent a modest increase over 2008 figures which were 33.4 and 29.2 percent for passenger cars and light duty trucks respectively of the GHG emissions expressed in CO_2 equivalents (calculated from US EPA April 2010, Table 2-15, p.2-24). Rail in contrast accounted for only 2.4 percent of the GHG emissions in 2009 (US EPA April 2011, p.2-22).

Looking at the patterns in another way, in all of the transportation sectors as is typical of GHG emissions in general, CO_2 accounts for by far the largest share of GHG emissions. These percentages are 95.2 percent, 93.4 and 96.6 percent for passenger cars, light duty trucks, and medium and heavy duty trucks respectively. N_2O was the second highest ranking GHG. For rail emissions, 93.8 percent were for CO_2, and HFCs were the second highest ranking GHG. (All figures calculated from US EPA April 2011, pp.2–22).

This pattern in transportation emissions varies geographically. As indicated above, NYC noted that the transportation sector as a whole accounted for only 21 percent of citywide emissions of CO_2 equivalents (11.4 million metric tons (MMT)) in 2010 (New York City 2011, p.12). Of the 2010 amount, passenger cars accounted for the largest share of CO_2 in the transportation sector, 69 percent (New York City 2011, p.12) which is almost double the share that passenger car CO_2 is of the transportation sector in the country as a whole. The rest of the shares in NYC are accounted for by light trucks 9 percent, heavy trucks 9 percent, subway 6 percent, bus 5 percent, and rail 2 percent. By fuel type gasoline accounted for 77 percent and diesel 14 percent (New York City November 2011, p.12).

How fuel is used: fuel economy

Fuel economy, defined as the amount of fuel used per mile of travel, is a significant factor in CO_2 emissions.

Several factors have led to the changes in fuel economy, primarily related to vehicle mix by age and type and VMT (US EPA April 2011, p.2-21). Auto emissions including conventional pollutants and those contributing to GHGs, however, typically vary by operating conditions such as speed and whether the car is starting from a hot or cold start (US EPA April 2011, pp.3–7). Annual CO_2 emissions nationwide are estimated at 4.2 tons at 45 miles per gallon (mpg) versus 12.4 tons at 15 mpg (US DOE and US EPA 2011, p.2). The Transportation Research Board (1995, p.50) cites studies indicating that grams per mile of CO_2 are highest at average trip speeds below about 20 miles per hour and above about 55 miles per hour.

Idling also affects fuel economy and emissions. Salt Lake City, Utah, for example, is funded for a VMT reduction program to reduce GHGs, and noted that idling is done on average for between five and ten minutes daily and identified the following effects of idling (Daley 2010): ten seconds of idling equals the amount of gas used to restart a car, two minutes of idling equals fuel used for a one mile trip, and one hour of idling uses about a gallon of gasoline. The American Transportation Research Institute (January 2012) gives examples of about 30 states and numerous localities within them in the US that have regulations to control idling usually designed, for example, in terms of time and temperature and vary according to these parameters. They also identify exemptions.

THE BACKLASH: CLIMATE CHANGE IMPACTS ON TRANSPORTATION

Introduction

Climate change entered the public agenda relatively recently compared with other environmental issues, yet it shares much in common with them. Initially thought to be a relatively slow moving crisis, it appears that new developments in the form of rapid release of water from ice melting and increased precipitation as well as projections of ongoing trends point to a hastening of the impacts. It is now a crisis. Relationships between weather extremes and climate change have become a key focus of climate change science and policy. Although not all extreme weather events originate from climate change and the connection has been considered by some to be difficult to make or make uniformly (Gillis 2011; Knutson et al. 2008), there is growing evidence that many are connected to climate change (Emanuel 2005; Emanuel et al. 2008). Wigley (2009), for example, examines the possibility of shorter return periods (time it takes a storm to return to a location) or more frequent extremes of warming with climate change.

An understanding of the kinds of climatic effects that are likely to occur is needed to assess the impacts on transportation and the associated effects on social and economic conditions related to transportation.

Based on climatic observations, the Intergovernmental Panel on Climate Change (IPCC) concluded for temperature impacts that, "Warming of the climate system is unequivocal" (IPCC 2007, p.2).

The impacts of climate change, their likelihood and the confidence levels in these likelihood assessments are also presented in the IPCC reports.

The expression of likelihood is based on the IPCC (Solomon et al. 2007 p.23) likelihood assessments. These are probabilities of occurrence equal to ">99% (virtually certain), >95% (extremely likely), >90% (very likely), >66% (likely), >50% (more likely than not), 33–66% (about as likely as not), <33% (unlikely), <10% (very unlikely), <5% (extremely unlikely), and <1% (exceptionally unlikely)" (Solomon et al. 2007 p.23). Solomon et al. (2007, p.22) also give confidence levels in terms of chance.

Given these categories, the IPCC rated the likelihood of specific occurrences based on when they did occur, would occur, and the likelihood of human contribution. The phenomena are (Solomon et al. 2007, p.52):

- "Warmer and fewer cold days and nights over most land areas
- Warmer and more frequent hot days and nights over most land areas
- Warm spells/heat waves. Frequency increases over most land areas
- Heavy precipitation events. Frequency (or proportion of total rainfall from heavy falls) increases over most areas
- Area affected by droughts increases
- Intense tropical cyclone activity increases
- Increased incidence of extreme high sea level (excludes tsunamis)."

Each phenomenon and its direction was then assigned a likelihood of occurrence (based on Solomon et al. 2007, p.52):

- All of the phenomena were either likely (in all or some regions) or very likely to have occurred in the latter part of the twentieth century.

- The observed trends were either likely or more likely than not to have been the result of human contributions.
- Through projected twenty-first century conditions, most were also likely or very likely to occur, but for some (cold and hot days and nights) it was virtually certain they would occur.

These categories have been adopted and adapted by individual cities, for example, for New York City (New York City Panel on Climate Change (NPCC) 2009, p.7).

This nomenclature provides a way of characterizing uncertainty by combining precise numerical estimates or ranges with a non-numeric scale. Its purpose is to provide a consistent mapping across the different kinds of GCC outcomes. However, Spiegelhalter et al. (2011, p.1394) point out that consistency in the application and interpretation is critical in order to make it work, which is difficult to achieve.

Though categorizing GCC impacts may be fraught with difficulties and uncertainties, the overall patterns and trends in GCC impacts have been formulated. We are now facing the extremes, and these have potentially serious ramifications for transportation and the services it provides.

- Wet areas will become wetter, dry areas drier (Karl et al. 2009, p.45). Moreover, recent studies show that these changes in precipitation are associated with human activity.
- Storms such as tropical cyclones and hurricanes are expected to increase in the more severe categories (Emanuel 2005).
- Increasing temperatures underway for decades are expected to continue and possibly become greater, and although trends indicate that temperature changes are not evenly distributed around the world, the global average is increasing (IPCC 2007). Moreover, looking at extremes the annual average temperature records show increases in temperature anomalies in the past decade with each of the years in the decade of the 2000s ranking from 1 to 11 over a 130-year period (NOAA NCDC 2012).
- All of these phenomena with the addition of rapid ice melt point to increasing sea level rise and other sources of potential inundation of exposed transportation systems by water. Since coastal areas are where the densest populations reside, house the majority of the population, and are the fastest growing areas of the US and elsewhere (Wilson and Fischetti 2010), they are particularly vulnerable to sea level rise. Given the history of cities, where coastal locations were sought for early industrial and maritime needs, the

infrastructure in coastal cities will become the most vulnerable to sea level rise.
- Within many of these cities, transportation infrastructure was traditionally located by the coast or in flood plains, thus transportation is vulnerable to the effects of sea level rise.

The Transportation Research Board (TRB) report on impacts of climate change on transportation identified the following similar aspects of climate change that are specifically of significance for transportation (TRB 2008, p.2-50, partial text, p.2. Copyright, National Academy of Sciences, Washington, DC, 2008. Reproduced with permission of the Transportation Research Board, Table 2-1):

- "Increases in very hot days and heat waves,
- Increases in Arctic temperatures,
- Rising sea levels,
- Increases in intense precipitation events, and
- Increases in hurricane intensity."

The first and fourth they regard as very likely, and others, for example, increased Arctic temperatures and increases in sea levels, are regarded as virtually certain (TRB 2008, p.3). The National Research Council (2011) also emphasized heat and precipitation extremes as climate change factors having major effects on transportation.

The previous section dealt with climate change and its manifestations. Climate changes have potentially severe implications for the integrity of transportation systems. These threats are now well-recognized (Kahn Ribeiro et al. 2007; Schmidt and Meyer 2009; TRB 2008; US Climate Change Science Program 2008; US Climate Change Science Program 2009; National Research Council 2011). The problem depends largely on where transportation systems are located relative to the manifestations of climate change. Although these threats may be seen as largely local problems the vast interconnections of both road and rail systems make them at least regional if not national in scope.

In the sections that follow, three types of effects are addressed: heat, sea level rise and rapid ice melt, and storms.

Heat

Increasing temperatures are a major driver of climate changes. The term global warming was used in 1975 by Broecker (1975, p.460; Harding 1995). Although it is difficult to identify any single temperature that is applicable to all transportation systems under different conditions, the impacts of excessive and at least extreme and persistent heat on transportation systems and their users is a reality.

Selected temperature patterns and trends

The IPCC (Solomon et al. 2007, p.37) indicates that average global mean temperature change "from the period 1850–1899 to the period 2001–2005 is 0.76 °C ±0.19 °C".

The heat effect is measured in a number of ways: as an absolute measure of temperature and the degree of change in that temperature disaggregated spatially and temporally. Global temperature is expressed in terms of means, anomalies and extremes. The National Oceanic and Atmospheric Administration (NOAA) defines an anomaly as a difference from some average or reference temperature (NOAA December 2011). Another definition is the number of degree-days exceeding a certain temperature. Yet another way is defining an extreme heat event as one in which temperatures (minimums, maximums and averages) exceed a given percentile defined over a certain period of time (Stone et al. 2010, p.1426). Heat has traditionally been measured in different ways for different purposes. Some aim at protecting human health and livelihoods such as the National Weather Service Heat Index Scale (NOAA NWS undated website) and the Heat Stress Index (NOAA NCDC undated website). Others aim at protecting materials and structures.

Jones (2010), citing Brohan et al. (2006) indicates that between 1850 and 2009 15 of the warmest years occurred in terms of global temperature and 14 of those occurred in the 1995 to 2009 time period.

NOAA NCDC (January 2011 updated September 2011) came to a similar conclusion, expressing it differently: "Each of the 10 warmest average global temperatures recorded since 1880 have occurred in the last thirteen years. The warmest years on record are 2005 and 2010." Moreover, NOAA reported that four states had attained record high temperatures in 2011 and three had attained such records in 2010. NOAA's *State of the Climate Global Analysis* report identified record temperatures across the globe in 2011 and the decade preceding that year (NOAA NCDC 2012).

Geographic, seasonal, and daytime versus nighttime variations are well-recognized. Seasonal differences depend on location with the northern hemisphere increasing in temperature in winter months and the southern hemisphere increasing but not as much (IPCC 2007).

Impact of heat on transportation

Heat can affect the facilities and operation of transportation by affecting materials. Materials such as concrete, asphalt, steel, and resins become less resilient to persistent heat. Commuter rail lines use overhead electric lines connected with catenaries that prevent sagging, but they have limited tolerances. When they sag too much from extreme heat, trains can lose power and also become entangled in them (US DOT, FTA 2011, p.23). Joints also may not operate as designed under extremes of heat.

Heat can have both structural effects and effects on materials that comprise transportation infrastructure as well as operational impacts on vehicles. Environmental factors play a key role in how severe the impacts are.

Materials are destroyed after prolonged exposure to heat, if they are not adapted to withstand that heat. The spreading of rail lines both along parallel and curved track, for example, due to heat can cause derailment. Rail joints are designed to accommodate a certain amount of expansion, but excessive heat can exceed those limits (US DOT, Federal Motor Carrier Safety Administration 2011).

(1) Steel buckles and bends   During extreme heat episodes various components of rail systems can become disrupted and in fact have done so. Such components include switches, track, track connections and joints, and power systems. Heat creates buckling, which is defined as a misalignment that can cause a derailment and buckles are also called "sun kinks" (Dobney et al. 2009, p.245, citing ORR 2008). US DOT, FTA (2011) has identified a number of the specific impacts of heat on rail lines as follows. One effect of buckling is expanding the distance between the rail lines so that train wheels can no longer connect to the rails. This can be more severe on curves. If switches are affected, the rail lines may not lock properly in position. Different materials will also have different heat tolerances. The operation of trains traveling over rail lines frequently and at high speed can probably add to the temperature impact on the rail lines. Trains are typically slowed down or stopped until rail lines can cool down (Kish and Clark 2009). The major impact of buckling or the threat of buckling in the short term is to delay or slow down travel, and a more extreme long term impact is damage to the rail requiring it to be replaced (US DOT, FTA 2011, p.22). The US DOT, FTA (2011, pp.20–21) identifies numerous cases for rail transit where buckling and other system aberrations occurred associated with heat in Boston, Washington, DC, Baltimore, and Philadelphia, particularly when temperatures exceed 90 degrees.

Some have attributed the vulnerability of rail to buckling to the replacement of rails with joints that used to allow expansion with welded rail lines that are not as flexible (Associated Press 2002). The US DOT Volpe Center (c2002) attributes buckling to "high compressive forces, weakened track conditions, and vehicle loads (train dynamics)", and point out that the distortion of rails can range from 6 to 12 inches for curved rail and 12 to 28 inches for parallel track.

Karl et al. (2009, p.65) underscore the problem also in the context of climate change pointing out that steel tracks can become deformed, producing reduced speed or at the extreme, derailments. They identify a 100 °F air temperature as a threshold that can produce equipment failure.

Dobney et al. (2009) derived a formula to convert air temperature to rail temperature in which air temperature was approximately equal to two-thirds of the rail temperature. Speed reduction was generally considered a measure to prevent increasing heat from the movement of trains. They mapped the delay times due to reductions in speed, and their findings indicate that delays begin to dramatically rise in the vicinity of 35 °C due to buckling.

Some data trends exist to determine whether or not the extent of the heat problem for transportation systems is changing. The US DOT Federal Railroad Administration (FRA) and the American Association of Railways have indicated that the incidence of heat-related derailments has declined from 174 accidents in 1980 to 44 in 2001 (Associated Press 2002). The US DOT Volpe Center (c2002) reported a low of 20 derailments to a high of over 40 derailments per year between 1992 and 2002 with costs continuing to rise to over $15 million by 2002. In 2008, however, the US DOT FRA (2008) statistics still indicated the persistence of the problem with 50 derailments occurring in 2006 and 34 in 2007 due to track buckling, resulting in $13 million and $14 million in reportable damages in each of the two years respectively.

Numerous incidents of the failure of transportation facilities due to the buckling of steel rail have been attributed at least in part to high temperatures. A few among many examples are given below. On July 29, 2002 a derailment of an Amtrak train in Kensington, Maryland was attributed to heat effects on the rail, resulting in over 100 injuries (Associated Press 2002). On July 18, 2006 temperatures in New York City created subway shutdowns due to the buckling of rail lines, for example, the A train from the Rockaways to Manhattan was shut down due to buckling of the third rail (Vasquez 2006). On October 12, 2006 a train derailed near Melbourne, Australia, which was attributed to buckling and generally to the conversion to welded rail (Office of the Chief Investigator 2006). In January 2009 extreme heat caused buckling of rail lines in Adelaide, Australia, resulting in closures, reduction in speed, and the use of old trams to substitute for those affected by the high temperatures (Railpage.com.au 2009). In the summer of 2011, train derailments due to heat in the Houston, Texas, area were reported to have delayed shipments there. The New York area commuter rail line, the New Haven line, experienced severe heat related impairment on July 22, 2011. Temperatures reached extremes and persisted. The report of the event went as follows (MTA 2011, p.6): "At 1:34 PM, a switch between Green's Farms and Southport became stuck in one position. The heat had so expanded the rails that they were unable to lock properly in any other direction." "At 1:42 PM, a Track Foreman reported that the heat had caused the rail to expand to such a degree that it disturbed the track alignment in the Rowayton area. While it was determined that trains could operate over this heat 'kink' in the rail, they were restricted to 30 mph. This speed restriction was later lowered to 10 mph and expanded to the area between Rowayton and South Norwalk" (MTA 2011, p.7).

(2) Concrete and asphalt   Concrete is a ubiquitous material. Wikipedia notes that "Concrete is used more than any other man-made material in the world (citing Lomberg 2001). As of 2006, about 7.5 cubic kilometers of concrete are made each year – more than one cubic meter for every person on Earth (citing the USG.S. 2007)." A large proportion of urban area is devoted to pavement. In Chapter 1 some initial numbers were cited, indicating that anywhere from a fifth to two-thirds of urban areas are paved for road-related uses.

Concrete and asphalt are commonly used as transportation materials for roadways, bridges, and rail. Although these materials are being adapted to increase their resiliency, they will be in common use for some time. Over land, Karl et al. (2009, p.65, citing Field et al. 2007) indicate that road materials such as asphalt can soften and become deformed from roadway traffic, and they identify a 90°F air temperature as a key threshold for these effects. In connection with rail tolerances, the US DOT, FTA (2011) also identifies this temperature level for the northeast with higher thresholds for warmer areas.

(3) Vehicle integrity   Heat can also affect vehicle operation. Vehicles can overheat and tires can deteriorate (Karl et al. 2009, p.65, citing National Research Council 2008). The rate of evaporation of transportation fuels is altered under extreme temperature conditions and emissions can also be affected. Other impacts pertain to commercial vehicles, in particular refrigeration trucks will require increased refrigeration to preserve perishable goods (Karl et al. 2009, p.65, citing Kafalenos et al. 2008). The US DOT FTA (2011, p.23) notes that air conditioning can fail on transit vehicles in heat waves. The severity of the impact of heat on materials is related to how vehicles operate. If a heavy vehicle or many vehicles in heavy traffic are sitting on a road bed or bridge for extended periods of time, the effect on road material is likely to be more severe than in fast moving traffic (Zimmerman 1996).

Hurricanes

The details of hurricanes and their impacts on transportation are presented in Chapter 6 in the context of natural hazards. Their association with global climate change, an ongoing debate as to whether or not hurricanes are an outcome of global climate change, is underway in the scientific literature (Emanuel 2005; Emanuel et al. 2008; Knutson et al. 2008). This is addressed in Chapter 6, and there is growing evidence for the connection (Environment 360, 2011).

Precipitation and Flooding

Two observations of the IPCC (2007), their supporting evidence regarding precipitation (Solomon et al. 2007), and research subsequent to the report (for example, Min et al. 2011), are significant for the relationship between precipitation and climatic change. These studies show that first, rainfall has been increasing and this in turn has been shown to be related to increasing warming, though the trend varies geographically. Second, human actions are likely to contribute to this increment of change or at least a significant part of it (Solomon et al. 2007, p.52).

According to the IPCC 2007 report (Solomon et al. 2007, Chapter 9, Section 9.5.4.1 citing Trenberth et al. 2005), it is anticipated that atmospheric moisture will increase as the climate warms. Trenberth et al. (2005, p.1) observe positive trends in precipitation (precipitable water) and ocean wide as averaging 0.40 ± 0.09 mm per decade or $1.3\pm0.3\%$ per decade, respectively, (with confidence intervals of 95 percent) between 1988 and 2003.

The role of human actions in increasing precipitation is pertinent to mitigation. Given that transportation accounts for a substantial portion of GHG emissions, in that sense it is also a contributor to increasing precipitation.

Min et al. (2011, p.380) tracked the trends in precipitation globally from 1951–99 for North America and Eurasia and concluded that extreme precipitation is becoming more intense, global models are underestimating the intensity, and that this trend is due to human contributions.

Pall et al. (2011, p.382) studied the year 2000 flooding episodes in England and Wales. Using models, they estimated that for nine out of ten of the severe events, anthropogenic inputs to GHGs contributed directly to about 20 percent of the flooding. For two out of three of the events the contribution was estimated to be 90 percent. Events were river runoff used to reflect flooding episodes.

Sachs and Myhrvold (2011) report on the results of the movement of the Intertropical Convergence Zone (ITCZ) which is a band of rainfall in the tropics that influences El Nino and La Nina, and predict, as have other studies cited above, that some areas will become wetter such as El Salvador and Manila while others in South America will become drier (Sachs and

Myhrvold 2011 p.65). As the rain band moves north, they indicate, it also pushes dry zones north that could affect the US, and the authors point to the southeastern US droughts as possible evidence of this. Thus, according to many of these studies, the movement of the band brings rain when it is directly over an area or drought when it moves drier air in front of it.

In addition to global studies pointing to the increasing trend in precipitation, a number of localized studies in the US have confirmed this trend as well, for example, for New York City (NPCC 2010) and Boston (Kirshen et al. 2008).

The vulnerability of transportation to increased precipitation potentially occurs in several ways. At one extreme, in areas with increasing or persistent drought, moisture is needed to retain the road structure. This could become more serious when combined with high temperatures. At the other extreme, flooding from excessive rainfall produces impairment of road and rail operations that can undermine their operations from intermittent closures, rerouting, and congestion, depending on the nature of the drainage conditions. Sudden or persistent precipitation can and already does cause massive flooding of road and rail networks and undermining of the supporting foundations. As the US DOT, FTA (2011, p.14) observes, the areas forecasted to become wetter, that is, northeastern and north central US, are also the areas in which some of the oldest and largest rail systems exist with the greatest amount of ridership. Many instances of flooding have already had severe impacts on transportation particularly for transit systems nationwide (Zimmerman 2005). One of the more noteworthy ones was the August 8, 2007 rainstorm in New York City that stopped transit throughout the City with 19 line segments identified as having reduced or no service (MTA 2007, p.28). During that event, record rainfall fell in the space of just a few hours. This has occurred periodically in the New York City system. On September 8, 2004, although only seven lines were listed as having reduced or no service (MTA 2007, p.28), these and other disruptions occurred at critical nodes in the system (MTA 2007, p.21). The impact of intense precipitation is compounded by the locational choices that have been made not only for operating rail and road systems but for vehicle storage areas as well. New Orleans buses, vital to emergency transport during Hurricane Katrina, were largely underwater (Litman 2006). The US DOT, FTA (2011, p.16) note the vulnerability of bus depots in Nashville, Honolulu, and Portland located at low elevations.

Precipitation during winter storms results in massive snowstorms that have similarly brought transportation to a halt. NOAA NWS data indicates that in NYC the snowstorm of 1998 was a record and the one in December 2010 ranked among the six highest snowfalls in the area. It brought transportation to a standstill. This case and its implications for transportation are covered in Chapter 6.

The persistence, increased frequency and intensity of precipitation events or the lack thereof illustrate the complexity and interrelatedness of actions that revolve around transportation and associated management and communication systems.

Sea Level Rise

Sea level rise has become a key focus of climate change impacts. According to the IPCC (2007) it is associated with many factors such as increasing temperature resulting in the thermal expansion of water and sea ice melting as well as increasing precipitation. In the long term, sea level rise has the potential for producing major changes in transportation routes. Changing road and rail routes will be particularly challenging given the often constrained transportation routes that exist in coastal and other areas in close proximity to waterways. On the other hand, water-based transit may become more feasible. These options are discussed more fully below; however, first, the extent of the problem and its consequences for transportation and the impacted populations are presented.

Estimates of sea level rise

Sea level rise from climate change is now estimated to be substantial in the twenty-first century. It can potentially produce persistent disruption of transportation facilities located in areas that are inundated.

Bindoff et al. (2007, p.419) and Solomon et al. (2007, p.50) summarize the IPCC's estimates of sea level rise globally. For the period 1961–2003, the observed average was 1.8 ± 0.5 mm/yr with the sum of thermal expansion, glaciers, ice caps and ice sheets estimated at 1.1 ± 0.5 mm/yr, and ice accounted for about two-thirds of the sum. They indicate an accelerating rate in the period from 1993 to 2003 to over double the 1961 to 2003 rate for the climate change contributions.

After these estimates were made, a number of studies appeared that also took rapid ice melt into account. Estimates reviewed by Nicholls and Cazenave (2010, p.1517) indicate that the approximately global average sea level rise estimated by the IPCC in 2007 of about 60 cm (Solomon et al. 2007), by 2100 would possibly be at least 1 meter if rapid ice melt were taken into account. Paul (2011, p.71) indicated that glaciers and ice caps alone would contribute about 0.5 meter. Ablain et al. (2009) cited by Nicholls and Cazenave (2010, p.1517) estimated a rise of 3.3 ± 0.4 mm/yr between 1993–2005. Jacob et al. (2012) using field measurement methods estimated the contribution of ice covered areas to sea level rise is 1.48 ± 0.26 mm/year.

Before addressing the issues that sea level rise pose directly for transportation, it is important to first understand the nature of the distribution of populations and transportation systems in areas that are more vulnerable to sea level rise. These are the direct human targets of sea level rise.

Worldwide estimates of populations and settlements vulnerable to sea level rise

McGranahan et al. (2007, p.17) estimated that "10 percent of the world's population and 13 percent of the world's urban population" live within what they call "low elevation coastal zones" (LECZs) within 10 meters above sea level. This area accounts for only "2 per cent of the world's land area". Six hundred million people are estimated to live in those zones of which 360 million are in urban areas, and this results in a relatively higher proportion of urban populations in the vulnerable zone (60 percent) relative to the population in general (50 percent) (McGranahan et al. 2007, p.22). They indicate that disparities exist with developing countries being more vulnerable than developed countries. About a 3 meter elevation is the lower bound of the US Army Corps of Engineers (USACE) et al. (1995) study for the New York area for the impact of a Category 3 hurricane. McGranahan et al. (2007) proceed to identify the regions and countries and the land and population in the total and urban portion within this boundary. For example, Asia, Australia and New Zealand and small island states exceed or are equal to the world average for percent urban land area within the 10 meter boundary (McGranahan et al. 2007, p.24).

The UN-Habitat report (2008, Overview, p.8) summarizes worldwide vulnerabilities in cities:

> 3,351 cities in low elevation coastal zones
> 384 million people at risk mostly developing world
> Asia alone will account for more than half of the most vulnerable cities
> Developed world: 35 of the largest cities are coastal or along a river bank.

McGranahan et al. (2007, p.19) citing Few and Matthies (2006) estimate that from 1994 to 2004, many of the flood disasters (a third), deaths associated with them (about half) and people affected (98 percent) were located in large population concentrations in major flood plains and coastal areas prone to cyclones in Asia.

Low lying land and potential sea level rise impacts by state

Based on tide gauge measurements, Tebaldi et al. (2012, Table 1) estimate for a 100-year storm return level projection for 54 areas across many states in the US, a range from 0.86 meters (Vaca Key, Florida Bay, FL) to 4.53

Table 3.3   Estimates of low lying land by state, US

	Low lying land area (0–3.5m elevation combined)* as a percent of state land area
Alabama	0.4
Connecticut	0.8
Delaware	8.7
District of Columbia	3.1
Florida	14.7
Georgia	1.8
Louisiana	21.7
Maine	0.6
Maryland	7.3
Massachusetts	2.7
Mississippi	0.8
New Hampshire	0.3
New Jersey	7.6
New York	0.4
North Carolina	7.0
Pennsylvania	0.0
Rhode Island	4.6
South Carolina	5.7
Texas	1.3
Virginia	1.8
Total	4.1

Sources: * Computed using elevations by state from US EPA-related research by Titus et al. (2009), and Titus and Richman (2001), Table 1 available at http://papers.risingsea.net/coarse-sea-level-rise-elevation-maps-article.html#table1. State land area was obtained from the US Bureau of the Census.

meters for Apalachicola, Apalachicola River, FL by 2050. Their estimated rate of increase based on 1959–2008 trends is a global average of 2.89 mm/yr, and 26 of the 54 areas in the US exceeded that rate.

Titus and Richman (2001) estimated the amount of land between 0–1.5 meters and 1.5 and 3.5 meters in elevation (expressed in square kilometers) for US Atlantic and Gulf of Mexico coastal states.

The Titus and Richman data was used to compute in Table 3.3 the sum of the 0–1.5 meter and 1.5–3.5 meter elevations, and then the percentage of total state land area that was low lying land.

Only a modest relationship exists between the amount of low lying land in the 0–1.5 meter category and in the 1.5–3.5 meter category. The correlation between these two is 0.66. That is, a state that has very low lying land (0–1.5 meters) may not necessarily have land in the 1.5–3.5 meter category.

The percentage of total land area in each state that is low lying (0–3.5 meters) varies considerably. The average for the 20 states is 4.1 percent with Louisiana having the most with 21.7 percent, Florida the second highest with 14.7 percent and Pennsylvania having the least with well under 1 percent. The other states have less than 10 percent of their land area below 3.5 meters. This information about the location of low lying areas and how low the areas are is significant for the flexibility that a given state might have in locating its transportation systems and in maintaining vigilance, emergency procedures, and thinking about adaptation in the face of severe flooding.

Titus et al. (2009, p.1) using a criterion of below 1 meter above sea level and based on a survey of 131 land use plans by state and local governments along the east coast of the US found that on average less than 10 percent of the land will be used for conservation. This varies by location. To the north of Delaware and in Florida 80 percent of the land is developed or in an intermediate development category. Between Georgia and Delaware, 45 percent is in that category and they attribute this to stricter laws or the location of development further inland (Titus et al. 2009 p.3). Titus et al. ranked the states according to development category using the 1 m criterion for high water (Titus et al. 2009 p.5): the amounts of developed low lying land (in square kilometers) averaged 42 percent and ranged from 82 percent for the District of Columbia to 19 percent for Maryland; the District of Columbia, Connecticut, New York, New Jersey, Florida, and Pennsylvania were above average and Virginia, Rhode Island, North Carolina, South Carolina, Delaware, Georgia, Massachusetts, and Maryland were below average.

Low lying land and potential sea level rise impacts by city

A report conducted by the Natural Resources Defense Council (NRDC) (Dorfman et al. August 2011) identifies sea level rise as one of nine water-related impacts of climate change on cities. Of the 12 cities in the US that they analysed, eight of them were identified as having highly likely increases in sea level. These were Boston, Los Angeles, Miami and the Keys, New Orleans, New York, Norfolk, San Francisco, and Seattle. Norfolk (at Sewell's Point) is considered to have the highest rate of sea level rise estimated at 4.5 mm/year (Dorfman et al. 2011, p.30). The report (Dorfman et al. 2011, p.25) shows clearly how sea level rise is fast approaching the 500-year flood. The data on sea level rise based on that report are organized in Table 3.4 below with year of the estimate. Most of the cities have a similar estimated maximum increase of about 4.5–5 feet by the year 2100. This range includes estimates since that report, for example, by the San Francisco Bay Conservation and Development Commission (2011, pp.2–3) of 55 inches by 2100, which without any adaptation is equivalent to 333 square miles of flooding.

Table 3.4   Amounts of low lying land by 2100 for selected cities, US

Location	Estimated additional sea level rise by 2100 over 2000 levels	References (from Dorfman et al. 2011)
Boston, MA	3.3–4.6′ (1–1.4 m)	Dorfman et al. (2011, pp.24–5) Vermeer and Rahmstorf (2009)
Los Angeles, CA	1.7–4.6′ (0.50–1.40 m)	Dorfman et al. (2011, p.92) Cayan et al. (2009)
Miami, FL	3–5′ (0.9–1.5 m)	Dorfman et al. (2011, p.42) Hoegh-Guldberg (2010)
New Orleans, LA	1–4.5′ (0.3–1.4 m)	Dorfman et al. (2011, p.50) Blum and Roberts (2009); Burkett et al. (2002)
New York, NY (2080s)	1.0–1.9′ (0.30–0.58 m)	Dorfman et al. (2011, p.12) Horton et al. (2010)
Norfolk, VA	1.3–5.2′ (0.39–1.6 m) Extremes: 7.4′ (2.3 m)	Dorfman et al. (2011, pp.30–31) Bryant (2008); Boon et al. (2010); Hampton Roads Planning (2010); Lentz (2010); Dwoyer (undated)
San Francisco, CA (calculated from 2000)	1.7–4.6′ (0.50–1.40 m)	Dorfman et al. (2011, pp.81–2) Cayan et al. (2009)
Seattle, WA	0.5–4.2′ (0.15–1.27 m)	Dorfman et al. (2011, p.70) Huppert et al. (2009)

Sources: Compiled from Dorfman et al. (2011) and sources cited by Dorfman et al. (2011) as indicated. The San Francisco estimate also includes the San Francisco Bay Conservation and Development Commission (2011, p.2) estimates subsequent to the NRDC report. Estimates were converted into the same units for comparability. Estimates do not generally include the potential effects of rapid ice melt unless indicated as extremes.

US coastal population and housing estimates for sea level rise impacts

The US Bureau of the Census (May, June 2011) and Wilson and Fischetti (2010) have identified increasing trends in population, population density, and housing growth in coastal areas, which will potentially increase their vulnerability unless steps are taken to protect them. A significant aspect of the vulnerability is the inability to protect transport networks that provide access to these populations often under very constrained geographic conditions.

NOAA and the US Bureau of the Census both provide detailed estimates of coastal area population. The two agencies include a different set of counties in their definitions of coastal counties, which must be taken into account in interpreting counties at risk from sea level rise (Wilson and Fischetti 2010, p.3). There are 3,142 counties in the US. Of those, the Census, according to Wilson and Fischetti (2010, p.1) defines coastal counties as those adjacent to salt water bodies, which includes the Atlantic coast, the Gulf Coast, and the Pacific Coast, totaling 254 counties. While these counties only account for 8.1 percent of the total number of US counties, they account for a far greater share of the population – 29 percent, and large concentrations of those areas' heavily populated cities and counties (Wilson and Fischetti 2010, p.1). In contrast, NOAA's definition of coastal counties also includes inland counties that are adjacent to inland waterways, and their total is 674 counties (Wilson and Fischetti 2010, p.3).

Using the Census definition of coastal counties, the following trends in population, population density and housing are apparent, pointing to a rapidly growing denser population though variations exist from county to county. Below is a summary from the US Bureau of the Census (May, June 2011) and Wilson and Fischetti (2010):

Population

- From 1960–2008, coastal population increased 84.3 percent or by 40 million people, which was larger than the growth rate of 64 percent for non-coastal counties (Wilson and Fischetti 2010, p.3; Zimmerman 2011).
- The percentage decadal increases for coastal areas from 1960 through 2008 range from 19.5 percent for 1960–70 to 6.5 percent for 2000–2008, and in each decade except for the 1990–2008 time period, the rate of increase for coastal areas exceeded that for non-coastal areas. Between 1950 and 2005, the overall rate for coastal counties was 106.1 percent and for non-coastal counties it was 75.8 percent. During many of the decades, coastal county population increased by about double the rate of growth of non-coastal counties, though the rates are slowing and the differences have diminished. The US Census indicates that the source of the increase between 2000 and 2008 was natural increase in population and international migration (US Census May, June 2011).

Population density (US Bureau of the Census May, June 2011)

- Population density is substantially greater in coastal versus non-coastal counties – coastal counties average about double the density of non-coastal counties (Wilson and Fischetti 2010, p.11).

- The rate of change of population density from 1960 to 2008 in coastal countries was 101.2 percent compared with 62.4 percent for non-coastal counties (Wilson and Fischetti 2010, p.11).

Housing (US Bureau of the Census May, June 2011)
The Census 2000 indicates that almost half of the US population, housing units and seasonal housing units were located within 50 miles from a coastline. Coastal areas contain a large proportion of seasonal housing.

- Coastal area housing contains a growing percentage share of seasonal housing. According to the US Bureau of the Census (June 2011) housing in coastal areas increased 126 percent compared to the US figure of 121 percent from 1960 to 1980.

The US Bureau of the Census bases these estimates on the Decennial Censuses of 1950, 1970, and 2000, Population Estimates Program's 2005 estimates, subject to nonsampling error from the questionnaires for obtaining Census data.

Estimates of the overall affected populations vary depending on assumptions about the areas to be inundated. For New York City, Aerts and Wouter Botzen (2011 pp.10–11) for example, summarize estimates for population exposure for the 100-year flood zone, shown in Table 3.5. Other studies have estimated populations at risk, for example, the San Francisco Bay Conservation and Development Commission (2011, p.3) estimates that a 55 inch sea level rise in the Bay Area would affect an estimated 270,000 people. Overpeck and Weiss (2009, p.21461) looked at the spatial impact of alternative sea level rise levels for ten cities on the Gulf and eastern US coasts. They estimated that a 6 meter increase in sea level would affect 98 percent or more of the areas of New Orleans, Miami, and Norfolk, 43 percent of Tampa and about a third of the

Table 3.5   Summary of estimates for population exposure to sea level rise, New York City

Nicholls et al. (2008)	1.54 million
with natural population increase by 2070	2.37 million
Addition of 50 cm scenario	2.93 million
Maantay and Moroko (2009)	
(Cadastral-based Expert Dasymetric System, CEDS)	0.4 million
Aerts and Wouter Botzen (2011, p.19)	0.2 million

Source: Compiled from Aerts and Wouter Botzen (2011), pp.10 and 19.

area of New York and Boston. They also estimated that a 1m increase would still affect quite a large portion of New Orleans (91 percent), whereas fewer than 20 percent of the other cities they selected would be affected.

Sea level rise impacts on transportation
Within this broad national perspective and focus on populations at risk, a number of regional studies provide specific sea level rise data not only region or locality wide but within those areas as well for transportation. Jacob et al. (2001; 2007; 2011) provided transportation specific findings for New York State. Suarez et al. (2005) focused on transportation impacts in the Boston metropolitan area. Borden et al. (2007) developed a method of overlaying physical systems, social conditions, and hazard areas at the level of urban areas. Though not specifically identifying sea level rise as a hazard, some of the consequences in the hazard index are similar to those attributed to sea level rise.

The US Climate Change Science Program (2008) analysed the Gulf Coast region, and the US Climate Change Science Program (2009) focused on the Mid-Atlantic areas (District of Columbia, Maryland, North Carolina and Virginia) co-locating transportation networks with land elevation.

A worst case scenario for sea level rise was developed by the US Climate Change Science Program (2008) for two major coastal US areas – the Mid-Atlantic and Gulf Coast regions. They measure eustatic sea level rise, defined as "a uniform change in sea level created by any volumetric increase in the oceans worldwide, primarily due to thermal expansion (caused by higher temperatures) and ice melt" (US DOT 2008, footnote 5). At each sea level rise point, infrastructure subject to both regular and temporary or "at-risk" inundation from storm surge is identified. The locations of rail and road networks as well as other transportation infrastructure components are included. A detailed estimate of the juxtaposition of transportation networks and low lying lands was provided by US DOT and ICF (2007) for highway, rail and other transportation facilities for eustatic sea level rise elevations ranging from 6 to 59 cm. For each level they estimate regular and at-risk inundation. Some examples are noteworthy at the extremes for 59 cm combining both regular and at-risk inundation as shown in Table 3.6. The estimates are for the infrastructure in the entire county bordering the coast.

The amount of transportation infrastructure has been estimated for individual areas as well, for example, for the Bay Area in California, the San Francisco Bay Conservation and Development Commission (2011, p.77) estimated some 99–196 miles of major roads and highways and

Table 3.6   Total inundation risks for selected coastal counties aggregated by state for a 59 cm sea level rise scenario, US

	Length affected (km)	Percent affected (%)
	Total inundation risk for a 59 cm sea level rise scenario	
Florida (Atlantic coastal counties) (US DOT 2008, p.60):		
"Interstates	41.7	4
Non-Interstate Principal Arterials	412.8	8
Minor Arterials	94.9	7
National Highway System (NHS)	199.0	6
Rails	176.4	5"
Georgia (US DOT 2008, p.57):		
"Interstates	16.5	1
Non-Interstate Principal Arterials	61.8	1
Minor Arterials	25.3	0
National Highway System (NHS)	59.0	1
Rails	69.4	1"
North Carolina (US DOT 2008, p.51):		
"Interstates	1	0
Non-Interstate Principal Arterials	130	2
Minor Arterials	209	4
National Highway System (NHS)	305	4
Rails	105	1"
New York (US DOT 2008, p.23):		
"Interstates	14.9	1
Non-Interstate Principal Arterials	159.2	2
Minor Arterials	21.3	0
National Highway System (NHS)	146.6	2
Rails	125.7	1"

Notes: This represents total estimated inundation ("regular" plus "at risk") at the 59 cm sea level rise scenario. Only selected states and transportation infrastructure are shown for illustration. For additional information see the full report.

Source: US DOT, Center for Climate Change and Environmental Forecasting (2008). "This report was produced under contract by ICF International for the U.S. DOT Center for Climate Change and Environmental Forecasting. The United States Government assumes no liability for its contents or use thereof. Contributing Authors: Kevin M. Wright, ICF International; Christopher Hogan, ICF International."

70–105 miles of rail lines could be vulnerable to flooding with 16–55 inches of sea level rise.

Canada has also identified areas sensitive to sea level rise as being concentrated along the coasts bordering the Atlantic and in portions of the Beaufort Sea (Natural Resources Canada website March 25, 2009). Overlays with rail and road networks have been mapped (Natural Resources Canada website May 25, 2011).

There are now numerous locally based estimates of sea level rise and its impacts on transportation. Dorfman et al. (2011, p.93 citing Heberger et al. 2009, Table 15) notes that if a 55 inch rise in sea level occurs in Los Angeles, 171 miles of roads and highways and 14 miles of railway will be impacted equivalent to a 100-year flood plain. Jacob et al. (2001) have produced similar types of estimates for the New York Region. The key factor in vulnerability of transportation infrastructure to flooding is through ventilation infrastructure. These accounted for a fifth of the facilities that are listed as vulnerable for the New York Region as Table 3.7 below shows in connection with a category 3 hurricane (summarized from USACE et al. 1995 and Zimmerman and Cusker 2001), but this vulnerability is applicable to other kinds of flooding. Stations rank as a close second as tunnels do but only if they are counted in conjunction with vents.

The MTA report on the August 2007 flash floods described above revealed some of the weaknesses of a rail system that has a large proportion of the mileage of its heavy rail system underground.

Ice Melt and Rapid Ice Melt

The phenomenon of ice melt significantly contributes to sea level rise and associated flooding that potentially affects transportation infrastructure, making many transportation arteries impassable or inoperable, requiring dramatic changes in transportation networks as we know them. It is generally agreed that ice melt is occurring and estimates over the decade of the 2000s reveal an increasing trend in many areas, including Greenland (Hamish 2009).

The discovery of rapid rates of ice melt has largely tipped the balance in the climate change crisis, since what was considered a gradual change may be more sudden and dramatic. This influence on sea level can affect much of the coastal infrastructure that supports transportation. These estimates are changing over time with new information and analyses.

The critical factors for transportation are regional differences in sea level rise from ice melt. Lemke et al. (2007, p.340) translated changes in ice into Sea Level Rise (SLR) Equivalents. Moreover, for Arctic sea ice from 1979 to 2005 the general trend was $-33 \pm 7.4 \times 10^3$ km^2 per year and the

Table 3.7   Estimates of transportation components exposed to low lying areas, New York City

Component	Equal to or less than		Total	
	10 ft NGVD	12 ft NGVD	Number	Percent***
Rail:				
Shafts	4		4	5.0
Tunnels	3*		3	3.8
Stations	13	1	14	17.5
Lines and line tracks	7**		7	8.8
Grates	2		2	2.5
Vents	9	8	17	21.3
Entrances	4	3	7	8.8
Other	1	1	2	2.5
Air and marine facilities:				
Airports	2**	2	4	5.0
Ports and piers	6		6	7.5
Roadways:				
Roads	8	1	9	11.3
Bridges	3	2	5	6.3
Total	62	18	80	100.0

Notes:
*   Tunnels that are vulnerable through vent shafts are tabulated under vents and are counted under the latter categories rather than in the tunnel category. Fourteen tunnels are actually mentioned without or in combination with vents or entrances.
**   Does not reflect the extent of the facility.
*** Percents may not add to the total due to rounding.

Source: Summarized from Zimmerman and Cusker (2001, Tables 9-6 and 9-7, pp.163–4, derived from USACE, FEMA, NWS (1995) and also appearing in Jacob, Edelblum and Arnold (2001).

minimum sea ice extent surviving the summer was $-60 \pm 20 \times 10^3$ km^2 per year and the same analysis was conducted for glaciers and ice caps and ice sheets (Lemke et al. 2007, p.351).

MEASURING THE CONNECTION: GREEN SCORES FOR TRANSPORTATION

A number of ways of capturing transportation's relationship to the environment largely motivated by climate change have rapidly emerged.

The need to measure the human impact on climate change and to motivate behavioral changes for mitigating climate change and other adverse environmental conditions gave rise to a wide range of measurement systems, collectively known, for example, as green or footprint calculators. These emerged at many different geographic scales, popularized, for example, by Wackernagel and Rees (1996), eventually as the "Global Footprint Network" (GFN). Measuring the footprint of nations was accompanied by subnational ranks, city ranking and scoring systems, down to individual and household ranking systems. Examples of some of those that have incorporated transportation in terms of its impact on carbon or carbon dioxide emissions are evaluated below.

Overall Footprint Calculations for Transport

Scoring at the level of individual types of infrastructure including several transportation sectors was conducted by the American Society of Civil Engineers (ASCE) (2005, 2009) aggregated by infrastructure type, states and metropolitan areas.

Carbon footprints for transportation were developed by Davis et al. (2011) defined for vehicles as "a vehicle's impact on climate change in tons of carbon dioxide (CO_2) emitted annually" (Davis et al. 2011, pp.11–12). Using 15,000 miles for average annual driving, the trend from 1975–2010 for short-tons of CO_2 emissions indicates slight average annual percentage declines of between 1.7 percent and 2.5 percent for cars depending on the car size and −1.2 percent to −2.1 percent for wagons; the footprints are weighted by sales (Davis et al. 2011, pp.11–13).

The American Public Transportation Association (APTA) (2007) addressed public transportation's contribution to greenhouse gas reduction:

- On average, the carbon footprint of American households is double that of European households, and the transportation related portion of a household's CO_2 emissions ranges from approximately 38 percent to 55 percent for one- and two-car households respectively.
- Transferring to public transportation reduces the carbon footprint of the single commuter by 20 pounds daily or 4,800 pounds annually which is about 10 percent of the footprint of the two-car household.
- If the two-car households eliminate one vehicle, the footprint can go down by between 25 and 30 percent, and if that household uses transit the footprint declines more by as much as 55 percent.

Ranking Cities: The Transportation Component

A number of urban area analyses incorporate transportation in their rankings, for example, those conducted by PricewaterhouseCoopers, The Economist Intelligence Unit (for specific cities and regions throughout the world covering Europe, Asia, North America, Africa, and Latin America), and the United Nations International Strategy for Disaster Reduction (UNISDR) for resiliency.

Transportation has been a key component of metropolitan area rankings by Brown et al. (2008) who developed separate city rankings for highways, automobiles, and trucks. When their city rankings for transportation and residential emissions are compared, a very different rank ordering of the cities emerged. Differences in the rankings occurred among the three transportation sectors and between the transportation and residential use sectors. The distribution of the higher emitting metropolitan areas was far more dispersed for residential use than for transportation even when emissions were standardized with per capita figures. "Walk Score", described below also provides city level rankings for 2,500 cities and 10,000 neighborhoods according to walkability (Walk Score 2011).

Carbon Calculators for Transportation: Individuals and Households

Many calculators specialize in particular modes of transportation, such as transit (MTA at http://www.mta.info/sustainability/index.html?c=calc), walking (Walk Score at http://www.walkscore.com/transit-score.php) and biking (Colorado DOT at http://www.metro.net/projects_studies/bikeway_planning/biketowork/images/bike_to_work_calculator.htm).

Types of calculators and relevance to transport
The following are examples of calculators that incorporate transportation along with other activities considered to influence carbon footprints.

1. Global Footprint Network (GFN) (2010)

The transportation-related questions contained in the GFN personal calculator include:

- Amount of food eaten that is grown within 200 miles;
- Distance traveled (in miles) by car, motorbike, public transportation weekly;
- Fuel efficiency – miles per gallon for each travel mode;
- Drive alone or with another person most often;

- Weekly travel by bus and train; and
- Annual hours traveled by air.

The travel characteristics are heavily aggregated by week or in the case of fuel efficiency and driving with others, are not aggregated at all. Peak and non-peak travel are not differentiated. The limitations are that no range of variability is requested. People in reality have many different patterns of consumption that vary over time and place. The advantages are that the calculator is scalable. They have calculated footprints for cities, states, and countries. Cases are also given.

2. Pew Climate Change Center, 'Make an Impact' (undated website c2010), http://makeanimpact.pewclimate.org/.

3. US EPA Household Emissions Calculator (undated website)

This calculator is one of the most quantitative ones using three components – transportation, household energy use and waste disposal. Transportation questions include number of vehicles a household owns and the number of miles per week or year the first vehicle travels relative to the US average of 240 miles per week per vehicle, and fuel economy relative to a US average of 20.4 miles per gallon ("Household Vehicles", citing fueleconomy.gov).

Ways of reducing transportation's contribution include reducing the amount of driving, regular maintenance on the car, and replacing the car with a more fuel efficient one.

4. Walk Score, Seattle WA (July 2011)

The calculator computes commuting time for the amenities that the calculator selects, and are adaptable to some extent by the user (Walk Score July 2011).

The transit score characterizes the quality of service by public transportation for selected cities (http://www.walkscore.com/transit).

Walk Score incorporates "The 'Street Smart' Walk Score" that calculates distances to amenities. The score improves on previous versions and other scores by taking into account travel conditions in the form of connections within the road network, average length of blocks and densities of intersections and weighting factors are used to reflect the number of trips to a given amenity (Walk Score July 2011).

5. Metropolitan Transportation Authority, MTA (undated website) "Transit Effect Calculator"

The calculator asks the user for mode of travel and how far the trip is over a defined time period that varies accordingly. For the main mode the time period for travel is per day. For occasional trips the time interval can be selected by the user. The inputs include a couple of housing characteristics. No combinations of modes are offered for the choice of transportation options. The results are expressed as metric tons of CO_2 emitted per year. The results are compared to the emissions of the average American which is 24.5 metric tons of CO_2 emitted per year. Oddly, it appears that if driving is entered as the mode of travel for both commuting and occasional trips, the footprint is still lower than that of the average American, probably because credit is given for the urban lifestyle and the amount of driving is less; however, transportation assumes a larger proportion of the footprint.

Evaluation of footprint calculator applications for transportation

The idea behind footprint or carbon calculators is to track resource usage and its impact on carbon emissions and its societal importance. The calculators are scalable ranging from individual to global footprint estimates. They are often used for comparative purposes, to ascertain changes over time in behavior and to evaluate alternatives.

Calculators are very valuable in making individuals sensitive to differences in travel choices and the implications of their actions in terms of resources consumed and environmental impact. They allow comparisons among alternative inputs such as location and levels of resource consumption. It is difficult to tell, however, given their simplifications, whether or not they distort the findings or mislead individuals.

Calculators are based on index construction. As such they share many of the drawbacks of indexing that include the fact that the actual differences between adjacent categories may not be equal and thus integer scales can oversimplify the relationships. While weighting systems can overcome some of these biases, such weighting systems need to be justified with sufficient empirical backing rather than based on the assessments of a small number of experts that may not reflect all of the conditions.

The calculators that were just described generally reflect concepts that are supported in the transportation literature. The calculators often do not take into account, however, traffic conditions, the speed, the nature of the conditions of travel such as idling and cold and hot starts, and age of vehicle, that often influence emissions of air pollutants. In order to compensate for the complexity of information that would be required to reflect these factors in a calculator, calculators usually aggregate detailed factors into three types of attributes of transport: type of mode, extent of use in terms of distance traveled, and for cars, fuel efficiency.

Individual or personal calculators rely on an "expressed preferences" approach or what the individual says. The reliance of calculators on user input creates biases such as recall bias, differences in interpretation, circumstantial and experiential influences, the tendency to overestimate some information and underestimate others, as well as other factors. These have been well-documented in the risk perception literature (see for example Slovic 2000). Calculators at larger scales such as citywide or countrywide may avoid this by relying on more objective data if available; however, the degree of aggregation may lead to other distortions. Some calculators can link users to websites that provide more specific information. For automobiles, the EPA calculator provides a link for the user to fuel efficiency tables by model.

In using multiple elements, the calculators are inevitably trading off one against another. One of the drawbacks of tradeoffs is that one can choose good behavior to trade off or cancel out bad behavior in another sector and those tradeoffs go unseen.

Comparing a half dozen calculators incorporating transportation, Padgett et al. (2008, p.111) found variations in the conversion factors used to convert gallons of gasoline into pounds of CO_2 and some calculators don't provide information on the conversion factors.

Only some of the calculators include public transportation, and those that do, usually do not disaggregate this into type of public transportation, which Padgett et al. (2008, p.111) also found.

The inputs used vary from one calculator to the next. Of the ten reviewed by Padgett et al. (2008, p.114), all used distance traveled per year, eight out of ten used fuel efficiency, and only two used more detailed information about driving such as the age, make and model of the vehicle and whether or not air conditioning was present.

For transportation, none of the calculators acknowledge that people often take multiple modes in their travel often in the course of one trip.

No variability is built into the calculators, that is, that there is really a minimum or maximum for travel characteristics over the course of travel periods and those ranges are usually not requested.

Unusual conditions such as hazards and congestion can dramatically alter people's choice of travel mode, change travel times, and the resources available, accessible, and used.

Jones and Niemeier (2009, p.12) critique 30 calculators including estimation of transportation emissions, and they point out that in their in-depth coverage of 12 calculators, six had detailed coverage of transportation emissions. They note a high degree of variability in the results, for example, for the same type of vehicle and for calculated emissions from mileage estimates at fueleconomy.gov versus emissions from actual fuel consumption. They underscore a lack of transparency in the way that some calculators are constructed, the assumptions that are made, and the extent to which assumptions reflect the factors that relate to emissions. They also evaluate the breadth of the calculators in terms of the number of sectors they include and their depth or levels of information within a given category. In order to evaluate the calculators they look at upstream and downstream and direct and indirect effects. Padgett et al. (2008) conducted a comparison among an older set of calculators and came to similar conclusions.

SETTING THE STAGE FOR SOLUTIONS THROUGH ADAPTATION

The foundation for planning in anticipation of climate change lies in the concepts of adaptation and mitigation and the international and US federal and state legislation that has emerged in response to these needs. The actual programs and plans by state and federal governments are covered in Chapter 4 since they share much in common with mechanisms for environmental planning and sustainability. This chapter focuses primarily on technology and land development related factors for climate change adaptation. Mitigation is only very briefly covered here from the technology and development perspectives since it has been more extensively covered relative to adaptation, for example, by Pacala and Socolow (2004), Kahn Ribiero et al. (2007), Greene et al. (2011) and in many climate plans covered in Chapter 4.

Adaptation to climate change encompasses many approaches that can be characterized as redesign (Meyer 2011), reinforcement and retrofit, relocation (of people and facilities), and redundancy. Adaptation concepts are briefly introduced and compared with mitigation, followed by examples of adaptive measures to illustrate the approaches mentioned.

The Concepts of Adaptation and Adaptive Capacity: Adaptation and Mitigation Compared

A two-pronged approach to climate change and its consequences involves mitigation and adaptation, which appears in numerous climate change studies and initiatives. Governmental efforts including plans by states and localities (discussed in Chapter 4), aim at both mitigation and adaptation and their relationship to one another and to environmental planning programs. A brief definition of these two concepts provides a foundation for plans and innovations for climate change. IPCC 2007 and references to IPCC 2001 are commonly cited as the source of the definitions for both of these terms with other variations introduced by the US White House Council on Environmental Quality and the National Research Council (Zimmerman and Faris 2011, p.181). Summarizing the gist of those definitions, mitigation involves reducing the sources of climate change and adaptation refers to intercepting the impacts of climate change once the effects are felt or are expected to occur.

Compatibility of adaptation and mitigation
The compatibility of adaptation and mitigation measures has been the subject of a longstanding debate. It has been argued that measures to pursue both adaptation and mitigation simultaneously produce synergies as well as conflicts depending on the timing, location, institutional and other factors, and many of these issues are relevant to transportation. Moser (2012 online, pp.2, 4), for example, identifies cases where the two are supportive pertaining to certain measures for resource management for coastal areas, energy production, soils, and forests, yet notes examples of where either adaptation undermines mitigation or vice versa. One notable example Moser cites of conflict is the removal of infrastructure from vulnerable areas (an adaptation) that can produce a one time or ongoing GHG emission increase depending on how it is done. Moser (2012 online, pp.8–9) identifies ways of seeking greater harmony between the two strategies by directing research to overcome the conflicts. Local Governments for Sustainability (ICLEI) (2008) suggests ways that localities can pursue both strategies through common planning. As more experience is gained in both areas and their interactions are understood better, effective and compatible strategies can emerge.

Mitigation examples
The more common engineering-related mitigation measures for transportation primarily focus on vehicular and transportation infrastructure design, operation, and maintenance. For road travel Kahn Ribiero et al. (2007) and TRB (2008, pp.226–9) identify extensive mitigation measures including reducing vehicular loads, increasing energy efficiency of existing fuels, use of alternative fuels, reducing tailpipe emissions and shifting to less energy demanding modes of travel and land uses that reduce vehicular use. For rail, they identify similar strategies such as reducing the vehicular

load and exploring different energy sources to economize on energy use such as regenerative breaking. Greene et al. (2011) provide a similar set of mitigation measures and also address various institutional mechanisms such as regulation and pricing. Pacala and Socolow (2004) created a set of scenarios that enabled the escalation in carbon emissions and their impacts to be intercepted in any number of ways, and transport was one of the options.

Adaptation and resiliency
The terms adaptation and adaptive capacity are commonly used in association with resiliency to portray the ability to change in response particularly to the adverse effects of climate change. The concept implies change to avoid the consequences of a negative condition. However, it could have a positive connotation where adaptation provides co-benefits with some other condition. It is a valuable way of portraying the ability of transportation systems and their users to change as they confront the adverse impacts of global climate change. Marshall (2010, p.37) citing a litany of studies, summarizes the concept of adaptive capacity, as a component of resilience and necessary to enable adaptation to occur by individuals, communities, industries, and nations and other social groupings and ecological systems. The concept of adaptive capacity, according to Marshall, includes flexibility and the ability to learn and change.

Are Adaptation Mechanisms Incorporating Transport?

Adaptation has long since been recognized as being understated in the planning process. Berrang-Ford et al. (2011, p.37) for example, citing other research, notes that although research on adaptation has been extensive with 1,741 articles alone appearing between 2006 and 2009, implementation is less apparent.

Many technological and development-related innovations are emerging that are provided below for two of the major climate change impact areas affecting transportation: heat and water.

Adaptation for heat-related impacts of climate change
Adaptation measures exist to reduce the impacts of heat that include design, operation and material modifications. For rail transportation, for example, redesign would involve placing rail ties closer together and using more heat resistant materials (US DOT, FTA 2011). Operational changes include altering the way that roadways and rail lines are used in times of extreme heat, such as reducing vehicle standing times and speeds. Maintaining and drawing upon stocks of vehicles less prone to

heat impacts, such as the trams used during the Adelaide, Australia 2009 heat wave described above, introduces flexibility for continuing service during high temperatures. Protecting and relocating vital transportation infrastructure such as bus storage facilities to locations less vulnerable to heat damage is vital (US DOT FTA 2011, p.63). Improvements in material technology are an ongoing effort to confront these problems. Ultra-high performing concrete that involves additives, special preparation, or structural adjustments is one example (Graybeal 2011). Better materials such as improved steel and wood that resist heating are being developed and some are already in use. Mehrotra et al. (2011, p.160) suggest adaptation measures such as "Milling out ruts; laying more heat resistant materials such as asphalt for roads and more heat tolerant metals for rail and rail connections." Finally, land use and urban form are essential to increasing the heat tolerance of areas by encouraging more compact development over sprawling low density development which has been shown to be more susceptible to heat extremes (Stone et al. 2010).

Adaptation for water-related impacts of sea level rise and precipitation
Permanent sea level rise from climate change poses a set of unusual problems for transportation infrastructure which may differ from the episodic inundations of intermittent weather events. The adaptive strategies for water-related problems associated with sea level rise take many different forms. They include changing design standards based on updated storm information, rerouting and removing water, installing barricades around vulnerable facilities, elevating structures above the vulnerable elevations, and reducing the vulnerability of land use (Meyer 2011). For roads and rail, one adaptation strategy has been elevation and improved drainage to reduce corrosion of structures which also avoids inundation of structures by water. Karl et al. (2009, p.65) point to such strategies that were used in the construction of a road in Kosrae, Micronesia by Hay et al. (2005). However, many of these approaches may be too modest to deal with storm surges and heavy precipitation. Some of the more elaborate methods for controlling flooding some of which are summarized in Dircke et al. (2012) and others are presented below with examples.

Updating weather related data used for facility design   The Massachusetts adaptation plan of 2011 emphasizes using updated weather information for the design of infrastructure. The report noted that rainfall intensity estimates in terms of return frequencies for precipitation are from the National Weather Service dating from 1977 and earlier. They are outdated and can underestimate such frequencies used for stormwater system design (Massachusetts Executive Office of Energy and Environmental Affairs, 2011, p.26). Some of the more catastrophic bridge failures reflect this need as well as adaptation to climate change.

Mechanical rerouting and removing water   Owners and operators of transportation facilities have pumping facilities to remove water from their systems for all eventualities. The MTA in New York City experienced serious flooding episodes that halted train service. Information from the agency indicates that they have 287 pump rooms throughout the system and 775 pumps. The pumping capacity is not easily measured given that flow meters are not present in all rooms. The estimate ranges from 8 to 13 million gallons per day when water enters the system from rainfall (personal correspondence, MTA, March 7, 2011). Alteration of conventional drainage structures to increase their capacity to capture and convey floodwaters is also a common means of managing water (US Environmental Protection Agency December 2009). Elevating transit structures is a common means of rerouting water, and the US DOT FTA (2011, p.67) points to many examples in Tokyo, Toronto and New York City where train tunnel grates, stations, and vents have been elevated to avoid flooding. The "Stormwater Management and Road Tunnel (SMART)" (undated website) was designed as a dual purpose structure developed to alternatively alleviate flooding and congestion in a road segment in Kuala Lumpur. Stormwater retention or storage has been a conventional technology to manage water release in conjunction with wastewater treatment capacity. Flexible or movable forms of such technology are in use. For example, in January 2012, NYC announced the use of movable storage facilities or inflatable dams to control stormwater flows capable of handling 2 million gallons of water for each rainfall event (New York City January 2012).

Artificial barriers and elevating structures   More permanent and heavily structural approaches were summarized by Tol et al. (2006) for the Rhine Estuary, the Thames Estuary, and the Rhone Delta and by Dircke et al. (2012). These include construction or raising sea walls, altering river flows, relocating population, and redesigning cities to elevate structures. Lead time would determine the feasibility of many of the options (Tol et al. 2006, p.478). In the US an extensive levee system is used to hold back and reroute riverine floodwaters thus potentially protecting the many low lying transportation networks. In extreme circumstances these may not hold. During the Mississippi floods of 1993 floodwaters overtopped the levees in many places trapping water behind them and requiring holes to be blown through them by the USACE to release some of the water (Zimmerman 1994). This situation has occasionally been repeated in subsequent flooding of the Mississippi River. The experience with the seawalls in the Japanese earthquake and tsunami of March 11, 2011 also demonstrated the limitations of floodwalls against the devastating tsunami. Those seawalls had actually been reconstructed prior to the event but weren't high enough to resist the height of the tsunami (Onishi 2011).

Barriers have been installed in Vienna, Taipei, and Istanbul transit areas (US DOT FTA 2011, pp.67–8). In contrast, an ambitious structure has been designed to control storm surges in the East River in New York City called the East River Tide Gates or East River Storm Surge Barrier (Abrahams 2009).

Natural water retardation methods   The movement toward green infrastructure for flood control has generated dozens if not hundreds of mechanisms to restore natural vegetation, drainage, and permeable structures to areas prone to flooding as a means of increasing the absorptive capacity of land surfaces and retarding overland runoff (US EPA 2009; New York City c2010).

Adaptation through behavioral change and land use changes   With enough warning and training, people can avert the consequences of rapid water inundation such as relocating over time to less vulnerable areas, incorporating evacuation strategies into their daily lives for short-term relocation, promoting more compact development, and adapting residential structures to extreme environmental conditions associated with climate change impacts. The ability to adapt land uses to support permanent relocation and the flexibility to reduce or avoid exposure through temporary relocation may require extensive modifications to the design and operation of transport networks. Adaptation through land use and transportation mechanisms has the advantage of being effective at very small and very large geographic scales.

NETWORKS, TRANSPORTATION AND CLIMATE CHANGE

Climate change is likely to produce large disruptions in transportation networks which differ from those produced by episodic disasters. As transport networks are currently designed and used it may take just one node to disrupt an entire system where economies dictate against redundancies. This is especially a problem in very dispersed areas. Although adaptation to heat by transportation networks may be possible through the introduction of new materials and operational changes, the ultimate test will be adapting to water inundation from intense precipitation, rapid water movement, and associated flooding by means of land use changes. Efforts to superimpose both road and rail transportation networks and the location of vulnerable areas are gradually spreading through local and regional mapping efforts. Together with case studies this is an important first step in connecting transportation to efforts to reduce the impact of climate change and toward implementation of both adaptation and mitigation measures.

REFERENCES

Ablain, M., A. Cazenave, G. Valladeau and S. Guinehut (2009), 'A new assessment of the error budget of global mean sea level rate estimated by satellite altimetry over 1993–2008', *Ocean Science*, **5**, 193–201.

Abrahams, M. (2009), 'Against the deluge: storm surge barriers to protect New York City', in J.S. Khinda (ed.), *East River Storm Surge Barrier*, Brooklyn, NY, USA: Polytechnic University of New York, March 30–31, pp.128–32.

Aerts, J.C.J.H. and W.J. Wouter Botzen (2011), 'Flood-resilient waterfront development in New York City: bridging flood insurance, building codes, and flood zoning', *Annals of the New York Academy of Sciences*, **1227** (1), 1–82.

American Public Transportation Association (APTA) (September 2007), Fact Sheet – Public Transportation's Contribution to US Greenhouse Gas Reduction, available at http://www.apta.com/mediacenter/pressreleases/2007/Documents/070926_fact_sheet.pdf.

American Rivers (undated), 'Estimated Stormwater and Direct Pollution from Federal-Aid Highways in Selected States', available at www.americanrivers.org/.

American Society for Civil Engineers (ASCE) (2005), *2005 Report Card for America's Infrastructure*, available at http://www.asce.org/reportcard/2005/index.cfm (accessed November 7, 2005).

American Society for Civil Engineers (ASCE) (2009), *2009 Report Card for America's Infrastructure*, available at www.asce.org/reportcard.

American Transportation Research Institute (January 2012), Compendium of Idling Regulations, available at http://www.atri-online.org/research/idling/ATRI_Idling_Compendium.pdf.

The Associated Press (2002), 'Heat-related rail "kinks" hard to prevent', available at http://www.chicagotribune.com/news/local/bal-heattracks30,0,7510272.story.

Bernstein, A. (2011), 'Survey: NYC residents more likely to walk or take transit', *WNYC*, September 2011, available at http://www.wnyc.org/blogs/

wnyc-news-blog/2011/sep/22/survey-nyc-   residents-more-likely-walk-or-take-transit/.

Berrang-Ford, L., J.D. Ford and J. Paterson (2011), 'Are we adapting to climate change?', *Global Environmental Change*, **21**, 25–33.

Bindoff, N.L., J. Willebrand, V. Artale, A. Cazenave, J. Gregory, S. Gulev, K. Hanawa, C. Le Quéré, S. Levitus, Y. Nojiri, C.K. Shum, L.D. Talley and A. Unnikrishnan (2007), 'Observations: oceanic climate change and sea level', in S. Solomon, D. Qin, M. Manning, Z. Chen, M. Marquis, K.B. Averyt, M. Tignor and H.L. Miller (eds), *Climate Change 2007: The Physical Science Basis, Contribution of Working Group I to the Fourth Assessment Report of the Intergovernmental Panel on Climate Change*, Cambridge, UK and New York, NY, USA: Cambridge University Press.

Blum, M.D. and H.H. Roberts (2009), 'Drowning of the Mississippi Delta due to insufficient sediment supply and global sea-level rise', *Nature Geoscience*, **2** (7), 488–91.

Boon, J.D., J.M. Brubaker and D.R. Forrest (2010), 'Chesapeake Bay land subsidence and sea level shange: An evaluation of past and present trends and future outlook', special report in applied marine science and ocean engineering, no. 425, Gloucester Point, VA, USA: Virginia Institute of Marine Science, The College of William & Mary.

Borden, K.A., M.C. Schmidtlein, C.T. Emrich, W.W. Piegorsch and S.L. Cutter (2007), 'Vulnerability of US cities to environmental hazards', *Journal of Homeland Security and Emergency Management*, **4** (2), Article 5, pp.1–21.

Broecker, W.S. (1975), 'Climate change: are we on the brink of a pronounced global warming?', *Science*, **189**, 460.

Brohan, P., J.J. Kennedy, I. Harris, S.F.B. Tett and P.D. Jones (2006), 'Uncertainty estimates in regional and global observed temperature changes: a new dataset from 1850', *Journal of Geophysical Research Atmospheres*, **111**, D12106.

Brown, M., F. Southworth and A. Sarzynski (2008), 'Shrinking the carbon footprint of metropolitan America', Washington, DC, USA: Brookings Institution.

Bryant, L.P. (2008), 'Final report: A climate change action plan', Climate Change in Hampton Roads, Virginia Governor's Commission on Climate Change, Norfolk, VA: Hampton Roads Planning District Commission (HRPDC).

Burkett, V.R., D.B. Zilkoski and D.A. Hart (2002), 'Sea-level rise and subsidence: implications for flooding in New Orleans, Louisiana', *US Geological Survey*, pp.63–71.

Cambridge Systematics, Inc. (2009), *Moving Cooler*, Washington, DC, USA: The Urban Land Institute.

Cayan, D., M. Tyree, M. Dettinger, H. Hidalgo, T. Das, E. Maurer, P. Bromirski, N. Graham and R. Flick (August 2009), 'Climate change scenarios and sea level rise estimates for the California 2009 climate change scenarios assessment', Berkeley, CA: California Climate Change Center, CEC-500-2009-014-F.

Cervero, R. and J. Murakami (2010), 'Effects of built environments on vehicle miles traveled: evidence from 370 US urbanized areas', *Environment and Planning A*, **42**, 400–418.

Daley, J. (September 2010), 'Salt Lake City to pursue idle-free ordinance', ksl.com, available at http://www.ksl.com/?nid=148&sid=12318246.

Dave, S. (February 2010), 'Life cycle assessment of transportation options for commuters', Cambridge, MA, USA: MIT, available at http://www.pietzo.com/storage/downloads/Pietzo_LCAwhitepaper.pdf (accessed September 4, 2011).

Davis, S.C., S.W. Diegel and R.G. Boundy (2010), *Transportation Energy Data Book: Edition 29*, ORNL-6985, Oak Ridge, TN, USA: Oak Ridge National Laboratory.

Davis, S.C., S.W. Diegel and R.G. Boundy (2011), *Transportation Energy Data Book: Edition 30*, ORNL-6986, Oak Ridge, TN, USA: Oak Ridge National Laboratory, available at http://cta.ornl.gov/data/tedb30/Edition30_Full_Doc.pdf.

Denman, K.L. et al. (2007), 'Couplings between changes in the climate system and biogeochemistry', in S. Solomon et al. (eds), *Climate Change 2007: The Physical Science Basis*, Cambridge, UK: Cambridge University Press, pp.499–587, available at http://www.ipcc.ch/pdf/assessment-report/ar4/wg1/ar4-wg1-chapter7.pdf.

Dircke, P., T. Jongeling and P. Jansen (2012), 'Navigable storm surge barriers for coastal cities: an overview and comparison', in J. Aerts, W. Botzen, M. Bowman, P. Ward, and P. Dircke (eds), *Climate Adaptation and Flood Risk in Coastal Cities*, London, UK: Earthscan, pp.197–221.

Dobney, K., C.J. Baker, A.D. Quinn and L. Chapman (2009), 'Quantifying the effects of high summer temperatures due to climate change on buckling and rail related delays in south-east United Kingdom', *Meteorological Applications*, **16**, 245–51.

Dorfman, M., M. Mehta, B. Chou, S. Fleischli and K. Sinclair Rosselot (2011), *Thirsty for Answers*, New York, NY, USA: The Natural Resources Defense Council, available at http://www.nrdc.org/water/files/thirstyforanswers.pdf.

Dwoyer, D. (undated), 'The impact of climate change on Hampton Roads', Norfolk, VA, USA: Hampton Roads Research Partnership.

Eby, M., K. Zickfeld, A. Montenegro, D. Archer, K.J. Meissner and A.J. Weaver (2009), 'Lifetime of anthropogenic climate change: millennial time scales of potential CO_2 and surface temperature perturbations', *Journal of Climate*, **22**, 2501–11.

Emanuel, K. (2005), 'Increasing destructiveness of tropical cyclones over the past 30 years', Letters, *Nature*, **436**, 686–8.

Emanuel, K., R. Sundararajan and J. Williams (2008), 'Hurricanes and global warming', BAMS, 347–67.

Environment 360 (2011), 'Is human-caused global warming contributing to more extreme weather events worldwide?', at *Forum: Is Extreme Weather Linked to Global Warming?* Yale Environment 360.

Ewing, R., K. Bartholomew, S. Winkelman, J. Walters and D. Chen (2007), *Growing Cooler: The Evidence on Urban Development and Climate Change*, produced by the Urban Land Institute, Smart Growth America, Center for Clean Air Policy, and the National Center for Smart Growth Research & Education, available at www.smartgrowthamerica.org/.

Few, R. and F. Matthies (2006), *Flood Hazards and Health: Responding to Present and Future Risks*, London, UK: Earthscan.

Gilbert, R. and A. Perl (2008), *Transport Revolutions*, London, UK: Earthscan.

Gillis, J. (December 2011), 'Harsh Political Reality Slows Climate Studies Despite Extreme Year', *The New York Times*, available at http://www.nytimes.com/2011/12/25/science/earth/climate-scientists-hampered-in-study-of-2011-extremes.html?_r=1&scp=1&sq=Climate%20Change%20December%2025%20 2011&st=cse.

Global Footprint Network (2010), Personal Footprint, Footprint calculator available at http://www.footprintnetwork.org/gfn_sub.php?content=calculator http://www.footprintnetwork.org/en/index.php/GFN/page/personal_footprint/.

Graybeal, B. (March 2011) 'Ultra-High Performance Concrete', Washington, DC, US DOT FHWA, available at http://www.fhwa.dot.gov/publications/research/infrastructure/structures/11038/11038.pdf.

Greene, D.L., H.H. Baker, Jr. and S.E. Plotkin (2011), *Reducing Greenhouse Gas Emissions from U.S. Transportation*, Washington, DC, USA: Pew Center on Global Climate Change.

Hamish D., R.J. Pritchard, D. Arthern, D.G. Vaughan and L.A. Edwards (October 2009), 'Extensive dynamic thinning on the margins of the Greenland and Antarctic ice sheets', *Nature*, **461**, 971–5.

Hampton Roads Planning District Commission (HRPDC) (2010), 'Climate change in Hampton Roads', available at http://hrpdc.org/Documents/Phys%20 Planning/2010/Climate_Change_Final_Report_All.pdf.

Harding, G.W. (1995), 'Broecker's warning', available at http://oto2.wustl.edu/bbears/trajcom/broecker.htm.

Hay, J.E., R. Warrick, C. Cheatham, T. Manarangi-Trott, J. Konno and P. Hartley (2005), *Climate Proofing: A Risk-Based Approach to Adaptation*, Manila, The Philippines: Asian Development Bank, available at http://www.adb.org/Documents/Reports/Climate-Proofing/default.asp.

Hoegh-Guldberg, H. (2010), 'Climate change and the Florida Keys', Socioeconomic Research and Monitoring Program, Florida Keys National Marine Sanctuary, NOAA.

Horton, R., C. Rosenzweig, V. Gornitz, D. Bader and M. O'Grady (May 2010), 'Climate risk information', Appendix A in *Climate Change Adaptation in New York City: Building a Risk Management Response, New York City Panel on Climate Change, Annals of the New York Academy of Sciences*, **1196** (1), 147–228, available at http://onlinelibrary.wiley.com/doi/10.1111/nyas.2010. 1196. issue-1/issuetoc.

Huppert, D.D., A. Moore and K. Dyson (2009), Washington Climate Change Impacts Assessment, 'Impacts of climate change on the coasts of Washington State', Seattle, Washington: Climate Impacts Group, University of Washington, available at http://cses.washington.edu/cig/res/ia/waccia.shtml.

ICLEI – Local Governments for Sustainability (2008), 'The Mitigation–Adaptation Connection: Milestones, Synergies and Contradictions', www.icleiusa.org.

Intergovernmental Panel on Climate Change (IPCC) (2007), *Climate Change 2007: Synthesis Report* available at http://www.ipcc.ch/pdf/assessment-report/ar4/syr/ar4_syr.pdf.

Intergovernmental Panel on Climate Change (IPCC) (November 2007), *Summary for Policymakers of the Synthesis Report of the IPCC Fourth Assessment Report*, Fourth Summary, available at http://www.ipcc.ch/pdf/assessment-report/ar4/syr/ar4_syr_spm.pdf.

Jacob, K., G. Deodatis, J. Atlas, M. Whitcomb, M. Lopeman, O. Markogiannaki, Z. Kennett, A. Morla, R. Leichenko and P. Vancura (2011), 'Transportation', in C. Rosenzweig, W. Solecki, A. DeGaetano, M. O'Grady, S. Hassol, and P. Grabhorn (eds), *Responding to Climate Change in New York State: The ClimAID Integrated Assessment for Effective Climate Change Adaptation in New York State*, New York, NY, USA: Columbia University.

Jacob, K.H., N. Edelblum and J. Arnold (2001), *Risk Increase to Infrastructure Due to Sea Level Rise*, MetroEast Coast (MEC) Regional Assessment, New York, NY, USA: Columbia University.

Jacob, K.H., V. Gornitz and C. Rosenzweig (2007), 'Vulnerability of the New York City metropolitan area to coastal hazards, including sea-level rise: inferences for urban coastal risk management and adaptation policies', in L. McFadden, R.J. Nicholls and E. Penning-Roswell (eds), *Managing Coastal Vulnerability*, Amsterdam, The Netherlands: Elsevier, pp.61–88.

Jacob, T., Wahr, J., Pfeffer, W.T. and Swenson, S. (2012 online), 'Recent contributions of glaciers and ice caps to sea level rise', *Nature*.

Jones, E. and D. Niemeier (2009), 'So you want to calculate your footprint? Quality of online carbon calculators', TRB 88th Annual Meeting Compendium of Papers DVD, Transportation Research Board Annual Meeting 2009 Paper 09-1361, 17.

Jones, P. (2010), 'Global temperature record', Climate Research Unit, University of East Anglia, available at http://www.cru.uea.ac.uk/cru/info/warming (accessed April 16, 2010).

Kahn Ribeiro, S., S. Kobayashi, M. Beuthe, J. Gasca, D. Greene, D.S. Lee, Y. Muromachi, P.J. Newton, S. Plotkin, D. Sperling, R. Wit and P.J. Zhou (2007), 'Transport and its infrastructure', in B. Metz, O.R. Davidson, P.R. Bosch, R. Dave and L.A. Meyer (eds), *Climate Change 2007: Mitigation. Contribution of Working Group III to the Fourth Assessment Report of the Intergovernmental Panel on Climate Change*, Cambridge, UK and New York, NY, USA: Cambridge University Press, pp.323–85, available at http://www.ipcc.ch/pdf/assessment-report/ar4/wg3/ar4-wg3-chapter5.pdf.

Karl, T.R., J.M. Melillo and T.C. Peterson (eds) (2009), *Global Climate Change Impacts in the United States*, Cambridge, MA, USA: Cambridge University Press, available at http://downloads.globalchange.gov/usimpacts/pdfs/climate-impacts-report.pdf.

King County, WA (2010), King County Energy Plan. King County, WA, available at http://your.kingcounty.gov/dnrp/library/dnrp-directors-office/climate/energy/2010-energy-plan-adopted.pdf.

Kirshen, P., M. Ruth and W. Anderson (2008), 'Interdependencies of urban climate change impacts and adaptation strategies: a case study of Metropolitan Boston USA', *Climatic Change*, **86**, 105–22.

Kish, A. and D.W. Clark (2009), 'Track buckling derailment prevention through risk-based train speed reductions', American Railway Engineering Maintenance-of-Way Association, available at http://www.arema.org/files/library/2009_Conference_Proceedings/Track_Buckling_Derailment_Prevention_Through_Risk-Based_Train_Speed_Reductions.pdf.

Knutson, T.R., J.J. Sirutis, S.T. Garner, G.A. Vecchi and I.M. Held (May 2008), 'Simulated reduction in Atlantic hurricane frequency under twenty-first-century warming conditions', *Nature Geoscience*, **1**, 359–64, available at www.nature.com/naturegeoscience (accessed May 21, 2008).

Lemke, P., J. Ren, R.B. Alley, I. Allison, J. Carrasco, G. Flato, Y. Fujii, G. Kaser, P. Mote, R.H. Thomas and T. Zhang (2007), 'Observations: changes in snow, ice and frozen ground', in S. Solomon, D. Qin, M. Manning, Z. Chen, M. Marquis, K.B. Avery, M. Tignor and H.L. Miller (eds), *Climate Change 2007: The Physical Science Basis. Contribution of Working Group I to the Fourth Assessment Report of the Intergovernmental Panel on Climate Change*, Cambridge, UK and New York, NY, USA: Cambridge University Press.

Lentz, K.M. (2010), *Flooding: Norfolk and the Region*, Norfolk, VA, USA: Norfolk Public Works.

Litman, T. (2006), *Lessons from Katrina and Rita: What Major Disasters Can Teach Transportation Planners*, Victoria, BC, Canada: Victoria Transport Policy Institute.

Maantay, J.A. and A. Maroko (2009), 'Mapping urban risk: flood hazards, race, and environmental justice in New York', *Applied Geography*, **29** (1), 111–24.

Marshall, N.A. (2010), 'Understanding social resilience to climate variability in primary enterprises and industries', *Global Environmental Change: Human and Policy Dimensions*, **20**, 36–43.

Massachusetts Executive Office of Energy and Environmental Affairs and the Adaptation Advisory Committee (2011), *MA Climate Change Adaptation Report*, available at http://www.mass.gov/eea/docs/eea/energy/cca/eea-climate-adaptation-report.pdf.

Matthews, H.D. and K. Caldeira (2008), 'Stabilizing climate requires near-zero emissions', *Geophysical Research Letters*, **35**, L04705.

McGranahan, G., D. Balk and B. Anderson (2007), 'The rising tide: assessment of the risk of climate change and human settlements in low elevation coastal zones', *Environment and Urbanization*, **19**, 17–37.

Mehrotra, S., B. Lefevre, R. Zimmerman, H. Gercek, K. Jacob and S. Srinivasan (2011), 'Climate change and urban transportation systems', in C. Rosenzweig, W.D. Solecki, S.A. Hammer and S. Mehrotra (eds), *Climate Change and Cities*

First Assessment Report of the Urban Climate Change Research Network, New York, NY, USA: Cambridge University Press, pp.145–77.

Metropolitan Transportation Authority (September 2007), 'August 8, 2007 storm report', New York, NY, USA: MTA.

Metropolitan Transportation Authority, Metro-North Railroad (August 2011), *A Review of the Actions Taken by Metro-North Railroad in Response to Multiple Heat-Related Incidents on the New Haven Line July 22, 2011*, New York, NY, USA: MTA.

Metropolitan Transportation Authority, MTA (undated website), 'Transit effect calculator,' New York, NY, USA: MTA, available at http://www.mta.info/sustainability/?c=calc.

Meyer, Michael (2011) 'Design Standards for U.S. Transportation Infrastructure: The Implications of Climate Change', commissioned paper for US DOT (2008), Special Report 290: 'The Potential Impacts of Climate Change on U.S. Transportation', available at http://onlinepubs.trb.org/onlinepubs/sr/sr290 Meyer.pdf.

Min, S.K., X. Zhang, F.W. Zwiers and G.C. Hegerl (2011), 'Human contribution to more-intense precipitation extremes', *Nature*, **470**, 378–81.

Moser, S.C. (2012 online), 'Adaptation, mitigation, and their disharmonious discontents: an essay', *Climatic Change*, published online January 21, 2012.

National Oceanic and Atmospheric Administration (NOAA), (August 2010), 'Second warmest July and warmest year-to-date global temperature on record', available at http://www.noaanews.noaa.gov/stories2010/20100813_globalstats. html.

National Oceanic and Atmospheric Administration (NOAA), National Climatic Data Center, (December 2011), 'Global surface temperature anomalies. Background Information – FAQ', available at http://lwf.ncdc.noaa.gov/cmb-faq/anomalies.php (accessed February 4, 2012).

National Oceanic and Atmospheric Administration (NOAA), National Climatic Data Center (January 2011), *2010 Annual State of the Climate Report – Supplemental Figures and Information*, available at http://www.noaanews.noaa. gov/stories2011/20110112_globalstats_sup.html (accessed June 29, 2011).

National Oceanic and Atmospheric Administration (NOAA), National Climatic Data Center (September 2011), *State of the Climate: Global Analysis for August 2011*, available at http://www.ncdc.noaa.gov/sotc/global/ (accessed September 16, 2011).

National Oceanic and Atmospheric Administration (NOAA), National Climatic Data Center (January 2012), *State of the Climate, Global Analysis*, Annual 2011, available at http://www.ncdc.noaa.gov/sotc/global/.

National Oceanic and Atmospheric Administration, National Weather Service (undated website), 'Heat: A Major Killer', available at http://www.nws.noaa. gov/om/heat/index.shtml.

National Oceanic and Atmospheric Administration, US Department of Commerce, National Climatic Data Center (undated website), 'US Heat Stress Index', available at http://www.ncdc.noaa.gov/temp-and-precip/heat-stress.html.

National Research Council (2011), *Climate Stabilization Targets: Emissions, Concentrations, and Impacts over Decades to Millennia*, Washington, DC, USA: National Academies Press.

Natural Resources Canada (March 2009), *The Atlas of Canada, Coastal Sensitivity to Sea Level Rise*, available at http://atlas.nrcan.gc.ca/auth/english/maps/climatechange/potentialimpacts/coastalsensitivitysealevelrise/1.

New York City (September 2010), 'PlaNYC inventory of New York City greenhouse gas emissions September 2010', available at http://nytelecom.vo.llnwd.net/o15/agencies/planyc2030/pdf/greenhousegas_2010.pdf.

New York City (September 2011), 'PlaNYC inventory of New York City greenhouse gas emissions September 2011', available at http://nytelecom.vo.llnwd.net/o15/agencies/planyc2030/pdf/greenhousegas_2011.pdf.

New York City (January 17, 2012), 'DEP installs two inflatable dams in Brooklyn to help improve New York harbor water quality', New York City Department of Environmental Protection Agency news release, available at http://www.nyc.gov/html/dep/html/press_releases/12-02pr.shtml.

New York City Panel on Climate Change (NPCC) (February 2009), 'Climate risk information', New York, NY, USA: NPCC, available at http://nytelecom.vo.llnwd.net/o15/agencies/planyc2030/pdf/nyc_climate_change_report.pdf.

New York City Panel on Climate Change (NPCC) (2010), 'Climate change adaptation in New York City, building a risk management response', *Annals of the New York Academy of Sciences*, **1196**.

Nicholls, R.J. and A. Cazenave (2010), 'Sea-level rise and its impact on coastal zones', *Science*, **328**, 1517–20.

Nicholls, R.J., S. Hanson, C. Herwijer, N. Patmore, S. Hallegatte, J. Corfee-Morlot, Jean Château and R. Muir-Wood (2008), 'Ranking port cities with high exposure and vulnerability to climate extremes exposure estimates', OECD Environment Working Papers No. 1, 19 November.

Office of the Chief Investigator (2006), 'Derailment V/Line passenger train 8432 11 km east of Traralgon 12 October 2006', available at http://www.transport.vic.gov.au/_data/assets/pdf_file/0019/30880/Derailment-of-Passenger-Train-at-Traralgon.pdf.

Onishi, N. (March 2011), 'In Japan, seawall offered a false sense of security', *The New York Times*, available at http://www.nytimes.com/2011/04/02/world/asia/02wall.html?ref=world (accessed November 16, 2011).

Overpeck, J.T. and J.L. Weiss (2009), 'Projections of future sea level becoming more dire', *National Academy of Sciences*, **106** (51), 21461–2.

Pacala, S. and R. Socolow (August 2004), 'Stabilization wedges: solving the climate problem for the next 50 years with current technologies', *Science*, **305** (5686), 968–72.

Padgett, J.P., A.C. Steinemann, J.H. Clarke and M.P. Vandenbergh (2008), 'A comparison of carbon calculators', *Environmental Impact Assessment Review*, **28** (2–3), 106–15.

Pall, P., T. Aina, D.A. Stone, P.A. Stott, T. Nozawa, A.G.J. Hilberts, D. Lohmann and M.R. Allen (2011), 'Anthropogenic greenhouse gas contribution to flood risk in England and Wales in autumn 2000', *Nature*, **470**, 382–6.

Paul, F. (2011), 'Sea level rise: melting glaciers and ice caps', *Nature Geoscience*, **4**, 71–2.

Pew Climate Change Center, (undated website circa 2010), 'Make an impact', Washington, DC, USA, Pew Climate Change Center, available at http://makean impact.pewclimate.org/; Center for Climate and Energy Solutions (undated website), 'Make an Impact', http://makeanimpact.pewclimate.org/about/make-impact (accessed February 5, 2012).

Railpage.com.au (January 29, 2009), 'Adelaide public transport in chaos amid heatwave', http://www.railpage.com.au/news/article-6385/.

Randolph, J. and G.M. Masters (2008), *Energy for Sustainability. Technology, Planning, Policy*, Washington, DC, USA: Island Press.

Sachs, J.P. and C.L. Myhrvold (2011), 'A shifting band of rain', *Scientific American*, **304** (3), 60–65.

San Francisco Bay Conservation and Development Commission (September 2011), '2011. Living with a Rising Bay: Vulnerability and Adaptation in San Francisco Bay and on its Shorelines', Draft, available at http://www.bcdc.ca.gov/BPA/LivingWithRisingBay.pdf.

Schmidt, N. and M.D. Meyer (2009), *Incorporating Climate Change Considerations Into Transportation Planning*, presented at 88th Annual Meeting of Transportation Research Board, Washington, DC, USA.

Slovic, P. (2000), *The Perception of Risk*, London, UK and Sterling, VA, USA: Earthscan.

Solomon, S., G.K. Plattner, R. Knutti and P. Friedlingstein (2009), 'Irreversible climate change due to carbon dioxide emissions', *Proceedings of the National Academy of Sciences of the United States of America*, **106**, 1704–9.

Solomon, S., D. Qin, M. Manning, R.B. Alley, T. Berntsen, N.L. Bindoff, Z. Chen, A. Chidthaisong, J.M. Gregory, G.C. Hegerl, M. Heimann, B. Hewitson, B.J. Hoskins, F. Joos, J. Jouzel, V. Kattsov, U. Lohmann, T. Matsuno, M. Molina, N. Nicholls, J. Overpeck, G. Raga, V. Ramaswamy, J. Ren, M. Rusticucci, R. Somerville, T.F. Stocker, P. Whetton, R.A. Wood and D. Wratt (2007), 'Technical summary', in S. Solomon, D. Qin, M. Manning, Z. Chen, M. Marquis, K.B. Averyt, M. Tignor and H.L. Miller (eds), *Climate Change 2007: The Physical Science Basis, Contribution of Working Group I to the Fourth Assessment Report of the Intergovernmental Panel on Climate Change*, Cambridge, UK and New York, NY, USA: Cambridge University Press.

Sperling, D. and J.S. Cannon (eds) (2009), *Reducing Climate Impacts in the Transportation Sector*, New York, NY, USA: Springer.

Spiegelhalter, D., M. Pearson and I. Short (2011), 'Visualizing uncertainty about the future', *Science*, **333**, 1393–400.

Stone, B., J.J. Hess and H. Frumkin (2010), 'Urban form and extreme heat events: are sprawling cities more vulnerable to climate change than compact cities?', *Environmental Health Perspectives*, **118**, 1425–8.

Stormwater Management and Road Tunnel (SMART) (undated website), available at http://www.smarttunnel.com.my/.

Suarez, P., W. Anderson, V. Mahal and T.R. Lakshmanan (2005), 'Impacts of flooding and climate change on urban transportation. A system-wide performance assessment of the Boston Metro area', *Transportation Research Part D* (10).

Tebaldi, C., B.H. Strauss and C.E. Zervas (2012), 'Modelling sea level rise impacts on storm surges along US coasts', *Environmental Research Letters*, **7** (1), 014032.

Titus, J.G. and C. Richman (2001), 'Maps of lands vulnerable to sea level rise: modeled elevations along the US Atlantic and Gulf coasts', *Climate Research*, **18**, 205–28; also available at http://papers.risingsea.net/coarse-sea-level-rise-elevation-maps-article.html#table1.

Titus, J.G., D.E. Hudgens, D.L. Trescott, M. Craghan, W.H. Nuckols, C.H. Hershner, J.M. Kassakian, C.J. Linn, P.G. Merritt, T.M. McCue, J.F. O'Connell, J. Tanski and J. Wang (2009), 'State and local governments plan for development of most land vulnerable to rising sea level along the US Atlantic Coast', *Environmental Research Letters*, **4**, available at http://papers.risingsea.net/downloads/plans-for-developing-land-vulnerable-to-sea-level-rise.pdf.

Tol, R.S.J., M. Bohn, T.E. Downing, M.L. Guillerminet, E. Hiznyik, R. Kasperson, K. Lonsdale, C. Mays, R.J. Nicholls, A.A. Olsthoorn, G. Pfeifle, M. Poumardere, F.L. Toth, A.T. Vafeidis, P.E. van der Werff and I. Hakan Yetkiner (2006), 'Adaptation to five metres of sea level rise', *Journal of Risk Research*, **9** (5), 467–82.

Transportation Research Board (1995), *Expanding Metropolitan Highways: Implications for Air Quality and Energy Use: Special Report 245*, Washington, DC, USA: National Academies Press.

Transportation Research Board, Division on Earth and Life Studies (2008), *Potential Impacts of Climate Change on US Transportation: Special Report 290*, Washington, DC, USA: The National Academy of Sciences, available at http://onlinepubs.trb.org/onlinepubs/sr/sr290.pdf (accessed August 2009).

Transportation Research Board (2011), *Policy Options for Reducing Energy Use and Greenhouse Gas Emissions from U.S. Transportation, Special Report 307*, Washington, DC: TRB.

Trenberth, K.E., J. Fasullo and L. Smith (2005), 'Trends and variability in column-integrated atmospheric water vapor', *Climate Dynamics*, **24**, 741–58.

UN-Habitat (2008), 'Overview', in *State of the World's Cities 2008/2009 Harmonious Cities*, London, UK and Sterling, VA, USA: Earthscan, available at http://www.clc.org.sg/pdf/UN-HABITAT%20Report%20Overview.pdf.

US Army Corps of Engineers (USACE), Federal Emergency Management Agency, National Weather Service, and NY/NJ/CT State Emergency Management (1995), *MetroNY Hurricane Transportation Study, Interim Technical Data Report*, New York, NY, USA: Federal Emergency Management Agency.

US Bureau of the Census (May 2011, June 2011), 'Census data & emergency preparedness', available at http://www.census.gov/newsroom/emergencies/add itional/additional_information_on_coastal_areas.html.

US Climate Change Science Program (CSP) (2008), *Impacts of Climate Change and Variability on Transportation Systems and Infrastructure: Gulf Coast Study, Phase I. A Report by the U.S. Climate Change Science Program and the Subcommittee on Global Change Research Synthesis and Assessment Product 4.7* [Savonis, M.J., V.R. Burkett and J.R. Potter (eds)], US Department of Transportation, Washington, DC, USA, available at http://www.climatescience. gov/Library/sap/sap4-7/final-report/sap4-7-final-all.pdf.

US Climate Change Science Program (USCCSP) (2009), *Coastal Sensitivity to Sea-Level Rise: A Focus on the Mid-Atlantic Region. A report by the U.S. Climate Change Science Program and the Subcommittee on Global Change Research* [James G. Titus (Coordinating Lead Author), K. Eric Anderson, Donald R. Cahoon, Dean B. Gesch, Stephen K. Gill, Benjamin T. Gutierrez, E. Robert Thieler and S. Jeffress Williams (Lead Authors)], US Environmental Protection Agency, Washington, DC, USA, available at http://www.climatesci-ence.gov/Library/sap/sap4-1/final-report/sap4-1-final-report-all.pdf.

US Department of Energy (DOE), Energy Information Administration (EIA) (December 2009), *Emissions of Greenhouse Gases in the United States 2008*, available at http://www.eia.doe.gov/oiaf/1605/ggrpt/pdf/0573(2008).pdf; http://www.eia.doe.gov/oiaf/1605/ggrpt/pdf/0573%282008%29.pdf; ftp://ftp.eia.doe.gov/pub/oiaf/1605/cdrom/pdf/ggrpt/057308.pdf.

US Department of Energy (DOE), Energy Information Administration (EIA) (April 2010), *Annual Energy Outlook 2010 with Projections to 2035*, available at http://www.eia.doe.gov/oiaf/aeo/pdf/0383%282010%29.pdf.

US Department of Energy (DOE), Energy Information Administration (EIA) (August 2010), *Annual Energy Review 2009*, available at http://www.eia.gov/oiaf/servicerpt/stimulus/pdf/sroiaf%282009%2903.pdf.

US Department of Energy (DOE), Energy Information Administration (EIA) (2011), *Alternative Fuel Station Counts by State*, available at http://www.afdc.energy.gov/afdc/fuels/stations_counts.html.

US Department of Energy (DOE), Energy Information Administration (EIA) (March 2011), *Emissions of Greenhouse Gases in the United States 2009*, available at http://www.eia.gov/environment/emissions/ghg_report/pdf/0573(2009).pdf.

US Department of Energy and US Environmental Protection Agency (2011), *Fuel Economy Guide 2011 Model Year*, available at http://www.fueleconomy.gov/feg/FEG2011.pdf.

US Department of Transportation (2008), *The Potential Increase of Global Sea Level Rise on Transportation Infrastructure, Methodology*, available at http://climate.dot.gov/impacts-adaptations/sea_level_rise/study_methodology.html.

US Department of Transportation and ICF International (2007), *The Potential Impacts of Global Sea Level Rise on Transportation Infrastructure, Phase 1 – Final Report: The District of Columbia, Maryland, North Carolina, and Virginia*, available at http://www.bv.transports.gouv.qc.ca/mono/0965210.pdf (accessed March 2008).

US Department of Transportation, Bureau of Transportation Statistics (various years), database, available at http://www.bts.gov/publications/national_transportation_statistics/2010/html/table_04_49.html.

US Department of Transportation, Center for Climate Change and Environmental Forecasting (2008), 'The potential impacts of global sea level rise on transportation infrastructure', Washington, DC: US DOT, available at http://climate.dot.gov/impacts-adaptations/pdf/entire.pdf and primary site: http://climate.dot.gov/impacts-adaptations/sea_level_rise.html.

US Department of Transportation, Federal Highway Administration (July 2008), *Integrating Climate Change into the Transportation Planning Process*, available at http://www.fhwa.dot.gov/hep/climatechange/climatechange.pdf.

US Department of Transportation, Federal Motor Carrier Safety Administration (April 2011), *Weather and Climate Impacts on Commercial Motor Vehicle Safety*, available at http://www.fmcsa.dot.gov/facts-research/research-technology/report/Weather-Impacts-on-CMV-Safety-report.pdf.

US Department of Transportation, Federal Railroad Administration (December 2008), *Research Results: Development of Rail Neutral Temperature Monitoring Device*, available at http://www.fra.dot.gov/downloads/research/rr0831.pdf.

US Department of Transportation, Federal Transit Administration (January 2010), *Public Transportation's Role in Responding to Climate Change*, Washington, DC, USA, available at http://www.fta.dot.gov/documents/PublicTransportationsRoleInRespondingToClimateChange2010.pdf.

US Department of Transportation, Federal Transit Administration (August 2011), *Flooded Bus Barns and Buckled Rails: Public Transportation and Climate Change Adaptation*, available at http://www.fta.dot.gov/documents/FTA_0001_-_Flooded_Bus_Barns_and_Buckled_Rails.pdf.

US Department of Transportation, Volpe Center (undated, c.2002), *Track Buckling Research*, Cambridge, MA, USA: US DOT, Volpe Center, available at http://www.volpe.dot.gov/coi/pis/work/archive/docs/buckling.pdf.

US Environmental Protection Agency (undated website), 'Household Emissions Calculator', available at http://www.epa.gov/climatechange/emissions/ind_calculator.html.

US Environmental Protection Agency (c2008), 'Reducing Urban Heat Island Effects. A Compendium of Strategies. Cool Pavements', available at http://www.epa.gov/heatisld/resources/pdf/CoolPavesCompendium.pdf.

US Environmental Protection Agency (December 2009), *Technical Guidance on Implementing the Stormwater Runoff Requirements for Federal Projects Energy Independence and Security Act Section 438*, available at http://www.epa.gov/owow/NPS/lid/section438/pdf/final_sec438_eisa.pdf.

US Environmental Protection Agency (April 2010), *Inventory of US Greenhouse Gas Emissions and Sinks: 1990–2008*, available at http://www.epa.gov/climate-change/emissions/downloads10/508_Complete_GHG_1990_2008.pdf.

US Environmental Protection Agency (April 2011), *Inventory of Greenhouse Gases and Sinks 1990–2009*, available at http://www.epa.gov/climatechange/emissions/downloads11/US-GHG-Inventory-2011-Complete_Report.pdf.

US Environmental Protection Agency (2011), *Fuel Economy Guide 2011 Model Year*, available at http://www.fueleconomy.gov/feg/FEG2011.pdf.

US Environmental Protection Agency, 'Household Emissions Calculator', Washington, DC, US EPA, available at http://www.epa.gov/climatechange/emissions/ind_calculator.html.

Vasquez, E. (2006), 'Think of It This Way: It Could Be 136', *The New York Times*, available at http://www.nytimes.com/2006/07/18/nyregion/18heat.html.

Vermeer, M. and S. Rahmstorf (2009), 'Global sea level linked to global temperature', *Proceedings of the National Academy of Sciences*, **106**, 21527–32.

Wackernagel, M. and W. Rees (1996), *Our Ecological Footprint*, Gabriola Island, BC, Canada: New Society Publishers.

Walk Score (2010, 2011), Seattle, WA, USA, available at http://www.walkscore.com and transit score http://www.walkscore.com/transit.

Walk Score, "street smart walk score" http://blog.walkscore.com/2011/01/preview-street-smart-walk-score/; http://www.walkscore.com/professional/street-smart.php (accessed 2011).

Walk Score (July 2011), White Paper 'Walk Score Methodology', available at http://www2.walkscore.com/pdf/WalkScoreMethodology.pdf.

Wigley, T.M.L. (2009), 'The effect of changing climate on the frequency of absolute extreme events', *Climatic Change*, **97**, 67–76.

Wikipedia, 'Concrete', available at http://en.wikipedia.org/wiki/Concrete (accessed September 11, 2011).

Wilson, S.G. and T.R. Fischetti (May 2010), 'Coastal population trends in the US: 1960–2008', available at http://www.census.gov/prod/2010pubs/p25-1139.pdf.

Zimmerman, R. (July/August 1994), 'After the deluge', *The Sciences*, **34**, (4), 18–23.

Zimmerman, R. (1996), 'Global warming, infrastructure, and land use in the metropolitan New York area: prevention and response', in D. Hill (ed.), *The Baked Apple? Metropolitan New York in the Greenhouse*, New York, NY, USA: New York Academy of Sciences, pp.57–83.

Zimmerman, R. (2005), 'Mass transit infrastructure and urban health', *Journal of Urban Health*, **82** (1), 21–32.

Zimmerman, R. (2011), Lecture presentations for the course 'Adapting the Physical City', New York University, Wagner Graduate School of Public Service.

Zimmerman, R. and M. Cusker (2001), 'Institutional decision-making', Chapter 9 and Appendix 10 in C. Rosenzweig and W.D. Solecki (eds), *Climate Change and a Global City: The Potential Consequences of Climate Variability and Change. Metro East Coast*, New York, NY, USA: Columbia Earth Institute and Goddard Institute of Space Studies, pp.9-1–9-25 and A11–A17.

Zimmerman, R. and C. Faris (2011), 'Climate change mitigation and adaptation in North American cities', *Current Opinion in Environmental Sustainability*, **3** (3), 181–7.

4. Planning, technology and behavior

Global climate change and other environmental issues have brought about new approaches to planning for and managing changes in transport in the form of technology for modes of transport and behavioral changes in how transport occurs. Each new environmental initiative brings with it a different set of planning and implementation programs. Climate change planning intersects with, builds on, and reinforces other major planning initiatives such as sustainability, smart growth and resilience that have forged extensive plans, partnerships, and consortiums, many of which potentially alter transport. The connections among these programs are often informal.

Transport networks will potentially be shaped by mitigation of greenhouse gas (GHG) emissions and adaptation to the many effects anticipated from the impact of climate change. Institutional mechanisms potentially play a key role in shaping the changes in these networks which will occur at many levels; at the level of the location and design of facilities, at larger scale land use changes, and as behavioral changes in the form of how people travel.

Existing planning and policy frameworks by many governments are presented and how the transportation focus has been incorporated, emphasizing climate-related plans. Selected new technologies and the infrastructure to support new modes of travel build upon those presented in the previous chapter. Finally, street systems are presented as a common denominator to integrate transportation and other urban functions, including those related to the environment and security.

PLANNING FOR AND MANAGING IMPACTS ON TRANSPORT

Climate Change Planning: Governmental Initiatives

International policies
International policy has underscored the need to control anthropomorphic climate changes. The United Nations Framework Convention on

Climate Change (UNFCCC) in 1992 was held in Rio de Janeiro, and the treaty marked a milestone for these policies (Matthews and Caldeira 2008, p.1). In 1988, the United Nations established the Intergovernmental Panel on Climate Change (IPCC) and it produced its reports in 1990, 1995, 2001 and 2007 (as well as numerous special studies) on the state of the science, the direction of climate change, mitigation, and many other themes, and the fifth assessment is due in 2013 (IPCC 2010). The definition of climate change used by the IPCC differs from that of the UNFCCC in that the former uses climate change to signify any change in climate whereas the UNFCCC specifically refers to climate change as being a consequence of human activity (IPCC 2007, p.30).

US actions
In the US, government regulatory initiatives for climate change have largely taken the form of numerous bills that have been introduced in Congress, many of which had different projected emission levels (Resources for the Future 2008). In June 2009 the Waxman-Markey bill, or the American Clean Energy and Security Act of 2009, which promoted clean energy and greenhouse gas reductions using a cap and trade program, was passed by the House of Representatives with a narrow vote of 219 to 212 (*The New York Times* October 2011; US House of Representatives 2009) and was not voted on by the Senate. The legislation in the year or so since the Waxman-Markey bill had moved in the direction of reducing the US role in climate change, such as the EPA Regulatory Relief Act of 2011 which would have reduced the EPA's authority to regulate greenhouse gases (Collins 2011).

Regional, multi-state initiatives
In the absence of clear programmatic efforts nationwide in the US, state and local governments and regional consortiums of governments have emerged as leaders in the planning and management of climate change initiatives in general. Most of these actions have incorporated transportation. They include the Regional Greenhouse Gas Initiative (RGGI) formed in 2009 (RGGI, Inc. undated website), the Mid-West Greenhouse Gas Reduction Accord developed in 2007 (Pew Center for Climate and Energy Solutions undated website), a Western Climate Initiative (WCI 2011), and Florida (Florida Governor's Action Team on Energy and Climate Change).

State legislation
States have addressed transportation and environmental concerns for many decades where their authority extends to municipal land use planning. These efforts date back at least to the growth control movement of

the 1970s accompanying the first Earth Day and the flurry of federal environmental regulations that followed. A number of states have taken direct action on climate change planning and some of those have emphasized transportation.

The Pew Center (c2010 undated web site) review of state legislation related to VMT highlighted the following actions for transportation as of 2010:

Florida (Pew Center 2010, p.2):
- HB 7135 (2008) provides strategies to reduce GHG for transportation and land use planning.
- HB 697 (2008) requires Local Government Comprehensive Plans to include transportation and land use measures to reduce GHG emissions.

New Jersey (Pew Center 2010, p.3):
- The New Jersey Department of Transportation (NJDOT) New Jersey Future in Transportation (FIT) program in conjunction with the Office of Smart Growth (OSG) and other agencies will combine land use and transportation.
- NJDOT's Transit Village program provides for growth near public transit.
- The Mobility and Community Forum Project provides for land use and transportation in development plans.
- 2008 Urban Transit Hub Tax Credit Act encourages growth around urban transit hubs by giving businesses tax credits if they are within a half-mile of a rail station.

New York (Pew Center 2010, p.3):
- The New York State Energy Plan under Executive Order 2 extensively addresses detailed transportation energy components.
- The draft Climate Action Plan (CAP) released in November 2010 contains extensive land use and transportation elements.

Oregon (Pew Center 2010, p.3):
- The Oregon Department of Land Conservation and Development statewide plan since 1973 contains land use and transportation goals.
- The Oregon Transportation and Growth Management Program (TGM) administered by both the Oregon Department of Transportation and Oregon Department of Land Conservation and Development also integrates transportation and land use, and guides local government in this area.
- Senate Bill 1059 (March 18, 2010) was signed that provides for "smart, sustainable, and cost-effective transportation systems" and

the creation of a state-level strategy for GHG reduction from transportation.

Virginia (Pew Center 2010, p.4) has ordinances that particularly address street networks:

- Virginia's Planning, Subdivision of Land and Zoning Code (Title 15.2, Chapter 22) specifically targets in a comprehensive plan "principles, including pedestrian-friendly road design, interconnection of new local streets with existing local streets and roads, connectivity of road and pedestrian networks, and mixed-use neighborhoods".

Washington (Pew Center 2010, p.4):

- HB 2815 of March 13, 2009 requires VMT reduction targets.

Climate Change Plans: Extent of Planning in States and Localities

Environmental planning has been a longstanding tradition, and climate change planning has been a recent form of it. While these planning efforts represent separate endeavors, philosophies, and policy streams and have different regulatory histories, they are now converging. A potential consequence is mutual reinforcement and economy from co-benefits. Often a forced marriage, the land use and transportation planning connection paved the way at least conceptually for what was to come in the form of sustainability plans and climate plans. Local climate action plans supplemented federal actions and regional initiatives and consortiums. Some argue that local government is an appropriate place for climate change initiatives (Rosenzweig 2011).

The most popular mechanism for state and local level action has been the Climate Action Plan. Climate action plans (CAPs) are but one mechanism that is used for climate change planning; others that have followed or have been incorporated into the plans have proven to be the drivers of much of the action. GHG inventories are one area; a second is best practices including energy plans, which in many ways provide more detailed implementation of planning goals. Some localities and states have begun to formulate detailed practices within their government's operations, and in that way, theoretically provide a model for other non-governmental entities to follow.

Best practices were perhaps the most influential set of actions for transportation, and were in part an outcome of the planning processes that preceded them. Such practices have been around since at least the early 1970s as part of mainstream environmental legislation. These provided technological innovations and design guidelines for resource use, land use and the physical form of human settlements, and human behavior.

Climate change plans are the latest wave of environmental planning. To a large extent they do not borrow extensively from earlier environmental planning traditions in either content or process. The plans cover a very large number of technologies and alternatives and the emphasis here is on where transport stands in these planning processes.

State Planning

Wheeler (2008, pp.491–5) reviewed and tabulated state and local climate change plans. He reviewed 29 state planning efforts through 2008 (Zimmerman and Faris 2011, p.182). Through 2011, the US EPA (2011) identified about the same – 31 states with climate action plans. Of those 31, according to the US EPA tabulation, 12 had state plans only (Arkansas, Iowa, Maine, Michigan, Montana, New Jersey, Nevada, Ohio, Rhode Island, Virginia, Vermont and Wisconsin) and 19 had both a state plan and at least one local plan (Alaska, Arizona, California, Colorado, Connecticut, Florida, Illinois, Maryland, Massachusetts, Minnesota, New Hampshire, New Mexico, New York, North Carolina, Oregon, Pennsylvania, South Carolina, Utah, and Washington). An additional five states had no state plans but at least one local plan (Georgia, Louisiana, Missouri, Tennessee, and Texas).

Wheeler (2008, p.492) identifies the following transportation initiatives targeted to emissions in the plans he reviewed: alternative fuels including biofuels and ethanol and incentive systems (17), California standards (11), smart growth (8), transit including greening of government fleets (6), and VMT reduction (1).

By August 10, 2011, the Pew Center on Global Climate Change (undated website) identified a number of transportation-related climate change programs discussed above and the states that had adopted them: Mandates and Incentives Promoting Biofuels (44), Medium- and Heavy-Duty Vehicle Policies including idling reduction, financial incentives and procurement of new or retrofitted alternative renewable fuel vehicles (40), Plug-in Electric Vehicles (37), VMT-related Policies and Incentives including smart growth (18), Vehicle GHG Emissions Standards (15), and Low Carbon Fuel Standard adopted or in development (14).

Local Planning

The Wheeler (2008, pp.493–6) review and tabulation of local climate change plans identified 18 large city and 17 small city plans by 2008 (Zimmerman and Faris 2011, p.182). The US Environmental Protection Agency State Climate and Energy Program (2011) listed 32 local (city or county) plans.

The development of local plans to achieve environmental goals has had a very long history (Saha and Paterson 2008; Toly 2008). The efforts have been mixed. In a statistical analysis of whether or not new communities had incorporated principles of green development, Berke et al. (2011, 2009) concluded that in fact many of these principles had not been incorporated. This complements an earlier evaluation by Berke and Conroy (2000) on sustainability plans.

Currently, local environmental planning tends to emphasize climate change and greening, and in some cases the two have merged. Many associations exist as clearinghouses and resources for local climate change planning. These associations, the size of their membership and the status of climate plans by their members are reviewed by Zimmerman and Faris (2011, pp.182, 184), are covered by Lindseth (2004), and the histories appear on the websites. They include:

> The US Conference of Mayors (USCOM)
> http://www.usmayors.org/climateprotection/ClimateChange.asp
> ICLEI (Local Governments for Sustainability)
> http://www.icleiusa.org/
> The C40 Cities http://www.c40cities.org/.

Extensive inventories of the jurisdictions engaged in this planning are maintained by these organizations (for example, ICLEI 2009a) and the US EPA (US Environmental Protection Agency State Climate and Energy Program http://epa.gov/statelocalclimate/).

The following local initiatives are examples that are specific to transportation.

The City of Seattle, Washington, transit vehicle fleet is a major target for GHG reduction in the county energy plan. Its transit vehicle fleet accounts for half of the municipal government's energy use and the use of renewables will be considered as a possibility to reduce this load (King County, WA, USA 2010; Zimmerman and Faris 2011, p.184)

The Metropolitan Transportation Authority (MTA 2007) in New York adopted a sustainability plan that supports a lot of the work already underway, such as using solar power for subway stations, regenerative breaking, and other measures. Bay Area Rapid Transit (BART) (2008) has also used solar power in its transit systems.

ICLEI (2009b, pp.43–5) reported the following examples of innovations by the end of 2009 in the transportation sector from 141 climate action plans and 56 sustainability plans:

- Olympia, Washington, Green Fleet Program. The vehicle fleet of the City of Olympia, Washington is a large energy consumer. In order to achieve VMT reduction, the city will reorganize work, reroute trips, make operational changes to reduce idling, and reduce the fleet size. Each agency operates under a Green Fleets Plan.

- Seattle, Washington, Transit Investments. As indicated above the King County Energy Plan aims at reducing energy consumption of its vehicles. In addition, the city will expand transit with a new Seattle Streetcar that expects an increase of 450,000 riders per year, a Central Link Light Rail that extends the existing transit system by 36 miles, and upgrading of its bus and commuter rail systems. This is expected to reduce GHG by 100,000–180,000 metric tons.
- Salt Lake City, Utah, Clear the Air Commute Challenge. This program aims at VMT reduction and a reduction in driving alone. Summer driving was reduced by 1.1 million miles with a reduction in carbon emissions of 1.87 million pounds.
- Chicago, Illinois, Promoting Cycling and Walking. The Chicago Pedestrian Plan and the Bike 2015 Plan provide for innovations such as bike racks and a bike network to encourage cycling and walking. The estimated GHG savings are 10,000 metric tons by 2015.

The US Conference of Mayors (USCOM) identified the following cases (USCOM 2009):

- San Francisco, California, SFGreasecycle is restaurant waste cooking oil recycled to create a biodiesel fuel for the City's 1,500 municipal buses and trucks. The grease is mixed with diesel to create B-20 biodiesel. It diverts 13.3 million pounds of carbon dioxide (USCOM 2009, p.12).
- Carmel, Indiana, Walkable Community involves shaping the street and sidewalk networks through design to encourage walking.

The US Housing and Urban Development (HUD) Sustainable Communities Regional Planning Grants often incorporate transportation elements which is a stated goal of the program. The City of Boston obtained a sustainability community planning grant that included funds for the development of a transit oriented development (TOD) along one of its transit corridors (the Fairmount corridor) and an expansion of one of its lines (the Green line in Somerville) without displacement.

The US Environmental Protection Agency (undated website) has a series of cases where the agency encourages green planning under its Green Power Community Challenge and Green Power Partnership initiative, and transportation agencies are occasionally partners in the effort.

CAPs and other environmental planning efforts are not the only way in which GHG emissions from transportation are controlled. Since the Supreme Court case Massachusetts versus EPA 549 US 497 (2007), GHG regulation under the Clean Air Act (CAA) has been strengthened. This affects other legislation such as the National Environmental Policy Act (NEPA). New York City, under its City Environmental Quality Review Act (CEQR), is reducing mobile sources of GHG through parking, vehicle charging stations and car sharing.

The public sentiment for local planning is also reflected in public opinion polls. Leiserowitz and Feinberg (2007) observed that action on global warming at the local level is preferred by most Americans, with local action being energy initiatives. The poll found that generally people supported development and local regulation initiatives but did not support as strongly measures that would require them to pay more money.

There are of course the many project-specific and even facility-specific systems such as Leadership in Energy and Environmental Design or LEED and US EPA's Energy Star program that pertain to transport facilities. For example, the NYC MTA Stillwell Avenue station was the first transit station to use solar cells and one of its maintenance facilities is a LEED facility (MTA NYC Transit undated website).

Planning for environmental goals that encompass transport has emerged under many programs. Planning is considered the first step toward implementation. Ultimately, these plans are locally based and located under the umbrella of a region, state, or country. The extent of adoption of such plans is mixed. In contrast to the findings of Berke et al. (2011, 2009) cited above that many communities do not incorporate environmental principles other studies find different types of progress following from CAPs. Boswell et al. (2010), for example, conducted a study of 30 cities with CAPs that had advanced to the next step of GHG emission inventories.

TECHNOLOGIES AND STRATEGIES FOR TRANSPORT ALTERNATIVES

Alternative Vehicles and Fuels

A profusion of alternative fuels for vehicular travel has emerged over the past century. The alternative technologies are well-known (Randolph and Masters 2008), and in part are driven by environmental goals. Yet the need to distribute these fuels and provide the infrastructure to support that requires considerable attention to transport networks. A brief overview of fuel alternatives is presented, followed by a focus on an analysis of alternative ways of locating places to provide fuel.

Renewables are usually obtained from a natural source, are replenishable and replaceable by natural sources, are inexhaustible, at least over a very long period of time, and are sustainable in the sense that they do not shift resource use from energy production to some other sector.

Renewable energy is usually defined by example, and includes a wide range of sources such as solar energy, energy from the movement of wind and water (including tidal and wave action), biomass, and heat from within the earth or geothermal heat (Randolph and Masters 2008, p.66). In total, by 2009 renewable energy contributed less than 10 percent of the supply of energy in the United States (US DOE, EIA 2010).

The flexibility of transportation vehicles to use alternative fuels has increased as vehicle design has adapted to new fuel types. The environmental and security tradeoffs and co-benefits of each of these different types of fuel, as well as their performance and degree of change required for vehicles, are noteworthy in looking to future choices. Adopting alternative fuels has considerable implications for the production and distribution systems associated with these fuels.

The types of alternative fuels and the environmental, performance and operational issues associated with them have been extensively covered (Kahn Ribeiro et al. 2007; Randolph and Masters 2008; US DOE, EIA 2010; Yacobucci 2010).

The value of renewable fuels has to be viewed not only in terms of the environmental benefits of the energy source, but also how these fuels fare over the cycle from extraction through production, distribution, disposal of residuals, and the transport of materials at each stage in the cycle. This assessment process is conventionally known as life cycle assessment (LCA), which has arisen to incorporate or internalize environmental impacts into the assessment of alternatives. Applied to transport, it is usually known as "Well-to-Wheels" assessments, and is a concept used worldwide (European Commission, Joint Research Centre 2007). This is usually divided into stages in the cycle called Well-to-Tank and Tank-to-Wheels assessments, or in order to be consistent with the need to evaluate air pollutants, Well-to-Pump and Pump-to-Wheels (Brinkman et al. 2005, p.11). Argonne National Laboratory has developed a model to conduct these assessments called the Greenhouse gases, Regulated Emissions, and Energy use in Transportation (GREET) model (Wang 2003).

By 2008, the US DOE, EIA listed five different types of alternative fuels used in vehicles in the US. According to EIA (US DOE, EIA 2010, p.295), the number of vehicles using those alternative fuels totaled 775,667: Ethanol (E85) accounted for 58 percent, Liquefied Petroleum Gases (LPG) 19.5 percent, Compressed Natural Gas (CNG) 14.7 percent, Electricity (not including hybrid vehicles) 7.3 percent, and Liquefied Natural Gas

(LNG) and Hydrogen each accounted for less than 1 percent. By far the fastest rates of growth have been experienced by cars using electricity and the use of E85. According to US DOE, EIA (2010, computed from p.295), between 1992 and 2008, E85 grew from 172 vehicles to 450,327 vehicles and electricity (not including hybrid vehicles) grew from 1,607 to 56,901 vehicles. The entire set of alternative fueled vehicles grew from 246,855 in 1995 (totals not available for earlier years) to 775,667 by 2008 about a tripling of the number. Three other types had been in use earlier but were listed as zero by 2008 by EIA (85 percent Methanol (M85), Neat Methanol (M100) and 95 percent Ethanol (E95)).

The ability to obtain rare earths for storage batteries continues to be a constraint for renewable energy, and these elements are concentrated globally in just a few countries. Gruber et al. (2011, p.766) estimate that a total of 38.68 million tons are available from over 40 different deposits from many different countries: Bolivia accounts for a quarter of the amount (but the deposits have a lower concentration than others), and the top ten resources including Bolivia account for 83 percent (Bolivia, Chile, China (2), United States (3), the Congo, Argentina, and Serbia). A number of other countries have begun to develop their lithium resources.

Electric vehicles
One of the vehicle categories, electricity, is noteworthy given its growth expectations. The electric car market is very diverse in terms of the number of products it offers, and Baum (2011) estimated about 100 to 120 products in this category by 2015. In September 2011, Baum estimated that the electric car market by 2015 would show sizable growth:

> Full electric vehicles: 200,000
> Plug-in hybrids: 200,000 (from about 15,000 in 2011)
> Regular hybrids: 500,000 (from about 300,000 in 2011).

According to Baum's estimates, for example, sales of two electric vehicles, the Chevy Volt and the Nissan Leaf that were introduced in December 2010, will by 2015 grow to 100,000 and 75,000 respectively from their base of sales through August 2011 of 3,500 and 6,200. Plug-in electric hybrids were expected to increase dramatically, following the effects of the Japan earthquake which slowed production.

The extent to which electric vehicles achieve a net reduction in carbon dioxide emissions from the energy they use depends on the source of electricity. That, in turn, will depend on the origin of the electric power which includes renewable energy as well as conventional fossil fuels.

In using solar power, some innovative uses include the placement of solar cells directly on to the vehicles (Patton 2012). Power from this source could be limited by the low density of the energy provided.

Alternative Fueling (or Fuel) Station (AFS) Infrastructure

The viability of alternative fueled vehicles in general, and electric vehicles in particular, depends on the availability of fueling stations. Although ethanol generally has accounted for the largest share of alternative fueling stations – about a third in the US – electricity has accounted for a larger percent in California (based on US DOE, National Energy Research Laboratory (NERL) 2010).

In some cases, putting in the required fueling infrastructure may be substantial. For example, the US Government Accountability Office (GAO) (2011, p.14) citing a US EPA study described the extensive network of transportation infrastructure required to support just ethanol, estimated at 22 billion gallons of ethanol, citing a cost of \$26 billion for rail, trucks, barges and wholesale terminals, almost half of which would be for the rail infrastructure.

Electric vehicles comprise an increasing portion of alternative vehicle technologies. In order for them to be viable, charging stations need to be close at hand. The network of regular gasoline stations provides insights into the road network and vehicular distribution that supports these alternatives. It also provides insights into how new fuel infrastructure, such as electric charging stations, might be distributed to the extent that it will make use of existing infrastructure networks.

Major types of alternative fuels and AFS
As discussed above, alternative fuels currently in use or being considered for transportation are compressed natural gas (CNG), Liquid Petroleum Gases (LPG), Ethanol, Liquefied Natural Gas, Electricity and Hydrogen. The fuel consumption and number of vehicles using each type of alternative fuel in 2008 and the number of alternative Fueling Stations (2010) provided by the US DOE, EIA (2010), are shown in Table 4.1.

Conventional gas station locations
The location of conventional gasoline stations primarily for petroleum are described and compared to the location of alternative fueling stations.

Two separate sets of figures are available for conventional stations, the US DOE and the National Petroleum News (NPN) *MarketFacts* (NPN 2011). According to NPN (2011), the number in 2010 was 159,006 and 162,350 in 2009 (assuming the drop of 3,344 cited in 2010). In 2008, the number was 161,768 (which they cite as a drop of 2,500 over 2007 figures)

Table 4.1 Alternative fuel characteristics

Fuel type	Million gasoline-equivalent gallons consumed* (2008)	Thousand vehicles* (2008)	Number of alternative fueling stations** (2010)	Number of incentives for production and use*** (2011)
CNG	189	114	898	not listed
LPG	148	151	2,603	283
Ethanol	62	450	2,429	418
LNG	26	3	44	360 (NG)
Electricity	5	57	2,920	302 (EVs)
Hydrogen	<1.0	<1.0	58	260 (H fuel cells)
Biodiesel (B20)			624	436

Sources:
* US DOE, EIA (2010), *Annual Energy Review 2009*, Washington, DC, USA: US DOE, EIA, Section 10, p.295.
** US DOE, NREL, available at http://www.afdc.energy.gov/afdc/fuels/electricity_locations.html (based on 9,576 station count through September 2011).
*** These are federal and state incentives. Davis, Stacey C., Susan W. Diegel and Robert G. Boundy (June 2011), *Transportation Energy Data Book*, 30th Edition, ORNL-6986, Oak Ridge, TN, USA: Oak Ridge National Laboratory, Table 10.9. Other incentives listed but not shown in the table are 43 for neighborhood electric vehicles (NEVs) and 60 for aftermarket conversions.

(NPN 2010). US DOE (2011) also reports the NPN database by year going back to 1996. In 1996 the total number of stations was 190,246 reflecting an even greater decline or consolidations over time.

In 2010, according to NPN, Texas led the states in the number of gas stations followed by California (Reid 2011). NPN *MarketFacts* attribute the decline in the number of stations to industry consolidation. Although this is a relatively small decline it may signal a growing concentration of gas stations.

The US DOE database lists 118,756 establishments as distinct from stations. As in the case of stations reported by Reid (2011), Texas also leads with about 9 percent of the establishments and California second with about 7 percent of the establishments. The US DOE (2011) tabulation of the NPN data includes state level station data but only through 2006 when the NPN no longer posted state data for stations on its public website.

Alternative fueling stations
The US DOE maintains a database of alternative fuel charging stations (AFS). In order to reflect the access to those

Table 4.2   Proximity of alternative fueling stations to interstate highways, US

Distance from interstate highways (in miles)	Percentage of stations (%)
0–0.15	7.2
>0.15–0.25	4.5
>0.25–5	47.1
>5–10	9.0
>10–20	10.1
>20–50	15.5
>50–75	4.6
>75–100	1.3
>100	0.8
Total	100.0

Source: Computed from US DOE Alternative Fuels and Advanced Vehicles Data Center, Alternative Fueling Stations, through October 2010, available at http://www.afdc.energy. gov/afdc/fuels/stations.html.

stations from major roadways, distances from interstates were calculated and mapped. Table 4.2 shows the distribution of the stations by distance from interstate highways using the stations that were in the database in October 2010 (computed from US DOE data). Figure 4.1 gives the location of stations 50 miles or more from an interstate highway.

The distribution of alternative fuel charging stations at the state level apparently is very similar to the distribution of regular gas stations. The correlation was high (r=0.78). Figure 4.2 shows this relationship for states in the US. Each of these types of stations is also highly correlated at the state level with vehicle miles of travel (VMT). This finding supports the idea that pre-existing infrastructure (for conventional fuel) is likely to be sought as a location for new infrastructure for alternative fuels.

The alternative fuel charging stations listed on the US DOE website change continually, since it allows for input from users. For example, in October 2010 the total was 7,068. By July 2011 the total was 9,576. In order to determine if any major re-distribution occurred at least at the state level, the distributions by state for the two time periods were correlated. The correlation was very high (r=0.97) indicating that very little redistribution at least at the state level had occurred. Through April 30, 2012 the US DOE website indicated 16,883 AFSs in the US.

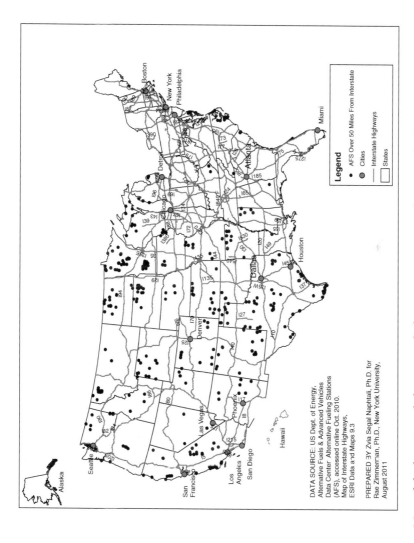

DATA SOURCE: US Dept. of Energy,
Alternative Fuels & Advanced Vehicles
Data Center Alternative Fueling Stations
(AFS), accessed online Oct. 2010.
Map of Interstate Highways,
ESRI Data a'nd Maps 9.3

PREPARED 3Y Zvia Segal Naphtali, Ph.D. for
Rae Zimmerman, Ph.D., New York University,
August 2011

Figure 4.1   Map of the location of alternative fueling stations greater than 50 miles from interstate highways, US, 2010

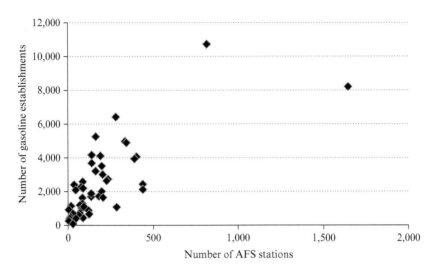

Sources: The number of gasoline establishments graphed from US Census Bureau (May 2011), '2007 Economic Census, gasoline stations by state 2007', available at http://fact finder.census.gov/servlet/IBQTable?_bm=y&-ds_name=EC0744A1&-geo_id=01000US&-dataitem=*.
The number of AFS Stations was graphed from US Department of Energy, Alternative Fuels and Advanced Vehicles Data Center, Alternative Fueling Stations, available at http://www.afdc.energy.gov/afdc/fuels/stations.html, as of October 2010.

Figure 4.2   Number of gasoline establishments and number of alternative fueling stations by state

BALANCING MULTIPLE MODES

The key factors in evaluating the distribution of transport types by mode are the inputs primarily in terms of the consumption of resources and the outputs in terms of emissions. Life cycle analysis (LCA) is a key approach to this problem.

Alternative Modes of Travel, Energy Use and Emissions

Dave (2010) developed calculations for the amount of energy consumed and CO_2 released by mode of travel. The work is based on two kinds of models, one is what Dave refers to as a process model, and the other is the Carnegie Mellon University Green Design Institute's Economic Input–Output Analysis (EIO-LCA).

Figures 1 and 2 in Dave's paper provide energy inputs and GHG outputs in terms of passenger mile traveled (PMT) by mode of travel. The modes included in increasing order of energy usage ranging from 102 to 8,837 KJ/PMT and GHG emissions ranging from 33 to 674 kg/PMT are walking, bicycling, electric bikes, buses during peak travel, transit as exemplified by Bay Area Rapid Transit, the Green Line, and MUNI, air travel exemplified by a Boeing 737, average bus travel, automobiles (sedan), SUVs, pickup trucks, and buses during off-peak hours (presumably expending the same amount of energy but with fewer passengers).

The conclusions suggested from a comparison of these per passenger miles of travel figures for inputs and outputs are:

- The correlation between energy use and GHG emissions is practically perfect (r=0.99) reflecting the fact that energy use is a critical determinant of emissions, at least given the way emissions are calculated.
- While walking and biking give the same amount of emissions per capita the energy usage for biking is greater.
- Sedans use 46 times more energy than walking and emit 12 times more GHG per passenger miles traveled (PMT).
- Sedans use 15 times more energy than biking and emit 12 times more GHG PMT.
- Electric bikes emit the same amount of GHG but use more energy than regular bikes (the ratio for energy is 1.2).
- Buses during off-peak hours suffer the greatest in terms of GHG PMT given that they have fewer passengers traveling fewer miles, yet since they travel the same routes, they expend the same amount of energy even though less congestion is involved.

Dave (2010, Figures 1 and 2) breaks down energy usage and GHG emissions according to the stage in the life cycle. In practically all cases, with the exception of walking and biking, operations account for the largest share of energy usage and with the exception of biking operations account for the largest share of GHG emissions. According to Dave (2010), for walking and biking, infrastructure accounts for the greater share of energy usage and GHG emissions except that for walking, operation accounts for the greater share counting the greater amount of CO_2 individuals emit while walking.

Walking

Southworth (2005) lists a number of criteria for making an area successfully walkable, many of which are similar to network concepts such as linkages, connections, and paths.

Walking is now connected with many other modes of travel,

including biking and transit as well as automobile travel, though accounting for those connections is not always available in data on commuting patterns. In Salt Lake City, Utah, an extensive pedestrian friendly boulevard, which consists of wide sidewalks above the streets, extends from the center of the city where the light rail system operates. Based on the analysis of the US DOT National Transit database (NTD), Salt Lake City currently leads other commuter rail systems in the size of its MSA served by commuter rail, accounting for 7 percent of the area served by such systems. However, it does not rank high in other respects such as population, trips, miles traveled or transit infrastructure.

Biking

Travel by bike has been tracked for some time (Kifer 2002) and its use is now growing substantially, primarily for commuting (US DOT, FHWA 2010) as described in Chapter 1 for individual cities. The American Community Survey makes it a formal part of their commuting database. This section briefly addresses some issues that have arisen in connection with the supporting street network for bicycle travel and its relationship to other modes of travel.

Bike travel can conflict with other modes of travel such as walking, auto travel, train travel and also with other bike travelers. There are a number of studies of incidents between bikes and other modes of travel. For example, Tuckel and Milczarski (2011, pp.3–4) in their study of biking accidents in New York State found that between 2007 and 2010 the number of accidents averaged about 1,000 annually. The authors suggest that this is an underestimation since it did not include people who had not gone to a hospital to treat their injuries (Tuckel and Milczarski 2011, p.12). They conclude that although the rate appeared to be going down slightly, the small sample size precludes such a conclusion (Tuckel and Milczarski 2011, p.4). The frequency of accidents appears to be higher during the late spring and summer months when cycling and pedestrian traffic are probably higher. The authors conclude that their findings are in sharp contrast with a previous study that estimated a nationwide number of 1,000 accidents, as reported by Goodman (2010). New York City (2006, p.2) reported that between 1995 and 2005, 92 percent of bike crashes occurred with motor vehicles and 89 percent of them were located at intersections. The Transportation for America and the Surface Transportation Policy Partnership (2011) cite road traffic-related pedestrian accident statistics. These findings suggest that it is critical to adapt street networks and their use to accommodate these multiple modes of travel.

RETHINKING STREETS

More and more demand is being placed upon streets in order to accommodate multiple travel modes and other activities in ways that minimize conflict. First, the safety of users is at stake. The statistics on automobile collisions and fatalities with cyclists cited briefly above and pedestrians are well-known. Second, is the convenience for different modes and other functions that streets perform. Third, are the environmental and security issues that streets pose given their ubiquitousness and accessibility.

The automobile had come to dominate streets and long distance roadways. The expansion in lane miles, described in Chapter 2, even with little change in route miles, contributed to this. Thus, the rethinking of how streets are designed, used and managed has become an imperative.

Deconstructing Streets

One of the more radical approaches has been to reduce the number of streets altogether. Cities such as Seattle, Buffalo, Toronto, and New Haven have torn down roadways that had divided communities and were land intensive, and Milwaukee stands out as an example of a city that demolished its freeway in 2003 to make way for development (Peirce 2008). In Madrid, Spain an old highway was replaced with a park (Kimmelman 2011).

Freemark and Reed (2009) identify the following cases of highway deconstruction: the Cheonggycheon highway in Seoul, South Korea in 2002, that was reported to have a capacity of 160,000 cars per day, Harbor Drive in Portland, Oregon in 1974, the Embarcadero Freeway in San Francisco which was destroyed in the 1989 Loma Prieta earthquake, and the Central Freeway in San Francisco later rebuilt as Octavia Boulevard. In 2010 the Congress for the New Urbanism (2010) identified a dozen freeways in seven states in the US and two areas in Canada as the "top teardown prospects" with the potential to be replaced by boulevards, often tree-lined and providing open space.

These freeways were typically damaged by natural hazards, were aging or in otherwise poor condition, or were barriers or divided communities. These deconstructed areas are usually replaced either with streets with greenery, natural areas such as watershed areas, or are used as parks.

"Complete Streets"

The wide range of uses now envisioned for streets has given rise to the "complete streets" movement backed by legislation and government policies. Complete streets primarily focus on the compatibility of bicyclists and pedestrians. According to the National Coalition of Complete Streets, the concept grew out of interests in biking and the term is attributed to David Goldberg (Goldberg undated website) of Smart Growth America, and the Coalition was formed in 2005 (McCann and Rynne 2010), though it is considered to date earlier in the context of bicycling actions. It is now backed by over 300 policies, guides and other government instruments from the federal government, 26 states, over 202 localities, Puerto Rico, the District of Columbia, and other geographic areas (National Coalition of Complete Streets undated web page; McCann and Rynne 2010).

Streets as Pedestrian Thoroughfares

There are ways of reshaping streets other than eliminating them. Parking can be moved off streets into buildings, and parking areas can be converted to usable commercial and recreational areas (Peirce 2008) to accommodate pedestrian traffic. Streets can be converted into pedestrian areas as New York City has done in some of the densest parts of the city. These conversions can be combined with the greening of streets described below to accomplish multiple objectives including environmental goals and water management. They also have the potential to minimize vehicle-related security problems.

Streets have been designed to be more pedestrian and traffic friendly using traffic controls to reduce congestion. For example, "Superstreets" is a term that Hummer et al. (2010) ascribe to an FHWA term "restricted crossing U-turns". According to Hummer et al. (2010) these are found in North Carolina, Maryland, Minnesota, and Michigan.

Greening Streets

The greening of streets involves a complex set of mechanisms to increase the amount of vegetation and permeability of pavement to water which accomplishes multiple objectives. The vegetation absorbs carbon dioxide, provides natural habitats for various species, retards water and thereby reduces flooding, and reduces the loss of energy by changing the reflectivity of land surfaces. In many ways it is not unlike the very extensive wetlands management programs that preceded it.

Streets for Stormwater Control

A key part of the greening of streets is water management. Streets inevitably channel large amounts of water. Many innovative ways of using streets for stormwater control and drainage now exist.

Some of the more common means of using streets to control the flow of water is altering their surfaces or providing plantings in adjacent areas to capture water. There is a profusion of such mechanisms varying in scale.

New York City's Greenstreets program began in 1996 and emphasizes the placement of vegetation, stormwater controls and permeable materials adjacent to streets (NYC 2010, p.62). The NYC Green Infrastructure Plan (NYC 2010, p.62) and its stormwater management plan (NYC 2008) use the City's agencies to implement green walkways. Porous concrete has been used for sidewalk material alongside one of its combined sewer overflow (CSO) detention basins in Paerdegat Basin, and the NYC Housing Authority is also adopting that approach.

Philadelphia's plan identifies 34 percent of its impervious surface as streets with even more than that in the public area category, and has put in place ideas for implementing the plan to reduce their impact (Philadelphia Water Department 2009, pp.10–12). Chicago is using reflective, permeable pavement (Dillow 2011).

Toronto has developed guidelines for greening parking lots (Toronto City Planning 2007). The US EPA has general guidance for street stormwater runoff control (US EPA 2009; August 2009).

Other approaches to using streets for stormwater control are more dramatic. In Kuala Lumpur, Malaysia a tunnel concept called the Stormwater Management and Road Tunnel (SMART) (undated website) project (mentioned briefly in Chapter 3) doubles as a relief for both road congestion and stormwater flooding. During periods of modest water accumulation, cars continue to use the tunnel both ways and water is channeled below the lower roadway. As water increases, one level is closed and is used to channel the excess water. In periods of severe flooding all lanes are completely closed to traffic, cars are removed from the tunnel, and the tunnel is then used to channel the increased floodwaters. According to the project's website, it is a 6 mile long project by the project developer MMC-Gamuda, a joint venture of two Malaysian engineering firms in cooperation with the highway and drainage authorities in Malaysia.

Streets for Waste Cleaning

Inevitably streets become receptacles for wastes generated on land, from pedestrians and vehicles using streets, or as an outcome of the debris accumulated after extreme events. Melosi, in his history of urban sanitation, pointed out that street sanitation was ahead of other forms of sanitation since it performed many functions (Melosi 2008, p.26), and street cleaning dates back many centuries even as an informal function performed by scavengers, becoming more formal in the mid-nineteenth century as traffic increased (Melosi 2008, p.26 footnote 74).

Even today, cleaning of transportation facilities is not an end in itself. In transit systems, the stairwells are cleaned to avoid slipping and falling. The tracks are cleaned to avoid track fires.

Streets and Waste Recycling

Street construction materials use recycled waste materials. One idea is to combine plastic bags with asphalt. According to Khullar (2009), the material extends road lifetime by one to two years, makes the material more resistant to higher temperatures due to the greater binding capacity provided by the plastic, increases the water resistance of the roadway due to the greater impermeability of the plastic, and overall reduces pothole formation and maintenance needs. Khullar notes that the amount of material used for 100 tons of the new bitumen material is eight tons of plastic, and for every lane mile, two tons of plastic are required. This technology may also have the effect of reducing the energy and hence environmental demands for street construction.

Another effort to use recycled material for roadway construction was Glasphalt. It was developed as a means of recycling glass, absorbing 167 tons of cullet per mile of road; however, the durability of the road surface and performance under heat came into question (Salter 1996). Others indicate that despite the disadvantages, there are advantages such as increased reflectivity and lower susceptibility to the effects of moisture (Lu et al. 2011). US DOT, FHWA (2011) reported in its history and use of Glasphalt that it requires pre-preparation and can deteriorate when glass separates from asphalt. New York City was known to have had one of the larger efforts given its extensive and continuous supply of glass and the need for an adequate supply of glass is a limitation that many areas face. A glass processing plant opened on Long Island in the 1980s and the use of glass for resurfacing within New York City from 1990 to 1995 was estimated at about 250,000 tons of glass.

Streets as Generators of Electric Power

The means to charge electric vehicles has been emerging in the form of very diverse technologies. Some technologies include using streets and parking areas to provide electric charging from solar panels. The National Renewable Energy Laboratory in Golden, Colorado and Dell Computer in Texas are being tested for using solar panels in a parking lot by Envision Solar in La Jolla, California (Woodyard 2010).

Brusaw and Brusaw (undated website) have developed a concept for interconnected solar panels that will initially be used at parking lots, and will eventually be driven on and used to charge cars (Woodyard 2010). They estimate the electricity generated per lane per mile is about 3.344 MW/hr. The surface is textured to prevent cars from slipping, and self-cleaning glass would keep the glass clean. Applied to sidewalks, the placement of rubberized tiles to generate electricity has been proposed to capture the energy from pedestrian traffic (Kateman 2011).

Streets as Communication Conduits

The growing use of sensors in travel vehicles and by users is expanding to its use along transport networks. Co-location of communication lines and roads and rail in utility corridors are common relationships between transportation and communication, and electric sensors have been used along rail lines to detect breaks in rails. Moreover, the location of sensors along road and rail lines provides a vital security function as well.

Streets for the Future

The end (or maybe it is a beginning) is a positive one. Though streets may have been built with single purposes in mind they hold promise for adapting to multiple needs for human transport as some of the new initiatives suggest. Ballon (2012), for example, portrays how the street grid of New York City planned in 1811 was able to adapt to the many diverse and ever-changing activities of the City for over two centuries.

Streets accommodate many forms of movement. Not including conventional automobiles and trucks, the list is very long. Other than pedestrians, there are the un-motorized walkers for people with disabilities, bikes, skates, horses, carriages, pedi-cabs, skateboards, and scooters! There are motorized scooters, motorcycles, mopeds, segways, electric bikes, and individually operated vehicles for the disabled such as motorized wheelchairs. All of these have different routes and different speeds, and all except walking and animal rides depend on the wheel. Many cities have programs underway to accommodate these needs on streets and sidewalks (NYC Department of Transportation 2009a, 2009b; Toronto City Planning 2007). There will inevitably be conflicts, and the adaptability of streets to some of the uses could require extensive construction time. Developing a process to resolve these issues will be a challenge in the context of a very diverse and ever-changing user population.

OBSERVATIONS ON PLANNING AND TECHNOLOGY

Planning mechanisms have proliferated with the onset of climate change and green infrastructure not unlike the predecessors for environmental and sustainability planning in general, and specialized areas such as coastal zones and flood plains. Ultimately, solutions are being tested at local levels as extensive networks of infrastructure to support innovative ways of providing energy for transport get underway. Some notable examples are the networks of fueling stations for charging vehicles with renewable fuels that range from locations at individual homes to larger facilities. Planning for a multitude of environmental and transport needs has come down to the street level which is the major infrastructure network to support transport of all kinds, as well as environmental and security needs. The many innovations will play out over the coming years as more uses of streets emerge. Instead of looking just at simultaneous usage options, the time dimension will be critical as well. Streets can be differentiated or become specialized according to when different uses occur, what the uses are, and who the users are. Plans and programs are moving forward at a rapid pace, and are the place where many of these innovations will be shaped.

REFERENCES

Ballon, H. (ed.) (2012), *The Greatest Grid: The Master Plan of Manhattan, 1811–2011*, New York, NY, USA: Columbia University Press.

Baum, A. (September 2011), 'Beyond first-year bumps, electric car market poised for growth', available at http://www.plugincars.com/beyond-first-year-bumps-electric-car-market-poised-growth-107919.html (accessed October 23, 2011).

Bay Area Rapid Transit (BART) (July 2008), 'BART goes solar, saving a projected $3.4 million over 20 years', available at http://www.bart.gov/news/articles/2008/news20080710.aspx.

Berke, P.R. and M.M. Conroy (2000), 'Are we planning for sustainable development? An evaluation of 30 comprehensive plans', *Journal of the American Planning Association*, **66** (1), 21–33.

Berke, P.R., Y. Song and M. Stevens (2009), 'Integrating hazard mitigation into new urban and conventional developments', *Journal of Planning Education and Research*, **28**, 441–55.

Berke, P., M. Stevens and Y. Song (September 2011), 'Are we placing smart growth in dumb locations?', *Natural Hazards Observer*, **XXXVI** (1), 1, 12–15, available at http://www.colorado.edu/hazards/o/archives/2011/sep11_observer-web.pdf.

Boswell, M.R., A.I. Greve and T.L. Seale (2010), 'An assessment of the link between greenhouse gas emissions inventories and climate action plans', *Journal of the American Planning Association*, **76** (4), 451–62.

Brinkman, N., M. Wang, T. Weber and T. Darlington (May 2005), *Well-to-Wheels Analysis of Advanced Fuel/Vehicle Systems – A North American Study of Energy Use, Greenhouse Gas Emissions, and Criteria Pollutant Emissions*, Argonne National Laboratories, available at http://www.transportation.anl.gov/pdfs/ TA/339.pdf.

Brusaw, S. and J. Brusaw (undated website), 'About', *Solar Roadways – A Real Solution*, available at http://solarroadways.com/about.shtml.

C40 Cities Climate Leadership Group (undated website), available at http://live. c40cities.org/.

Collins, S. (2011), 'EPA Regulatory Relief Act', 112th Congress 1st Session, S. 1392, July 20, 2011, available at http://www.govtrack.us/congress/bill. xpd?bill=s112-1392.

Congress for the New Urbanism (2010), 'Freeways without futures', available at http://www.cnu.org/highways/freewayswithoutfutures2010 (accessed October 2, 2011).

Dave, S. (February 2010), *Life Cycle Assessment of Transportation Options for Commuters*, Cambridge, MA, USA: MIT, available at http://files.meetup. com/1468133/LCAwhitepaper.pdf (accessed March 4, 2012).

Davis, S.C., S.W. Diegel and R.G. Boundy (2011), *Transportation Energy Data Book: Edition 30, ORNL-6986*, Oak Ridge, TN, USA: Oak Ridge National Laboratory.

Dillow, C. (2011), 'Preparing for permanent climate change, Chicago invests in warm-weather-ready infrastructure', *Popsci*, May 24, available at http://www. popsci.com/environment/article/2011-05/preparing-climate-change-chicago-adapting-itself-warmer-weather.

European Commission, Joint Research Centre (2007), *Well to Wheels Analysis of Future Automotive Fuels and Power Trains in the European Context*, available at http://ies.jrc.ec.europa.eu/uploads/media/WTW_Report_010307.pdf.

Florida Governor's Action Team on Energy and Climate Change (undated website), available at http://www.flclimatechange.us/documents.cfm; Background at http://www.flclimatechange.us/background-ccagrole.cfm.

Freemark, Y. and J. Reed (July 2009), 'Huh?! 4 cases of how tearing down a highway can relieve traffic jams (and save your city)', *The Infrastructurist*, available at http://www.infrastructurist.com/2009/07/06/huh-4-cases-of-how-tearing-down-a-highway-can-relieve-traffic-jams-and-help-save-a-city/.

Goldberg, D. (undated website), 'Who we are', *National Coalition of Complete Streets*, Smart Growth America, available at http://www.completestreets.org/ who-we-are/ (accessed October 2, 2011).

Goodman, J.D. (September 2010), 'The cyclist–pedestrian wars', *The New York Times*, available at http://cityroom.blogs.nytimes.com/2010/09/18/spokes-the-cyclist-pedestrian-wars.

Gruber, P.W., P.A. Medina, G.A. Keoleian, S.E. Kesler, M.P. Everson and T.J. Wallington (2011), 'Global lithium availability, a constraint for electric vehicles?', *Journal of Industrial Ecology*, 15 (5), 760–75.

Hummer, J.E., R.L. Haley, S.E. Ott, R.S. Foyle and C.M. Cunningham (November 2010), *Superstreet Benefits and Capacities*, Raleigh, NC, USA: North Carolina Department of Transportation.

ICLEI – Local Governments for Sustainability, 'About ICLEI', available at http:// www.iclei.org/index.php?id=about (accessed October 25, 2011).

ICLEI – Local Governments for Sustainability (2009a), 'US local sustainability plans and climate action plans', available at http://www.warmtraining.

org/gov/pdf/SustainabilityClimatePlans_USA.pdf (accessed October 25, 2011).

ICLEI – Local Governments for Sustainability (2009b), *Measuring Up: A Detailed Look at the Impressive Goals and Climate Action Progress of US Cities and Counties*, Boston, MA, USA: ICLEI USA, available at http://www.icleiusa. org/action-center/affecting-policy/ICLEI%20USA%20Measuring%20Up%20 Report%202009.pdf.

Intergovernmental Panel on Climate Change (IPCC) (2007), *Climate Change 2007: Synthesis Report*, available at http://www.ipcc.ch/pdf/assessment-report/ar4/syr/ ar4_syr.pdf.

Intergovernmental Panel on Climate Change (IPCC) (November 2010), *Understanding Climate Change, 22 Years of IPCC Assessment*, Geneva, Switzerland: IPCC Secretariat.

Kahn Ribeiro, S., S. Kobayashi, M. Beuthe, J. Gasca, D. Greene, D.S. Lee, Y. Muromachi, P.J. Newton, S. Plotkin, D. Sperling, R. Wit, and P.J. Zhou (2007), 'Transport and its infrastructure', in B. Metz, O.R. Davidson, P.R. Bosch, R. Dave and L.A. Meyer (eds), *Climate Change 2007: Mitigation. Contribution of Working Group III to the Fourth Assessment Report of the Intergovernmental Panel on Climate Change*, Cambridge, UK and New York, NY, USA: Cambridge University Press, pp.323–85, available at http://www. ipcc.ch/pdf/assessment-report/ar4/wg3/ar4-wg3-chapter5.pdf.

Kateman, B. (October 2011), 'Green sidewalk is electrifying', available at http:// blogs.ei.columbia.edu/2011/10/14/green-sidewalk-is-electrifying/.

Khullar, M. (November 2009), 'Plastic roads offer greener way to travel in India', *The New York Times*, available at http://www.nytimes.com/2009/11/14/ business/global/14plastic.html?_r=1&scp=1&sq=India%20roads%20from%20 plastic&st=cse.

Kifer, K. (May 2002), 'How many bicycle commuters are there in the USA', available at http://www.kenkifer.com/bikepages/survey/commuter.htm (accessed January 3, 2010).

Kimmelman, M. (December 26, 2011), 'In Madrid's Heart, Park Blooms Where a Freeway Once Blighted', *The New York Times*, available at http://www.nytimes. com/2011/12/27/arts/design/in-madrid-even-maybe-the-bronx-parks-replace- freeways.html?_r=1&hp.

King County, WA, USA (2010), '2010 King county energy plan', available at http://www.kingcounty.gov/environment/climate.aspx.

Leiserowitz, A. and G. Feinberg (2007), *The GfK Roper Yale Survey on Environmental Issues – Fall 2007: American Support for Local Action on Global Warming*, New Haven, CT, USA: Yale School of Forestry & Environmental Studies, available at http://environment.yale.edu/news/5323/.

Lindseth, G. (2004), 'The Cities for Climate Protection Campaign (CCPC) and the framing of local climate policy', *Local Environment*, **9** (4), 325–36.

Lu, H., W. Huang, K. Li, L. Liu, and L. Sun (2011), *Glasphalt Mixtures' Performance Research and Analysis*, American Society of Civil Engineers Proceedings of the Third International Conference on Transportation Engineering.

Massachusetts versus EPA 549 US 497 (2007).

Matthews, H.D. and K. Caldeira (2008), 'Stabilizing climate requires near-zero emissions', *Geophysical Research Letters*, **35**, L04705.

McCann, B. and S. Rynne (2010), *Complete Streets: Best Policy and Implementation*

Practices, Chicago, IL, USA: American Planning Association, Planning Advisory Service.

Melosi, M.V. (2008), *The Sanitary City. Environmental Services in Urban America from Colonial Times to the Present, Abridged Edition*, Pittsburgh, PA, USA: University of Pittsburgh Press.

Metropolitan Transportation Authority (2007), *Greening Mass Transit and Metro Regions: The Final Report of the Blue Ribbon Commission on Sustainability and the MTA*, New York, NY: MTA.

Metropolitan Transportation Authority (undated website), New York City Transit and the Environment, available at http://www.mta.info/nyct/facts/ffenvironment.htm.

National Coalition of Complete Streets, available at http://www.completestreets.org/.

National Petroleum News (NPN) (2010), *NPN MarketFacts 2008 Highlights*, Bev-Al Communications Inc., available at http://www.npnweb.com/ME2/dirmod.asp?sid=A79131211D8846B1A33169AF72F78511&type=gen&mod=Core+Pages&gid=CD6098BB12AF47B7AF6FFC9DF4DAE988.

National Petroleum News (NPN) (2011), 'Station Count Shows Big Drop', State of the Industry 2011, *NPN Magazine*, Digital Issue p.19. http://read.dmtmag.com/issue/24948/18.

New York City (various agencies) (2006), Bicyclist Fatalities and Serious Injuries in New York City 1996–2005, available at http://www.nyc.gov/html/dot/downloads/pdf/bicyclefatalities.pdf.

New York City (2008), plaNYC 2030: Sustainable Stormwater Management Plan 2008, available at http://nytelecom.vo.llnwd.net/o15/agencies/planyc2030/pdf/nyc_sustainable_stormwater_management_plan_final.pdf.

New York City (September 2010), *NYC Green Infrastructure Plan*, New York, NY, USA: City of New York, available at http://www.nyc.gov/html/dep/html/stormwater/nyc_green_infrastructure_plan.shtml.

New York City Department of Transportation, 'Bicyclists, bicycle network development', available at www.nyc.gov/html/dot/html/bicyclists/bikenetwork.shtml.

New York City Department of Transportation (2009a), *2009 Sustainable Streets Index*, available at http://www.nyc.gov/html/dot/downloads/pdf/sustainable_streets_index_09.pdf.

New York City Department of Transportation (2009b), *Street Design Manual*, available at http://www.nyc.gov/html/dot/html/about/streetdesignmanual.shtml.

The New York Times (October 2011), 'House vote 477 – H.R.2454: On passage', available at http://politics.nytimes.com/congress/votes/111/house/1/477.

Patton, P. (2012), 'It's Electric. Should it look electrifying?', *The New York Times*, available at http://www.nytimes.com/2012/01/08/automobiles/its-electric-should-it-look-electrifying.html?_r=1&hpw.

Peirce, N. (August 2008), *City Curbs on Cars: Now Accelerating*, Washington, DC, USA: Citiwire, available at http://citiwire.net/post/144/.

Pew Center on Climate and Energy Solutions (undated website), 'Midwest Greenhouse Gas Reduction Accord', available at http://www.pewclimate.org/what_s_being_done/in_the_states/mggra.

Pew Center on Global Climate Change (undated website), 'US climate policy maps', available at http://www.pewclimate.org/what_s_being_done/in_the_states/state_action_maps.cfm, (accessed October 24, 2011).

Pew Center on Global Climate Change (September 2010), 'VMT-related policies and incentives', available at http://www.pewclimate.org/sites/default/modules/usmap/pdf.php?file=6638.

Pew Center on Global Climate Change (2010), 'Climate action plans', available at http://www.pewclimate.org/what_s_being_done/in_the_states/action_plan_map.cfm.

Philadelphia Water Department (September 2009), *Green City, Clean Waters*, Philadelphia, PA.

Randolph, J. and G.M. Masters (2008), *Energy for Sustainability. Technology, Planning, Policy*, Washington, DC, USA: Island Press.

Regional Greenhouse Gas Initiative (RGGI) (undated website), 'RGGI documents', available at http://rggi.org/rggi/documents.

Reid, K. (2011), National Petroleum News (NPN) Magazine's 2010 MarketFacts Industry Survey, available at http://www.npnweb.com/me2/dirmod.asp?sid=A79131211D8846B1A33169AF72F78511&nm=Market+Data&type=MultiPublishing&mod=PublishingTitles&mid=8F3A7027421841978F18BE895F87F791&tier=4&id=846DBB41B759447D91F1B479DFFCEC80.

Resources for the Future (January 2008), 'Timeline of emissions targets of bills introduced into the 100th Congress', Washington, DC, USA: Resources for the Future.

Rosenzweig, C. (September 2011), 'All climate is local', *Scientific American*, **305** (3), 70–73.

Saha, D. and R.G. Paterson (2008), 'Local government efforts to promote the "Three Es" of sustainable development survey in medium to large cities in the United States', *Journal of Planning Education and Research*, **28**, 21–37.

Salter, R. (September 1996), 'A second look at glasphalt the glittery paving material made from recycled glass has lost some of its sparkle. With pieces of glass coming out of glasphalt-paved roads, questions about durability and safety are being raised', *Lehigh Valley's Newspaper The Morning Call*, available at http://articles.mcall.com/1996-09-08/news/3101919_1_paving-glass-glasphalt.

Southworth, M. (December 2005), 'Designing the walkable city', *Journal of Urban Planning and Development*, **131** (4), 246–57.

Stormwater Management and Road Tunnel (SMART) (undated website), available at http://www.smarttunnel.com.my/.

Toly, N.J. (2008), 'Transnational municipal networks in climate politics: from global governance to global politics', *Globalizations*, **5** (3), 341–56.

Toronto City Planning (2007), Design Guidelines for 'Greening' Surface Parking Lots, Toronto City Planning, available at http://www.toronto.ca/planning/urbdesign/pdf/greening_parking_lots_dg_update_16nov07.pdf.

The Transportation for America and the Surface Transportation Policy Partnership (2011), *Dangerous by Design*, available at http://t4america.org/docs/dbd2011/Dangerous-by-Design-2011.pdf.

Tuckel, P. and W. Milczarski (September 2011), *Pedestrian–Cyclist Accidents in New York State: 2007–2010*, available at http://www.hunter.cuny.edu/communications/repository/files/Pedestrian%20Cyclist%20Accidents_3.pdf.

US Census Bureau (May 2011), '2007 Economic Census, gasoline stations by state 2007', available at http://factfinder.census.gov/servlet/IBQTable?_bm=y&-ds_name=EC0744A1&-geo_id=01000US&-dataitem=*.

US Conference of Mayors (June 2009), *Mayors Climate Protection Center: Taking*

Local Action: Mayors and Climate Protection Best Practices, The United States Conference of Mayors, available at http://www.usmayors.org/pressreleases/uploads/ClimateBestPractices061209.pdf.

US Department of Energy (2011), 'Public retail gasoline stations by state and year', available at http://www.afdc.energy.gov/afdc/data/docs/gasoline_stations_state.xls.

US Department of Energy, Alternative Fuels and Advanced Vehicles Data Center (undated website), Alternative Fueling Stations, available at http://www.afdc.energy.gov/afdc/fuels/stations.html.

US Department of Energy, Energy Information Administration (2010), *Annual Energy Review 2009*, Washington, DC, USA: DOE, EIA, available at http://www.eia.gov/emeu/aer/pdf/pages/sec10.pdf.

US Department of Energy, Energy Information Administration, Office of Coal, Nuclear, Electric, and Alternate Fuels (April 2010), 'Table V1. Estimated number of alternative fueled vehicles in use in the United States, by fuel type, 2004–2008', in *Alternatives to Traditional Transportation Fuels 2008*, available at www.eia.gov/cneaf/alternate/page/atftables/afv-atf2008.pdf (accessed October 23, 2011).

US Department of Energy, National Renewable Energy Laboratory (2010), 'Electric charging station locations', available at http://www.afdc.energy.gov/afdc/fuels/electricity_locations.html.

US Department of Housing and Urban Development (HUD) (undated website), *Sustainable Communities Regional Planning Grants*, Washington, DC, USA: US Department of Housing and Urban Development, available at http://portal.hud.gov/hudportal/HUD?src=/program_offices/sustainable_housing_communities/sustainable_communities_regional_planning_grants.

US Department of Transportation, Federal Highway Administration (May 2010), *The National Bicycling and Walking Study: 15-Year Status Report*, available at http://drusilla.hsrc.unc.edu/cms/downloads/15-year_report.pdf.

US Department of Transportation, Federal Highway Administration (June 2011), *User Guidelines for Waste and Byproduct Materials in Pavement Construction*, available at http://www.fhwa.dot.gov/publications/research/infrastructure/structures/97148/wg2.cfm.

US Environmental Protection Agency (undated website), available at http://www.epa.gov/owow/NPS/lid/section438/pdf/final_sec438_eisa.pdf.

US Environmental Protection Agency (undated website), 'Green Power Community Challenge and Green Power Partnership', available at http://www.epa.gov/greenpower/communities/gpcchallenge.htm.

US Environmental Protection Agency (2009), *Technical Guidance on Implementing the Stormwater Runoff Requirements for Federal Projects under Section 438 of the Energy Independence and Security Act*, Washington, DC, USA: US Environmental Protection Agency.

US Environmental Protection Agency (August 2009), *Green Streets*, available at http://www.epa.gov/npdes/pubs/gi_arra_green_streets.pdf.

US Environmental Protection Agency (July 2011), *State Climate and Energy Program*, available at http://www.epa.gov/statelocalclimate/ (accessed October 24, 2011).

US Government Accountability Office (GAO) (June 2011), *Biofuels. Challenges to the Transportation, Sale and Use of Ethanol Blends*, Washington, DC, USA: US GAO, available at http://www.gao.gov/new.items/d11513.pdf.

US House of Representatives (June 2009), 'H.R. 2454 American Clean Energy and Security Act of 2009 Final vote results for roll call 477', available at http://clerk. house.gov/evs/2009/roll477.xml.

Wang, M. (2003), *Well-to-Wheels Energy and Emission Impacts of Vehicle/Fuel Systems Development and Applications of the GREET Model*, Argonne National Laboratory, Center for Transportation Research, presented at Sacramento, CA, USA, California Air Resources Board, available at http://www.transportation. anl.gov/pdfs/TA/273.pdf.

Western Climate Initiative (2011), 'History', available at http://www.western climateinitiative.org/history.

Wheeler, S.M. (2008), 'State and municipal climate change plans', *Journal of the American Planning Association*, **74** (4), 481–96.

Woodyard, C. (July 2010), 'Turning parking lots into vast urban solar farms', *USA Today*, available at http://content.usatoday.com/communities/driveon/ post/2010/07/turning-parking-lots-into-vast-urban-solar-farms/1.

Yacobucci, B.D. (2010), *Alternative Fuels and Advanced Technology Vehicles: Issues in Congress*, Washington, DC, USA: Congressional Research Service, September 22, available at http://www.cnie.org/NLE/CRSreports/10Oct/ R40168.pdf.

Zimmerman, R. and C. Faris (2011), 'Climate change mitigation and adaptation in North American cities', *Current Opinion in Environmental Sustainability*, **3** (3), 181–7.

5. Environmental networks and transport: air, water and ecosystems

INTRODUCTION

The relationships between transportation and the environment have a very long history and have been the centerpiece of environmental legislation since at least the mid-twentieth century. Going far back in history, prior to motorized transport, the use of horse-drawn vehicles created sanitation conditions that dominated public health concerns (Melosi 2008) and motorized transport created its own set of environmental conflicts. The environmental review process assumed a central role in integrating transport and environment, since that was among its intended purposes, and is presented here first. Although security would potentially be incorporated into environmental review, it was not originally very pronounced, though since the World Trade Center attacks of September 11, 2001, it has been addressed to a greater extent.

Following the environmental process for transport, a few selected environmental themes are presented for air, water and ecology, focusing on how they change and shape transport.

Environmental Impact Assessment as an Integrator of Environment and Transport

The National Environmental Policy Act (NEPA) passed in 1969 became the backbone for the review of the compatibility of transportation projects with the environment incorporating the mandates of the Clean Air Act and other federal environmental legislation. The NEPA process with a full disclosure mandate gradually became integrated and incorporated into mainstream environmental legislation. For many years transport projects, primarily road construction, dominated federal environmental impact statements (EISs) prepared under NEPA. State and local EISs or environmental review processes have also encompassed transport projects.

By the late 1990s transportation projects still accounted for a large share of federal EISs, ranging from about 16 percent to 24 percent in any given year (Council on Environmental Quality 2011a), but the number of EISs prepared by other agencies began to exceed those of the US Department of Transportation (Council on Environmental Quality 2011a). Since the 1990s, the US DOT EISs have been about a fifth of all federal EISs (Council on Environmental Quality 2011a).

The US Department of Transportation (DOT) has usually ranked third among agencies for NEPA EIS filings. It also usually averages about 10 percent of the NEPA related court cases filed annually, with variations from year to year (Council on Environmental Quality 2011b). According to the Council on Environmental Quality (2009), of the 543 federal EISs filed in calendar year 2008 104 were filed by the US DOT. Highway projects typically dominate the number of transportation EISs though there is some variation. Of the 104 transportation EISs in 2008, 64 were filed by the Federal Highway Administration (FHWA) and 21 by the Federal Transit Administration (FTA), reflecting the relative dominance of highway projects over rail in the EIS process. These figures only reflect EISs for which the US DOT was designated as a lead agency, and underestimate transportation issues in the EIS process, since transportation is a part of all EISs.

Each agency is required to develop and implement its own procedures under NEPA. FHWA's procedures for highway projects are in 23 CFR § 771 (US DOT, FHWA undated website). The US DOT Federal Transit Administration provides guidance for transportation projects generally, including rail, noting the exemption of plans and programs from NEPA under the Transportation Efficiency Act for the 21st Century (TEA 21) (US DOT, FTA 2005, p.1). The guidance suggests ways that transportation planning can contribute to project level reviews under NEPA. The type of information identified is very much targeted to the networked properties of transportation systems: mode, "termini, approximate length, and general alignment; number of lanes or tracks; and degree of grade separation and access control" (US DOT, FTA 2005, p.2) but activity flows are included also, such as congestion, and the factors that shape them such as management and financial practices (US DOT, FTA 2005, p.7).

The issues addressed by EISs have evolved over time. Regulations, guidance, and practice have changed, reflecting emerging issues arising with changing technology for transport and detection of environmental conditions, public sentiment and political will, and changes in priorities and standards for environmental protection that accompanied or soon followed those technological developments.

One of the newer issues emerging within the environmental review process in the late twentieth century was climate change. Climate change and GHG emissions are now incorporated into EISs. On February 18,

2010, the CEQ issued draft guidance for the consideration of GHG emissions in EISs (Sutley 2010). The guidance had broad applicability, including programs that affect transportation (US White House 2007). A compilation by the Columbia University Center for Climate Change Law identified nine states and seven localities as initiating guidance to incorporate GHG in EIS requirements as of early 2012 (Columbia University Center for Climate Change Law 2012), and the federal government has guidance for transportation (US DOT FHWA May 13, 2010). Gerrard (2012) addressed the question of whether EISs consider impacts of climate change on projects (as distinct from project impacts on climate change) and indicated that only four highway projects out of 18 project EISs since 2009 took climate change impact into account on the projects.

Within the EIS process, mobile source air toxics (MSAT) have emerged as another newer issue relevant to transportation in EISs. Over the years, the number of toxic air pollutants regulated under the federal Clean Air Act (CAA) has grown from about a half dozen to about two hundred. The history is summarized in US DOT, FHWA (September 2011). The FHWA issued interim guidance for the incorporation of MSAT in highway projects into NEPA documents. As summarized in the FHWA guidance (2009, p.1):

> Controlling air toxic emissions became a national priority with the passage of the Clean Air Act Amendments (CAAA) of 1990, whereby Congress mandated that the US Environmental Protection Agency (EPA) regulate 188 air toxics, also known as hazardous air pollutants. The EPA has assessed this expansive list in their latest rule on the Control of Hazardous Air Pollutants from Mobile Sources (US EPA 2007) and identified a group of 93 compounds emitted from mobile sources that are listed in their Integrated Risk Information System (IRIS) [US EPA, IRIS undated website]. In addition, EPA identified seven compounds with significant contributions from mobile sources that are among the national and regional-scale cancer risk drivers from their 1999 National Air Toxics Assessment (NATA) [US EPA 1999]. These are acrolein, benzene, 1,3-butadiene, diesel particulate matter plus diesel exhaust organic gases (diesel PM), formaldehyde, naphthalene, and polycyclic organic matter.

Streamlining the Environmental Review Process for Transport

In order to manage an increasing number of issues to be addressed in EISs, streamlining, exemption procedures, and expedited reviews were developed. The opportunity for streamlining is pervasive in environmental and land use areas that affect transportation, for example, for the fuel and transport routes that are allowed. In Chapter 6 the exemption process is discussed in the context of emergency response conditions. Federal transportation agency environmental streamlining procedures for roads and rail are from US DOT, FHWA (undated website Environmental Review Toolkit) and US DOT, FTA (undated website Environmental Decision-making).

Streamlining expedited the rebuilding of Lower Manhattan following the World Trade Center attacks on September 11, 2001. Just after the attacks, during response and recovery, streamlining occurred for the rapid collection and removal of debris. Soon after the attacks, cumulative effects analysis under NEPA, which allows the aggregation of projects with similar effects, was used to conduct a single review for a number of the transportation projects for the area, namely, the Permanent Port Authority Trans-Hudson Port Authority (PATH) Station Terminal at the World Trade Center, Fulton Street Transit Center, and the South Ferry Subway Terminal. The projects were considered to be making upgrades to what had been serving the area before (US DOT, FTA 2003).

On August 31, 2011, the federal government set up expedited reviews including but not limited to EISs for projects that would create jobs, had funding identified, were within the federal government's jurisdiction, and could be completed in 18 months (US White House, Office of the Press Secretary August 2011). On October 11, 2011, five road and rail transportation projects were selected as part of the process – two rail projects, two bridge projects, and one highway project (US White House October 2011) – with estimated time savings of a few months to a number of years:

- The Crenshaw/LAX in California will extend a light rail system in the LA Metro. The time saving is estimated to be several months.
- The Baltimore Red Line in Maryland is a rail transit line that connects downtown Baltimore and other nearby areas with suburbs to the west over a 14 mile distance. Permit expediting would save an estimated two years.
- The new Tappan Zee Bridge in New York State is to replace the existing deficient bridge that is a major link in the New York region's transportation system and the environmental review process streamlining would save a number of years.
- The Whittier Bridge along I-95 in Massachusetts will incorporate multi-modal transportation through the addition of pedestrian and bicycle lanes, and permit and other document review streamlining would enable project approvals to occur within six months.
- The Provo Westside Connector is a highway project in Utah for a new arterial from Provo Airport to Interstate 15 that will improve road linkages, and expedited permits could save six months or more.

MAINSTREAM TRANSPORTATION-RELATED ENVIRONMENTAL CONCERNS: AIR AND WATER QUALITY

Air and water quality concerns associated with transportation have a very long history and predate much of the attention to climate change. Just a few aspects of air and water quality are reviewed very briefly here primarily emphasizing some selected and illustrative relationships to transport networks. Included are selected patterns and trends relevant to transport, some issues specifically shaping the way transport services are provided, and some planning mechanisms affecting transport other than those previously discussed for climate change and sustainability.

Air Quality

The US EPA has indicated that the average concentration of many conventional air quality pollutants in the atmosphere, regulated under the Clean Air Act as National Ambient Air Quality Standards (NAAQS), have declined or stabilized since 1980. Localized pockets, however, still persist that exceed NAAQS: 124 million people lived in counties exceeding at least one or more of the NAAQS (US EPA 2012a; 2012b, p.1). The US EPA notes that NAAQS pollutants are generally not included as contributing to global warming, since according to the IPCC 1996, a method of doing so has not been agreed upon (US EPA 2011, p.ES-3).

According to the US DOE (Davis et al. 2011, p.12-2) transportation emissions in 2008 accounted for the following US share of NAAQS criteria pollutants relative to other sectors of the economy:

- Carbon monoxide (CO) 73.2%
- Nitrogen oxides (NO_x) 57.9%
- Volatile organic compounds (VOC) 37.7%
- Particulate Matter PM-2.5 7.2% (less than 2.5 microns in diameter)
- Sulfur dioxide (SO_2) 4.5%
- Particulate Matter PM-10 3.2% (less than 10 microns in diameter).

In contrast, for Europe in 2009, the European Environment Agency (2011, p.29) indicated the share of CO from transport as 34 percent, NO_x 56 percent, VOC 18 percent, PM-2.5 25 percent, and SO_x 17 percent.

Air quality, land use and transportation connections have been emphasized in US federal legislation since at least the 1990s, in the form of State Implementation Plans (SIPs) (US DOT, FHWA 2011a) and their conformity with air quality requirements for congestion mitigation (US DOT,

FHWA 2011b). Transportation network connectivity was identified as a key component of that effort and The Louis Berger Group Inc. (2004), for example, applied a connectivity index to street layouts for the purpose of characterizing land use and air quality relationships in terms of transportation. In the late 2000s, air quality and transportation linkages were expanded to GHGs. The regulations of certain parts of the transportation industry and vehicle emissions under the Clean Air Act are now converging with GHG regulation. This is a result of the EPA seeking approval authority over GHGs under the CAA. SIPs are the central mechanism for managing air quality impacts from transportation, and are the basis for the issuance of permits that affect emissions. In a final rule issued by the EPA on December 1, 2010, the US EPA required SIP changes to incorporate GHGs for all or part of Arizona, Arkansas, California, Connecticut, Florida, Idaho, Kansas, Kentucky, Nebraska, Nevada, Oregon, and Texas (US EPA 2010, pp.1, 5 and 23–4).

Applications and exemptions within the rule pertain to transportation, for example, for "transportation equipment manufacturing" and a "Vehicle Rule", the latter is considered to be the first application of the GHG provisions in that area (US EPA 2010, p.16).

The American Lung Association (ALA) measures year-round particle pollution, short-term particle pollution and ozone at the metropolitan and county level. In its 2010 *State of the Air* report, the ALA found that although there were air quality improvements in the 2009 levels for these three pollutants, 25 cities were still ranked as having the most severe pollution; the number of unhealthy days increased in ten of these 25 cities for ozone and in seven of them short-term particle pollution increased (American Lung Association 2011, p.6). On a more national scale, the ALA estimated that about 175.3 million people in 445 counties, or 58 percent of the population were living in areas considered unhealthy with respect to either ozone or particle pollution, and transportation (vehicles using dirty diesel) is one of the areas they recommended improving to attain healthier air (American Lung Association 2011, p.7).

Another air quality related environmental issue that has emerged in the transport area is the impact of gasoline additives and combustion on human health and the environment. Lead additives, initially used as an anti-knock substance in gasoline, were later withdrawn since they caused catalytic converters, devices used to clean exhaust, to malfunction. In the course of withdrawing lead for that reason, lead levels in human blood, particularly children, plummeted as the concentration of lead in air declined (US Executive Office of the President 2000). The Methyl Tertiary Butyl Ether (MTBE) substitute is described below under water quality.

Air quality issues are pervasive throughout the life cycle of transportation systems. Many cases that initially appear as air quality issues often cross the boundaries of other environmental areas. One case was a rehabilitation or maintenance operation involving the removal of lead-based paint on the Williamsburg Bridge in New York City. The case led to a transformation in maintenance operations for bridges and elevated roadways, and also influenced other infrastructure as well. Although it started out as an air quality issue it eventually generated water, solid waste, health and community quality concerns. It brought to light the large number of air quality and other environmental standards that exist for lead, yet none was suitable for the paint removal operation (Zimmerman 1999).

Water Quality

A few brief examples of how transportation intersects with water quality issues not addressed elsewhere are presented here. Direct water quality impacts from transportation primarily pertain to fuel discharges that enter runoff waters and migrate into adjacent areas and water supplies. Extensive stormwater management techniques have targeted such problems, very similar to those described earlier for climate change adaptation, and transportation facilities, particularly roadways, are often the place where initiatives to control these water problems occur. These innovations were covered in Chapter 4.

However, indirect water quality problems originate along the entire production cycle for vehicles and fuels. For example, for petroleum the bulk of the fuel used by road-based vehicles covers exploration through ultimate disposal, and potential water quality problems exist at each stage.

Part of this life cycle for fuels involves the introduction of additives, with often unforeseen effects on water. Lead additives in gasoline contaminate areas adjacent to roadways. MTBE became the additive of choice for increasing the oxygen content of fuel until it was withdrawn, because it was polluting water supplies and confronting water supply and underground storage regulations. MTBE was attractive because it increased fuel combustion, enabling it to burn more cleanly and reduce tailpipe emissions as well as displace some of the more harmful components (US EPA 2008, 2009). In the late 1990s the federal government and a number of states issued advisories and standards for MTBE, and ethanol replaced it (Zimmerman 2004, p.193).

ECOLOGICAL IMPACTS AND SOLUTIONS: ENVIRONMENTAL CORRIDORS AND TRANSPORTATION

Network Concepts and Environmental Corridors

Connecting transportation to the environment is key to achieving many environmental policies. In Chapter 1, various modes of transportation were discussed that connect or disconnect transportation and the environment, and the conflicts that occur. Road ecology is a science that deals with many of these conflicts. MassDOT (2006, p.14-2) indicates that the science addresses environment and transportation linkages (citing the work of Forman et al. 2003). The science has subfields depending on the type of ecological processes engaged, such as "corridor ecology" or "connectivity conservation" (ScienceDaily 2008).

The extent of land area devoted to roadways is significant and a number of estimates were presented in Chapter 1. As significant is the larger area affected by environmental impacts on wildlife from discharges, noise, light, and collisions with passing vehicles. The ecological areas that surround transport networks and their characteristics have their own networks. One of the more intriguing ways of managing ecological impacts is through wildlife corridors. By superimposing environmental networks and transport networks one can begin to understand conflicts and begin to formulate synergistic solutions. What makes this a viable approach is the common use of network concepts or the ability to map ecological concepts onto transportation network characteristics, as outlined in Chapter 1.

Cook (2002) identifies many of the components of ecological networks and the conditions that lead to their vulnerability or viability. These provide an important basis for understanding the interaction with road systems. Other studies have provided applications of primarily corridor concepts specific to road systems that are integrated here with the theoretical ecological network concepts provided by Cook (2002) and others.

Cook (2002) defines species habitats in ecological systems in terms of patches (identical to nodes) and corridors. Patches are then described in terms of the kind, extent, the ratio of the boundary to the area, how natural they are, the degree of isolation and other factors (Cook 2002, p.269). Corridors are described in similar terms plus connectivity (Cook 2002, p.269). Corridors provide important transmission routes, buffering and filtering.

First, some fundamental and overarching principles of habitats are that: fragmentation should be reduced otherwise the habitat can no longer support itself; the naturalness should be maintained or improved; and the landscape's matrix should be compatible with the overall ecological area of concern (Cook 2002, p.270).

Second, Cook derives or summarizes principles from the basic patch and corridor concepts. Beneficial characteristics of patches and corridors include (Cook 2002, p.271-4, citing Forman (1995) and others):

- *Type*. Original, enriched or ones that are consistent with surroundings.
- *Size*. Large patches; however, smaller more scattered habitats have some benefits as well where species require that for protection and where species are dense and confined to a small area; wider corridors or at least wide enough to accommodate runoff and vegetation (Cook 2002, p.274).
- *Character or Quality*. Vegetative cover, vegetative diversity extending over multiple dimensions or structure (for example, tree canopies versus ground cover), and native vegetation.
- *Context*. Compatibility with adjacent areas or buffers, connectivity (absence of isolation) in terms of proximity to other patches or distances among patches.
- *Accessibility*. Number of connections.
- *Naturalness*. Reducing or eliminating human impact.

Then the patch and corridor measures are combined into a network structure analysis which produces another set of integrated indexes and measures. Some highlights of the analysis are:

Linkages or connectivity among patches and corridors are key to ecosystem viability; they pertain to patch and corridor density and the extent of the linkages between the two types of components (Cook 2002, p.275).

Flexibility is key to providing alternative routes for migration and is reflected in the existence of loops and the pattern of nodes and links that promote such alternatives, and are referred to in part as "circuitry".

Cook begins to get into the nature of the nodes and links, not only their prevalence, in the concept of "link suitability" exemplified by vegetation or lack of human impact.

Context as isolation or connectivity or the proximity of patches to one another is analogous to the centrality concept of betweenness. Accessibility defined as number of connections among patches is analogous to the centrality concepts of betweenness and closeness.

Patches and corridors have their own spatial structures and characteristics defined by the characteristics of the patches or habitats and the species that inhabit them.

Grunbaum (2011, p.1515) points out that habitats can exhibit patchiness or the condition in which food resources are unevenly distributed, which makes the ecological dynamics more complex and these dynamics are not easily predicted by density.

In Europe, a biodiversity index is used for transport impacts related to patches called "mesh size", which is a measure of the probability that two areas in a patch are connected (European Environment Agency (EEA) 2011, p.37). The higher the mesh density, the greater the fragmentation of the habitat, and 29 countries in Europe have been ranked by density with Luxembourg and Belgium having the highest and Sweden and Norway the lowest (European Environment Agency (EEA) 2011, pp.38–40).

The Vulnerabilities: Ecological and Transportation Conflicts

Safety of humans and wildlife

The convergence of transport routes and ecological migration routes can have positive or reinforcing benefits that are unidirectional or mutual (bidirectional) as well as negative effects. Conflicts occur when wildlife is attracted to roadways, resulting not only in the death of wildlife but also endangering humans. US DOT FHWA (2008) reports trends in collisions.

The MassDOT (2006 p.14-1) estimates that "in northern New England, one in every 75 motor vehicle collisions with moose (*Alces alces*) results in a human fatality, as does one in every 2,500 collisions with white-tailed deer (*Odocoileus virginianus*)" . . . "In Massachusetts, there were 33 moose–vehicle collisions in 2003, resulting in one human fatality. In 2004, the number of collisions increased to 52" (MassDOT 2006, p.14-8).

Vulnerability to road collisions is positively related to both attributes and behavior of species and the design and use of roadways. MassDOT (2006, p.14-8) states that the larger the range or distance over which a species migrates the more likely it is to be threatened by collisions with road vehicles; species with low regeneration rates or long reproductive cycles may find it more difficult to compensate for losses. The type of wildlife whose routes of travel intersect with roads extends to smaller animals. Airport runways (given their proximity to coastlines) often find themselves being corridors for aquatic wildlife. For example, runway activity at John F. Kennedy airport in New York City has been stopped, for almost as long as four hours, to accommodate the annual migration of diamondback terrapin turtles (Newman 2011). MassDOT (2006, p.14-3) also notes this area of conflict: "Female Blanding's turtles may travel up to a mile in search of a suitable nest site, and are likely to cross at least one road to do so."

Transportation factors that contribute to negative impacts on wildlife due to collisions include the traffic volume and speed and roadway design.

MassDOT (2006, p.14-8) reports that "Research suggests that roads with less than 1,000 vehicles per day (vpd) may cause road avoidance in smaller species, but crossing movements will still occur frequently. Roads with greater than 10,000 vpd are likely pose an impenetrable barrier to wildlife, deterring most wildlife from crossing and killing many that do attempt to cross."

Other road-related impacts on wildlife include noise, heat, and the movement of water or drainage.

Some Solutions: Integrating Environmental Protection Areas with Transportation

Transportation networks can conflict with natural ecosystems in ways other than direct collisions. When these occur, there are innovative ways to reduce or even eliminate the conflict. Nature will seek and make paths of its own where none exist. The case of the diamondback terrapins, described above, is one example. Many ecological corridor strategies adopted by states include the protection of turtle crossings, though they address a wide range of species.

Classification of Ecological Corridors

There are many ways to classify corridors (see for example Kintsch and Cramer 2011, pp.36–47). The categories below, for the purpose of categorizing cases, are broken down into four major types, reflecting much of the literature: those that avoid conflict and injury by

- enhancing wildlife movement along transportation corridors,
- preventing entry or movement,
- protective measures, and
- human behavioral changes.

More description and examples of the first two categories are provided below, though all four categories are covered in the section on cases.

(1) Supporting wildlife movement with vegetation to enhance "patches" in ways that promote the habitation of wildlife or enable wildlife to move safely reflects a node/link network framework. Vegetating areas adjacent to roads is one such method for wildlife preservation, as well as having other environmental co-benefits for transportation. It is well-established that vegetation creates numerous environmental benefits for transportation such as drainage control in the form of

absorbing water and reducing runoff and moderating heat. Vegetative cover is also key to absorbing carbon dioxide thus reducing climate change impacts. Given the relatively large amount of land devoted to transportation, designing vegetative cover as green corridors is advantageous and may not necessarily add to the demand for land.

Road construction not only disrupts that vegetation if not designed properly but operational practices such as mowing can result in the destruction of ecological habitats. MassDOT (2006, p.14-15) noted the following example and mitigation effort from Wisconsin: wild lupine (*Lupinis perennis*) usually growing next to roads is critical for the Karner blue butterfly (*Lycaeides melissa samuelsis*), an endangered species in Wisconsin, and the Department of Defense has changed mowing procedures in one location to avoid the plant.

Vegetation is now a common part of street planning. The green streets movement described in Chapter 4 emphasizes the incorporation of environmental areas into transportation networks. Its historical precedence is the many tree-lined thoroughfares built over the last century in cities around the world, and greenery appeared both at roadsides and between lanes.

Passageways are important to enhance wildlife migration. Fish passage was an early wildlife corridor process where electric power plant water was discharged to natural waterways and threatened fish migration routes. Fish ladders and other means of rerouting fish passage were common. Passageways by roads for terrestrial species have coincided with the need to reroute water to prevent flooding caused by roads. Culverts and tunnels are used for amphibians, for example, "One of the first amphibian tunnels was constructed beneath Henry Street in Amherst, Massachusetts to minimize road kill of spotted salamanders as they migrated to and from breeding sites. . . . Another larger tunnel, greater than 10-feet wide was constructed under Route 57 in Agawam" (MassDOT 2006, Figure 14-2 and p.14-18). MassDOT points out that culverts and tunnels are more common in Europe than in the US, and the structures come in many different shapes and sizes:

> *Ecopipes over Land.* Ecopipes are small, dry tunnels (1-foot to 1.3-foot diameter) used to facilitate movements of small and medium-sized mammals. They have been installed in the United Kingdom and the Netherlands, and appear to be successfully used by badger (*Meles meles*) and otter (*Lutra lutra*).
> *Wildlife Culverts over Water.* Wildlife culverts are similar to ecopipes but are installed over waterways. They are up to four feet wide and have raised dry ledges, or shelves, on one or both sides of the waterway that

allow wildlife to cross under the road and adjacent to the river or stream. The shelves also ensure that the appropriate stream channel configuration is maintained, which prevents possible morphological streambank degradation (MassDOT 2006, p.14-19).

The design of passageways and corridors in general is an art. The researchers Holland and Hastings at UC Davis suggest that such corridors should be random and uneven to respond to the behavior of wildlife (ScienceDaily 2008).

(2) Preventing entry or movement. Jersey barriers and other similar structures are usually invoked for security and safety. MassDOT (2006, p.14-16) notes that these can often be made porous to enable small species to pass through the barriers, and point out that these are in use in Massachusetts "along Route 6A on Cape Cod and sections of Route 24 and Route 3". Ironically, barriers are a central part of security measures as well.

Case Studies of Innovative Wildlife Management in Transportation Projects

The FHWA (2006a, b, c, d) has documented innovative cases for areas near bridges, along waterways and wetlands. Examples of cases for roads and rail are categorized below in terms of the four areas of enhancing wildlife movement along transportation corridors, preventing entry or movement, protective measures, and human behavioral changes.

In addition to the FHWA cases that are cited below, a number of guidebooks exist for the development of corridors (Venner 2010; MassDOT 2006, 2010; Kintsch and Cramer 2011). An extensive academic literature analyses and in many cases supports the combination of ecological and transport networks. One set of studies pertains to the effect of wildlife corridors on the behavior of various species and the characteristics of corridors that should be considered (Aars and Ims 1999; Bennett 1999; Dole et al. 2004; Mech and Hallett 2001; Roach 2006; Simberloff et al. 1992; Sutcliffe and Thomas 1996; and Tewksbury et al. 2002). Others identify wildlife corridor attributes (Beier and Loe 1992; Beier and Noss 1998; Rosenberg et al. 1997). Another set of studies focuses on how to design effective corridors (Fleury and Brown 1997; Wald 2011).

Roads cases
Some specific applications of the four components of the wildlife corridor concept have occurred for roads (many terms are those used in or summarized from US DOT FHWA 2006a):

(1) Enhancing wildlife movement along transportation corridors
- Passageways
  - Ramps: tortoises (Arizona);
  - Median barrier gaps: various (California);
  - Toad walls: toads (Colorado);
    Ledges: various (Florida), phoebes (Illinois);
  - Guide fence – old guard rail: salamanders (New York); and
  - Tunnels.
- Attraction of wildlife to transportation corridors: habitat creation or enrichment
  - Rights of way modification: woodpecker (Louisiana);
  - Limited maintenance/clearance to avoid disturbance: game birds (South Dakota), bats (Texas);
  - Rock brush piles: snakes (Kansas);
  - Habitat modification: kit fox (California) ;
  - Clearance: ground nesting birds (New York);
  - Natural fiber matting for erosion control (to prevent entrapment): snakes (Vermont);
  - Plantings: quail (Virginia), various (West Virginia, Wisconsin, Wyoming);
  - Nest boxes: various (New York);
  - Perch poles: bald eagles (Oklahoma);
  - Provision of food (from road-killed deer): white wolves (Oregon);
  - Conversion of culverts into homes: bats (Texas); and
  - Enlargement drainage pipes and culverts: various (Virginia).

(2) Preventing entry or movement
- Relocation
  - Nest relocation, modification: ferruginous hawks (Montana), osprey (Montana).
- Barriers
  - Fences: elk (Montana), tortoise (Arizona), turtle (Arkansas), various animals (Iowa), gopher tortoises (Mississippi);
  - Electrified walks: elk (Montana); and
  - Vegetative barriers: snow fences – various (New York).
- Repellants
  - Use of composted deer remains to repel other species (New York).
- Lighting alteration

- Shorebirds (Hawaii); and
- Bats (Indiana).

(3) Protective Measures
- Water
  - Catch basins for chemical removal: various (Iowa);
  - Trenches for runoff protection: lake fish (Maine);
  - Culvert clearance: desert tortoise (California);
  - Narrow berms: fish (Maine); and
  - Traplines – buckets and silt fences: salamanders (Maryland).
- Noise
  - Quiet guardrails: spotted owl (Oregon).
- General
  - Creation of special management areas: butterflies (Oregon); and
  - Wood topped rails to prevent injury: deer (Wyoming).

(4) Human behavior modification
- Reduce attractants: prevention of trash buildup;
- Keep away: red-legged frog (California);
- Warnings – signs: elk (Arizona);
- Warning to dim lights: migrating turtles (South Carolina); and
- Fish markers: salmon, oyster beds (Washington).

Rail

In Massachusetts crossings constructed under rail lines along 17 miles of the Greenbush Line Commuter Railroad protected spotted turtles and provided a migration route for the connectivity of the turtle habitats. The concept is being extended to up to 17 other species: FHWA (2006e).

Bridges

Bridges pose unusual advantages for wildlife protection in being geographically concentrated or localized. Measures for roads also fit into the four generic categories and subcategories and are applied to bridges also. These can be found in US DOT FHWA (2006b). One of the main differences in protective measures between roads and bridges is the ability to construct beneath the roadbed of bridges, for example, the construction of netting under bridges to protect birds.

International cases of ecological corridors

In France and other French speaking parts of Europe, "écoducs" are wildlife corridors. An écoduc example is the écoduc Hsueh on the

Brussels–Luxembourg highway entering the city of Luxembourg for the purpose of enabling toads to move under roads rather than being in danger along the roads themselves (Wikimedia Commons 2006; Wikimedia undated website).

Ecological corridors are incorporated into some countrywide plans in Europe. The concept of the écoduc was identified as part of France's national biodiversity strategy adopted in February 2004 (Sétra 2005). These target not only the road system but also the TGV rail network. Germany has developed a plan to protect wildlife along transportation corridors (Herrmann et al. 2007).

Various terms are used to reflect the particular type of animal that uses the corridors. For example, "capraducs" provide corridors for connectivity to enable amphibians to meet for the purpose of mating.

In Qatar, routes are provided along transportation corridors for camels. According to the Hukoomi (Third Quarter 2008), the Public Works Authority in Qatar has planned 20 camel crossings to avoid collisions which are exacerbated by high speed limits set at 120 km. In 2008, they were being planned in four separate phases. According to the article, studies of the effect of speed reduction signs have been undertaken in Saudi Arabia; however, although the signs resulted in reduced speeds, the reduction was not sufficient to prevent accidents.

Non-road Based Corridors

Non-road based ecological corridors parallel non-road based transport routes. Ecological corridors that allow migration are not always along roads or rail lines, and can cover non-road areas as well. Robbins (2011), citing the Wildlife Conservation Society of North America, notes that existing migration routes can become corridors whether they cross transportation networks or not. He indicates that this was the case in western Wyoming for the pronghorn. Non-road based corridors for fish and wildlife were designated in Montana (Weaver 2011). One early instance of a non-road corridor was the elevation of the Alaska pipeline to avoid blocking caribou migration paths.

Off-road vehicles such as all-terrain vehicles and snowmobiles can result in considerable environmental damage by opening up new transport corridors where guidelines either do not exist or are not followed. Vehicles that combine off-road and on-road transport, for example, mountain bikes, expand the formal transport networks. Snowmobiles reflect many of the issues that these forms of travel pose for the environment by opening up new transport networks.

Snowmobiles

Snowmobiles travel over open snow covered areas or along trails marked within such areas. In 2011, the International Snowmobile Manufacturers Association (ISMA) (2011a, 2011b) reported about 4 million snowmobile riders with 1.55 million snowmobile registrations in the US and 602,902, traveling over an estimated 225,000 miles of trail in North America. The ISMA recorded the registrations for about half of the states in the US and three states, Minnesota, Michigan and Wisconsin (in that order) account for about half of the US registrations. At the state level, registrations for the states that have them are not at all correlated with either population or population density – the correlations are practically zero. This probably reflects the variability in environmental conditions within states as well as population characteristics of snowmobile users.

Snowmobiles are to non-road areas as automobiles are to roads. They are an extension of the auto culture, being private, individually based, and gasoline based. The snowmobile dates back roughly to the emergence of the automobile, with a similar type of propulsion, and the original development is ascribed to Bombardier (MacDonald 2001).

Snowmobiles are known to have adverse effects on air quality, water quality, ecology, and noise in the areas they traverse. The weight of a snowmobile can potentially trigger an avalanche (US Forest Service, undated, accessed October 2011) and the way it is driven can also contribute to that risk (Gardner 2009).

Yellowstone National Park and other similar public park areas have been active forums for the environmental impact controversy. Yellowstone showed a dramatic rise in the number of snowmobiles, with less than 5,000 over-snow vehicles in general in use in the park in the 1960s, increasing to an annual 76,000 during the 1990s and tapering off to 25,000 in the latter 2000s (US Department of the Interior (DOI), National Park Service (NPS) 2011a, 2011b, p.5), though a peak was cited for that earlier period of 140,000 vehicle-days (US DOI, NPS 2011a, 2011b, p.104).

In 2011, Yellowstone National Park passed a one-year rule to restrict the number of snowmobiles allowed in the park at a given time. This followed an extensive environmental review process under NEPA which had been ongoing for a number of years as interest groups made their voices known (US DOI, NPS 2011a).

The air quality impacts in Yellowstone were initially very substantial, with the highest emissions rates of carbon monoxide (CO) reported in the US in 1995 (Layzer 2012, p.216). The results of findings under the Yellowstone National Park Winter Use Plan Environmental Impact Statement documents in 2011 show measurable concentrations of the National Ambient Air Quality Standards (NAAQS) pollutants. Though according to the

NPS, the concentrations don't appear to be violating standards, concentrations are higher around congestion points and CO and Particulate Matter (PM2.5) exceed summer concentrations from road-based vehicles and nitrogen dioxide (NO_2) concentrations are more of a concern than CO and PM2.5. Moreover, snowcoaches are accounting for a significant portion of the pollutants, and the implication is that snowcoaches will have to follow improvements in technology that snowmobiles did (US DOI, NPS 2011b). Noise along transportation corridors has been shown to displace wildlife and can affect their distribution, though it depends on the species, their size, and the conditions (US DOI, NPS 2011b, p.120)

According to Layzer (2012) snowmobile effects in winter were over and above the effects of summer time use of Yellowstone, when visitors to the park during the summer months escalated. Moreover, contributing to greater air pollution was the shift over time in travel from train travel to the more environmentally demanding automobile travel, for example, in 1915 80 percent of visitors traveled to the park by train and by 1930 that amount was only 10 percent (Layzer 2012, p.215). The growth in and control of land by concessions and other amenities made the park more attractive for year-round use also adding to pollution problems (Layzer 2012, p.214). Apparently, changes in snowmobile technology, for example moving from a two-stroke to a four-stroke technology, have reduced emission generation.

A number of states have regulations governing the use of snowmobiles similar to those governing Yellowstone, such as Maine and Ohio (State of Maine 2010, Ohio Department of Public Safety, undated website).

The mechanism of control seems to be to regulate operational conditions, encourage and even mandate best available technologies to improve the technology and design in an environmentally friendly manner, and to restrict the times, frequency and location of use, encouraging group travel.

The social implications of the snowmobile controversy have been substantial. Conflicts for example arose among recreational users of Yellowstone. Hikers who opposed the snowmobiles were regarded as being from a more privileged class relative to snowmobile users who were considered to be from average families (Layzer 2012, p.221). The ISMA (2011a, 2011b) notes that the average snowmobile user has a typical annual income of $65,000.

CONCLUDING COMMENTS

Environmental networks and transport networks converge and the intersections can be either catastrophic or mutually beneficial. The environmental areas covered here emphasized only examples of those where networks were in conflict and where some improvements were possible to reduce conflict. It is difficult in general to link environmental conditions to the configuration of transport corridors. The corridors and "patch" enhancements make improvements at an extremely site-specific level. Other controversies are larger. The snowmobile controversy exhibits much of the same "issue enlargement" phenomenon as the lead-based paint removal on the Williamsburg bridge case did where these networks converged and produced conflicts. These seemingly localized concerns often connect with much larger issues going on at the time. In the case of lead-based paint removal, it was the growing concern about lead-based paint in general as a national issue. For snowmobiles it was the growing environmental movement and NEPA process that occurred at the time the growth in snowmobile use was occurring.

REFERENCES

Aars, J. and R.A. Ims (1999), 'The effect of habitat corridors on rates of transfer and interbreeding between vole demes', *Ecology*, **80** (5), 1648–55.

American Lung Association (2011), *American Lung Association State of the Air 2010*, Washington, DC, USA: American Lung Association, available at http://www.lungusa.org/assets/documents/publications/state-of-the-air/state-of-the-air-report-2010.pdf.

Beier, P. and S. Loe (1992), 'In my experience: a checklist for evaluating impacts to wildlife movement corridors', *Wildlife Society Bulletin*, **20** (4), 434–40.

Beier, P. and R.F. Noss (1998), 'Do habitat corridors provide connectivity?', *Conservation Biology*, **12** (6), 1241–52.

Bennett, A.F. (1999), *Linkages in the Landscape: The Role of Corridors and Connectivity in Wildlife Conservation*, Gland, Switzerland: The World Conservation Union.

Columbia University Center for Climate Change Law (2012), 'NEPA and State NEPA EIS Resource Center, Environmental Assessment Protocols for the Consideration of Climate Change', available at http://www.law.columbia.edu/centers/climatechange/resources/eis.

Cook, E.A. (2002), 'Landscape structure indices for assessing urban ecological networks', *Landscape and Urban Planning*, **58**, 269–80.

Council on Environmental Quality (2009), 'Calendar year 2008 filed EISs', available at http://ceq.hss.doe.gov/nepa/Calendar_Year_2008_Filed_EISs.pdf.

Council on Environmental Quality (2011a), 'Current developments', available at http://ceq.hss.doe.gov/nepa/nepanet.htm (accessed October 10, 2011).

Council on Environmental Quality (2011b), 'NEPAnet, NEPA litigation', available at http://ceq.hss.doe.gov/nepa/nepanet.htm (accessed October 10, 2011).

Davis S.C., S.W. Diegel and R.G. Boundy (June 2011), *Transportation Energy Data Book: Edition 30*, Oak Ridge, TN, USA: Oak Ridge National Laboratory, available at http://cta.ornl.gov/data/tedb30/Edition30_Full_Doc.pdf.

Dole, J.W., S.J. Ng and R.M. Sauvajot (2004), 'Use of highway undercrossings by wildlife in southern California', *Biology Conservation*, **115** (3), 499–507.

European Environment Agency (EEA) (2011), *Laying the Foundations for Greener Transport*, Copenhagen, Denmark: EEA.

Fleury, A.M. and R.D. Brown (1997), 'A framework for the design of wildlife conservation corridors with specific application to southwestern Ontario', *Landscape and Urban Planning*, **37** (8), 163–86.

Forman, R.T.T. (1995), *Land Mosaics*, New York, USA and Cambridge, UK: Cambridge University Press.

Forman, R.T.T., D. Sperling, J.A. Bissonette, A.P. Clevenger, C.D. Cutshall, V.H. Dale, L. Fahrig, R. France, C.R. Goldman, K. Heanue, J.A. Jones, F.J. Swanson, T. Turrentine and T.C. Winter (2003), *Road Ecology: Science and Solutions*, Washington, DC, USA: Island Press.

Gardner, A. (January 2009), 'Snowmobile "high-marking" triggers avalanches', Sierra Social Hub, available at http://hub.sierratradingpost.com/blogs/agardner/snowmobile-%22high-marking%22-triggers-avalanches-528/.

Gerrard, M.R. (2012), 'Reverse environmental impact analysis: effect of climate change on projects', *New York Law Journal*, **247** (45).

Grunbaum, D. (2011), 'Why did you levy?', *Science*, **332** (6037), 1514–15.

Herrmann, M., J. Enssle, M. Süsser, J.-A. Krüger (February 2007), 'Der nabu-bundeswildwegeplan', NABU Bundesverband, available at http://www.nabu.de/imperia/md/content/nabude/naturschutz/wildwegeplan/4.pdf.

Hukoomi, Qatar Government (Third Quarter, August 2008), 'Camel crossing tunnels on highways to reduce accidents, Ashghal plans to build camel crossing tunnels on highways to reduce accidents', *The Peninsula*, Doha, Qatar, available at http://www.iloveqatar.net/forum/read.php?28,3414.

International Snowmobile Manufacturers Association (2011a), 'Quick facts', available at http://www.snowmobile.org/pr_snowfacts.asp.

International Snowmobile Manufacturers Association (2011b), 'Snowmobile statistics', available at http://www.snowmobile.org/stats_registrations_us.asp (accessed October 18, 2011).

Kintsch, J. and P.C. Cramer (2011), *Permeability of Existing Structures for Terrestrial Wildlife: A Passage Assessment System*, Seattle, WA, USA: Washington State Department of Transportation, available at http://ntl.bts.gov/lib/42000/42000/42081/777.1.pdf.

Layzer, J.A. (2012), 'Playground or paradise? Snowmobiles in Yellowstone National Park', in J.A. Layzer (ed.), *The Environmental Case. Translating Values into Policy*, Washington, DC, USA: CQ Press, pp.209–39.

The Louis Berger Group, Inc. (2004), 'Emissions benefits of land use planning strategies', Washington, DC, USA: US DOT, FHWA, available at http://www.fhwa.dot.gov/environment/air_quality/conformity/research/emissions_benefits/.

MacDonald, L. (2001), *The Bombardier Story: Planes, Trains, and Snowmobiles*, Toronto, Canada: John Wiley & Sons.

Massachusetts Department of Transportation (MassDOT) (January 2006), 'Wildlife accommodation', in *Project Development and Design Guide*, available at http://www.mhd.state.ma.us/downloads/designGuide/CH_14.pdf.

Massachusetts Department of Transportation (MassDOT) (December 2010), *Design of Bridges and Culverts for Wildlife Passage at Freshwater Streams*, available at http://www.mhd.state.ma.us/downloads/projDev/Design_Bridges_Culverts_Wildlife_Passage_122710.pdf.

Mech, S.G. and J.G. Hallett (2001), 'Evaluating the effectiveness of corridors: a genetic approach', *Conservation Biology*, **15** (2), 467–74.

Melosi, M.V. (2008), *The Sanitary City. Environmental Services in Urban America from Colonial Times to the Present, Abridged Edition*, Pittsburgh, PA, USA: University of Pittsburgh Press.

Newman, A. (June 2011), 'Delays at J.F.K.? This time, blame turtles', available at http://cityroom.blogs.nytimes.com/2011/06/29/turtles-force-runway-closure-at-kennedy-airport/?ref=kennedyinternationalairportnyc.

Ohio Department of Public Safety, Bureau of Motor Vehicles (undated website), 'All-purpose vehicles (APVs), off-road motorcycles, and snowmobiles', available at http://bmv.ohio.gov/registration_titling_apv_usv.stm.

Roach, J. (2006), 'First evidence that wildlife corridors boost biodiversity, study says', National Geographic Society, available at http://news.national geographic.com/news/2006/09/060901-plant-corridors.html.

Robbins, J. (July 2011), 'Preserving land for northward migration', *The New York Times*, available at http://green.blogs.nytimes.com/2011/07/03/preserving-land-for-northward-migration/?hp.

Rosenberg, D.K., B.R. Noon and E.C. Meslow (1997), 'Biological corridors: form, function, and efficacy', *BioScience*, **47** (10), 667–87.

ScienceDaily (October 2008), 'Designing wildlife corridors: wildlife need more complex travel plans', available at http://www.sciencedaily.com/releases/2008/10/081020135221.htm.

Sétra (August 2005, translated May 2007), *Technical Guide: Facilities and Measures for Small Fauna*, Paris, France: French Ministere de l'Ecologie et du Developpement Durable.

Simberloff, D., J.A. Farr, J. Cox and D.W. Mehlman (1992), 'Movement corridors: conservation bargains or poor investments?', *Conservation Biology*, **6** (4), 492–504.

State of Maine (2010), 'Maine snowmobile laws and rules effective December 1, 2010', available at http://www.maine.gov/ifw/laws_rules/pdf/2010-2012Snow &ATV.pdf.

Sutcliffe, O.L. and C.D. Thomas (1996), 'Open corridors appear to facilitate dispersal by ringlet butterflies (*Aphantopus hyperantus*) between woodland clearings', *Conservation Biology*, **10** (5), 1359–65.

Sutley, N.H. (February 2010), 'Memorandum for heads of federal departments and agencies, draft NEPA guidance on consideration of the effects of climate change and greenhouse gas emissions', Council on Environmental Quality.

Tewksbury, J.J., D.J. Levey, N.M. Haddad, S. Sargent, J.L. Orrock, A. Weldon, B.J. Danielson, J. Brinkerhoff, E.I. Damschen and P. Townsend (2002), 'Corridors affect plants, animals, and their interactions in fragmented landscapes', *Ecology*, **99** (20), 1223–6.

US Department of the Interior, National Park Service (2011a), '2011 winter use draft environmental assessment reports', available at http://www.nps.gov/yell/parkmgmt/reports.htm.

US Department of the Interior, National Park Service (2011b), 'Scientific assessment of Yellowstone National Park winter use March 2011', available at http://www.nps.gov/yell/parkmgmt/loader.cfm?csModule=security/getfile&PageID=550776.

US Department of the Interior, National Park Service (September 2011), 'Yellowstone National Park news release: NPS to implement one-year rule for 2011–2012 winter use plan', available at http://www.snowmobile.org/docs/ NPS_One-Year_Rule_2011-2012_Winter_Use_Plan.pdf.

US Department of the Interior, National Park Service (October 2011), 'Snowmobile best available technology (BAT) list snowmobiles meeting Yellowstone and Grand Teton National Parks' best available technology (BAT) requirements', available at http://www.nps.gov/yell/parkmgmt/current_batlist.htm.

US Department of Transportation, Federal Highway Administration (undated website) *Environmental Guidebook*, available at http://www.environment. fhwa.dot.gov/guidebook/results.asp?selSub=17   http://www.fhwa.dot.gov/envi ronment/; http://www.environment.fhwa.dot.gov/guidebook/index.asp.

US Department of Transportation, Federal Highway Administration, 'Environmental review toolkit – streamlining/stewardship', available at http:// www.environment.fhwa.dot.gov/strmlng/index.asp.

US Department of Transportation, Federal Highway Administration (2006a), 'Along roads', available at http://www.fhwa.dot.gov/environment/wildlife protection/index.cfm?fuseaction=home.viewTopic&topicID=1.

US Department of Transportation, Federal Highway Administration (2006b), 'On or near bridges', available at http://www.fhwa.dot.gov/environment/wildlife protection/index.cfm?fuseaction=home.viewTopic&topicID=2.

US Department of Transportation, Federal Highway Administration (2006c), 'On or along waterways', available at http://www.fhwa.dot.gov/environment/wild lifeprotection/index.cfm?fuseaction=home.viewTopic&topicID=3.

US Department of Transportation, Federal Highway Administration (2006d), 'Near wetlands', available at http://www.fhwa.dot.gov/environment/wildlife protection/index.cfm?fuseaction=home.viewTopic&topicID=4.

US Department of Transportation, Federal Highway Administration (21 August 2006e), 'On Track with "Turtle Tracks"', available at http://www. fhwa.dot.gov/environment/wildlifeprotection/index.cfm?fuseaction=home.view Article&articleID=119.

US Department of Transportation, Federal Highway Administration (June 2008), 'Wildlife strikes to civil aircraft in the US 1990–2007', available at http://wildlife. pr.erau.edu/BASH90-07.pdf.

US Department of Transportation, Federal Highway Administration (September 2009), 'Interim guidance update on mobile source air toxic analysis in NEPA', available at http://www.fhwa.dot.gov/environment/air_quality/air_toxics/ policy_and_guidance/100109guidmem.cfm.

US Department of Transportation, Federal Highway Administration (13 May 2010), 'Climate Change – Model Language in Transportation Plans', available at http://climatechange.transportation.org/pdf/climate%20change%20and%20 planning%20-%20model%20language%205-13-10.pdf.

US Department of Transportation, Federal Highway Administration (updated September 2011), 'Air Quality', available at http://www.fhwa.dot.gov/environ ment/air_quality/index.cfm.

US Department of Transportation, Federal Highway Administration (2011a), 'Air quality planning and SIPs', available at http://www.fhwa.dot.gov/environment/ air_quality/conformity/research/sips.cfm.

US Department of Transportation, Federal Highway Administration (2011b), 'Congestion mitigation and air quality improvement (CMAQ) program', avail- able at http://www.fhwa.dot.gov/environment/air_quality/cmaq/.

US Department of Transportation, Federal Transit Administration,

'Environmental decision making and transit – streamlining/stewardship', available at http://www.environment.fta.dot.gov/Streamlining/default.asp.

US Department of Transportation, Federal Transit Administration (July 2003), 'Approach to the cumulative effects analysis for the Lower Manhattan recovery effort', available at http://www.environment.fta.dot.gov/Streamlining/environ.asp.

US Department of Transportation, Federal Transit Administration (February 2005), 'Linking the transportation planning and National Environmental Policy Act (NEPA) processes', available at http://www.fta.dot.gov/documents/05-04NEPAGuidanceattachment.pdf.

US Environmental Protection Agency, Integrated Risk Information System (IRIS), available at http://cfcpub.epa.gov/ncea/iris/index.cfm.

US Environmental Protection Agency (1999), 'Technology transfer network: 1999 National-scale Air Toxics Assessment (NATA)', available at http://www.epa.gov/ttn/atw/nata1999/.

US Environmental Protection Agency (February 2007), *Federal Register*, **72** (37), 8430.

US Environmental Protection Agency (July 2008), 'Methyl tertiary butyl ether, gasoline, MTBE in gasoline', available at http://www.epa.gov/mtbe/gas.htm (accessed May 7, 2011).

US Environmental Protection Agency (February 2009), 'Methyl tertiary butyl ether, drinking water', available at http://www.epa.gov/mtbe/water.htm.

US Environmental Protection Agency (April 2010), *Inventory of US Greenhouse Gas Emissions and Sinks: 1990–2008*, available at http://www.epa.gov/climatechange/emissions/downloads10/US-GHG-Inventory-2010_Report.pdf.

US Environmental Protection Agency (December 2010), 'Final rule: 40 CFR part 52 6560-50-P [EPA-HQ-OAR-2010-0107; FRL-xxxx-x] RIN-2060-AQ08', *Action to Ensure Authority to Issue Permits under the Prevention of Significant Deterioration Program to Sources of Greenhouse Gas Emissions: Finding of Substantial Inadequacy and SIP Call* (this version will be removed when final version published), available at http://www.epa.gov/nsr/documents/20101201finalrule.pdf.

US Environmental Protection Agency (2011), *Inventory of Greenhouse Gases and Sinks 1990–2009*, available at http://www.epa.gov/climatechange/emissions/downloads11/US-GHG-Inventory-2011-Complete_Report.pdf.

US Environmental Protection Agency (2012a), 'Air quality trends', available at http://www.epa.gov/airtrends/aqtrends.html.

US Environmental Protection Agency (2012b), 'Our Nation's Air – Status and Trends through 2010', available at http://www.epa.gov/airtrends/2011/report/fullreport.pdf.

US Executive Office of the President, President's Task Force on Environmental Health Risks and Safety Risks to Children (February 2000), *Eliminating Childhood Lead Poisoning: A Federal Strategy Targeting Lead Paint Hazards*, Washington, DC, USA: US Government Task Force.

US Forest Service, National Avalanche Center (undated), 'Snowmobiles surviving in avalanche country', available at http://www.fsavalanche.org/Default.aspx?ContentId=10&LinkId=16 (accessed October 19, 2011).

US White House (January 2007), 'Executive order 13423 – strengthening federal environmental, energy, and transportation management', available at http://nepa.gov/nepa/regs/E.O._13423.pdf.

US White House, Office of the Press Secretary (August 2011), 'Presidential memorandum: speeding infrastructure development through more efficient and effective permitting and environmental review', and 'Memorandum for the Heads of Executive Departments and Agencies – subject: speeding infrastructure development through more efficient and effective permitting and environmental review'.

US White House, Office of the Press Secretary (October 2011), 'Obama Administration announces selection of 14 infrastructure projects to be expedited through permitting and environmental review process', available at http://www.whitehouse.gov/the-press-office/2011/10/11/obama-administration-announces-selection-14-infrastructure-projects-be-e?utm_campaign=TWIW%20-%201014&utm_medium=email&utm_source=Eloqua.

Venner, M. (June 2010), 'Environmental corridor management. NCHRP 2525/63', Washington, DC, USA: Transportation Research Board, available at http://onlinepubs.trb.org/onlinepubs/nchrp/docs/NCHRP25-25%2863%29_FR.pdf.

Wald, M.L. (January 2011), 'Design picked for wildlife crossing', *The New York Times*, available at http://www.nytimes.com/2011/01/24/science/earth/24overpass.html?_r=1&hp.

Weaver, J.L. (April 2011), *Conservation Value of Roadless Areas for Vulnerable Fish and Wildlife Species in the Crown of the Continent Ecosystem*, Bozeman, MT, USA: Wildlife Conservation Society, available at Weaver_MontanaRoadlessReport.pdf.

Wikimedia, écoduc Hsueh before the city of Luxembourg, on the highway Brussels–Luxembourg, 'Toad tunnels that enable toads to travel under roadways to avoid getting hit', available at http://commons.wikimedia.org/wiki/Image:Toad_tunnel.jpg?uselang=fr.

Wikimedia Commons (2006), 'File: Toad tunnel.jpg', available at http://commons.wikimedia.org/wiki/Image:Toad_tunnel.jpg.

Zimmerman, R. (1999), 'Community, city, state and nation: integrated decision-making for infrastructure maintenance: lead-based paint removal from bridges (The Williamsburg Bridge, NYC), Report to the National Science Foundation', in *Integrated Decision-making for Urban Infrastructure Performance*, funded by the National Science Foundation (NSF) under grant number 9526057.

Zimmerman, R. (2004), 'Social and environmental dimensions of cutting-edge infrastructures', in R.E. Hanley (ed.), *Moving People, Goods and Information in the 21st Century*, Oxford, UK: Routledge, pp.189–210.

6. Natural hazards and accidents that disrupt transportation networks

TRANSPORTATION AND NATURAL HAZARDS

Overview of Significant Natural Hazards Affecting Transportation

Transportation is affected by emergencies and affects the recovery from them. Of the numerous hazards that exist, some affect transportation and its users similarly while others have very different consequences. Many of the impacts share in common those that occur in deliberate attacks on the system that will be addressed in Chapter 7. In addition, many of the hazards and impacts are similar to those that were covered in Chapter 3 on global climate change. Differences between the impacts of global climate change and natural hazards occur with respect to the duration and timing of the effects although that distinction is becoming less clear. Flooding may occur with great suddenness in a natural hazard and then recede. In contrast, flooding from a rise in sea level associated with global climate change (GCC) generally takes longer, allowing more time to adapt, but may last longer, and is usually permanent, though the recognition of rapid ice melt may counter these differences. This section begins with an identification of some of the patterns and trends in natural hazards in general, and then focuses primarily on hurricanes, precipitation extremes, and earthquakes as case areas.

Categorizing natural hazards

Natural hazards can be categorized in many ways. The Centers for Disease Control and Prevention uses "Natural Disasters and Extreme Weather" (Centers for Disease Control and Prevention, undated web page), which they subdivide further as various categories for weather and geophysical events. Weather includes extreme heat, floods, drought, hurricanes, landslides and mudslides (water/precipitation induced), tornadoes, wildfires, winter weather, and sandstorms. Geophysical events include earthquakes, tsunamis, and volcanoes. Guha-Sapir et al. (2011, p.7) use more major categories, but generally arrive at a similar list. Woo (1999, pp.7–9) notes the difficulty of categorizing natural hazards, for example, a given natural hazard can cause others, making them difficult to separate.

Incidence and vulnerability

Natural hazards seem to be growing, both in number and severity of impact. This chapter begins with a discussion of these patterns and trends, followed by a more in-depth analysis of examples that provide insights into key impacts on transportation and the people who depend on it. According to the Federal Emergency Management Administration (FEMA 2012) the year 2011, with 99 major disaster declarations, ranked first since 1953 in the number of annual major disaster declarations (not including emergency declarations). This was almost three times the annual average and accounted for almost five percent of all disasters in that time period. After 2011, 2010 with 81 declared disasters and 2008 with 75 declared disasters (tied with 1996) ranked second and third respectively. In fact, the first decade of the twenty-first century (including 2011) with a total of 741 disaster declarations accounted for over a third of the total from 1953 through 2011. By the end of 2011, the top six states in terms of disaster declarations from 1953 through 2011 were Texas (86), California (78), Oklahoma (70), New York (65), Florida (63), and Louisiana (58) (FEMA 2012).

Texas, California and New York not only rank highest in population, but also rank highest in terms of transportation infrastructure usage. For road mileage California and Texas ranked first and second in the US respectively in terms of vehicle miles of travel in 2009 with 11 percent and 8 percent respectively of the US total (calculated from US DOT FHWA data). In terms of transit, New York State's heavy rail system concentrated in New York City accounts for 37 percent of the track miles, 45 percent of stations and 68 percent of passenger trips for heavy rail nationwide, and a substantial share of the miles of track and stations for commuter rail. In California, if New York City is not included in the NTD US data set, Oakland's heavy rail accounts for 19 percent of the track mileage, 8 percent of the stations, and 10 percent of the heavy rail trips nationwide. Several of the California cities together account for over 10 percent of the commuter rail track mileage (calculated from the US DOT, FTA (undated website), National Transit Database 2009; see Chapter 2 for details).

For hazards, internationally, the International Strategy for Disaster Reduction (ISDR) (2010) reported that:

- The annual average number of disasters between 1975 and 2010 began peaking in 2000 and peak values have persisted through 2010.
- The average annual number of deaths between 2000 and 2009 was 78,087, but the Haiti earthquake of January 2010 brought the 2010 total alone to 296,818. The Haiti earthquake fatalities at the time

of their accounting were still being verified. The effect of the Haiti earthquake is also seen in the distribution of deaths from natural disasters by world region. Between 2000 and 2009, Asia ranked first by far in terms of the average number of deaths accounting for 85 percent, but in 2010, the Americas ranked first accounting for 76 percent primarily because of the Haiti earthquake.

- According to ISDR, the total number of people affected is many times more than the number of deaths putting the 2000–2009 average at 227,378,014.

According to ISDR's accounting, earthquakes and hurricanes are among the most devastating, and often coincide with other hazards. These two natural hazards almost invariably disrupt transport and often place the lives of the people it serves in jeopardy.

NOAA (2012) reported that after generally increasing but somewhat uneven trends in the cost of weather events, 2011 exceeded every other year in terms of the number of events exceeding a billion dollars in damages and a total damage estimate of $200 billion.

Earthquakes

Two scales are commonly used to measure earthquakes. The Richter scale consists of nine levels that measure magnitude as ground motion over time (USGS 2009a). The Modified Mercalli Intensity Scale consists of twelve levels of increasing intensity based on the effects that are observed (USGS 2009b).

Earthquakes are among the most severe of the natural hazards and may in fact be the worst in terms of the numbers of lives they claim and the amount of destruction they create. Although according to ISDR (2010) numbers, earthquakes only rank third far behind floods and storms in terms of the total number of natural hazard events in the 2000–2010 time period, earthquakes are the highest ranking in terms of numbers of deaths between 2000 and 2009; with the exception of Hurricanes Katrina, Rita and Wilma, earthquakes were highlighted by ISDR as accounting for seven out of the eight selected largest annual average dollar losses (in 2009 dollars) in any given year between 1980 and 2010.

The destructiveness of earthquakes is due in part to their suddenness, the short duration of the effects often lasting only seconds preventing people from seeking relief quickly, and the relatively limited ability to predict them. Earthquakes are among the least predictable natural phenomena, other than locating general areas of vulnerability from physical conditions and historical trends. Thus, the ability to give advance warnings for earthquakes tends to be more limited than for other kinds of hazards. Are we able to have any advance warning of earthquakes? Some of the approaches to prediction include analysing foreshocks and slippage or slip instability (nucleation) (Bouchon et al. 2011) but how much time these actually give and for which earthquakes is still uncertain. Animals give warnings. Behavior of animals in zoos changed just prior to the earthquake centered in Virginia on August 23, 2011 (Achenbach 2011).

Tsunamis can be associated with earthquakes as well as volcanoes. They are also measured by magnitude and intensity scales. Although like earthquakes tsunamis are difficult to foresee, the amount of time between their formation and effect can be a little longer than that of earthquakes, if the distances they travel are long enough. Given the short distance between earthquake epicenter and shoreline, however, in the devastating Japan earthquake of March 11, 2011, there was little warning of the onset of the tsunami because of how close it was to the shore. The 2004 Asian tsunami brought to light numerous problems in emergency communications, resulting in the establishment of tsunami warning centers to enable warnings to be given at least a few hours in advance.

Hurricanes and Flooding

Severe storms take a number of different forms, and among the most destructive are hurricanes. One of the common ways of measuring the severity of hurricanes is based on wind speed as defined by the Saffir-Simpson Hurricane Wind scale of 1 through 5 (Schott et al. undated website). Other attributes or ways of measuring severity are the return period, which is the frequency that a storm of a given intensity recurs within 86 miles of a given location (National Oceanic and Atmospheric Administration (NOAA), undated website; search "return period"), and storm surge or the movement of wind-driven water (NOAA, undated website, search "storm surge"). Hurricane damage produces both coastal and inland waterway flooding. Differences in NOAA and US Census accounting of coastal counties occur, since NOAA takes into account inland counties that potentially are also at risk of flooding (Wilson and Fischetti 2010, p.3).

Severe storms and associated flooding and wind damage have been viewed in the context of climate change. The National Research Council (NRC) (2011) reviewed the debate over this connection and concluded that although climate modeling indicates increased precipitation and evaporation from warming, environmental evidence is less consistent with this finding given the dynamics and instabilities in land and water changes (NRC 2011 pp.1–2). Emanuel et al. (2008) differ in some of their findings with Knutson et al. (2008) about the extent to which climate (greenhouse gas emissions) is linked to tropical storms and hurricanes, with Knutson et al. (2008) finding no evidence of a link between GHG emissions and hurricane frequency based on modeling for the Atlantic basin.

Nevertheless, hurricanes represent a threat to the social and economic fabric of society. Pielke et al. (2008, p.29) observe that: "The decade 1996–2005 has the second most damage among the past 11 decades, with only the decade 1926–1935 surpassing its costs." The Blake et al. (2011, p.9, 11) update through 2010 indicates that nine out of the ten most costliest hurricanes exceeding $7 billion in damages occurred since 2000 (without adjusting for inflation) and six out of the top ten exceeding $11 billion occurred since 2000 when adjusting for inflation using a 2010 deflator. Blake et al. (2011, p.7) figures also show that of the 52 Atlantic and Gulf Coast hurricanes between 1851 and 2010 with 25 or more deaths, three occurred after 2000.

Blake et al. (2011, p.6) provide other insights directly by combining hurricane intensity and outcomes:

> (1) Fourteen out of the fifteen deadliest hurricanes were category three or higher. (2) Large death totals were primarily a result of the ten feet or greater rise of the ocean (storm surge) . . . (3) A large portion of the damage in four of the twenty costliest tropical cyclones (Table 3a) resulted from inland floods caused by torrential rain. (4) One-third of the deadliest hurricanes were category four or higher. (5) Only seven of the deadliest hurricanes occurred during the past twenty five years while over two-thirds of the costliest hurricanes occurred during the same period.

Some categories of hurricanes and related storms have been increasing, and this trend is expected to continue. Bender et al. (2010, p.454) use a model that predicts that the most intense storms will double in frequency but overall frequency of storms will decrease as the twenty-first century ends. Webster et al. (2005) have also examined this relationship.

Impacts of Natural Hazards on Transportation

Natural hazards relate to transport in a number of ways. Several are emphasized here; the direct danger to human life from the collapse of structures, the lessons learned in terms of the management of infrastructure (illustrated by the Loma Prieta earthquake of 1989), and the nature of the transportation disruptions and their effect on welfare and the economy. One important observation is that multiple points of failure of human and natural origins contribute to the magnitude of these consequences through the intersection of transport and natural hazard networks.

First, the direct destruction of transport infrastructure is considered a major contributor to deaths and injury for some types of hazard, given that people are often in close proximity to the physical structures. Numerous studies have supported this in connection with earthquakes (Bourque et al. 2007, p.103). The Loma Prieta earthquake is a major example that occurred in the San Francisco Bay area on October 17, 1989, measuring 7.1 on the Richter scale. As a consequence of the earthquake, the upper section of the Cyprus Viaduct fell upon the lower section killing approximately 42 people. A US Geological Survey (USGS) professional paper on the earthquake and its effect on transportation infrastructure and its users concluded that: "Failure of highway systems was the single largest cause of loss of life during the earthquake. Forty-two of the 63 earthquake fatalities occurred when the Cypress Viaduct in Oakland collapsed" (Holzer, ed. October 1998).

Second, the effect of natural hazards on transportation structures is often the result of the interplay of both natural and man-made actions at many points, not just a single point. The case of the collapse of the Cypress Street Viaduct of the Nimitz Freeway in California during the Loma Prieta earthquake illustrates not only the devastating effect of earthquakes but also how decisions about infrastructure affect the severity of the damage. The collapse of the viaduct during the Loma Prieta earthquake reflected the interplay of factors in the design and financing of transportation infrastructure.

Yashinksy describes the Cypress Street Viaduct as a long connector between I-80 south and I-880 in Oakland, which was the transportation structure that suffered the most damage in the earthquake (Yashinksy 1998 p.19). By November 7, 1989 temporary repairs to the connector were completed and it was open to traffic (Yashinksy 1998 p.31). Several separate transportation incidents occurred in the earthquake. The San Francisco Oakland Bay bridge lost a section, disrupting traffic for miles, and requiring users to take a 75 mile detour around the bridge until the repair was made about a month later. The Cypress Street Viaduct collapsed, and rail lines were disrupted which were later put back in service.

Pre-event conditions and characteristics illustrate underlying problems with the way transportation infrastructure can withstand the effects of natural hazards. Several features are worthy of consideration: design, standards, and practices for maintenance, rehabilitation and reconstruction (adapted from Pollack and Bishop 1989; Yashinsky 1998):

- *Design.* The Cypress Street Viaduct section of the Nimitz Freeway was designed as a double decker roadway, with hinge joints connecting the roadway to the supporting columns. Steel supporting rods through the concrete differed on either side of the roadway, and concrete columns were not reinforced uniformly with horizontal steel rings.

- *Standards*. At the time of its design and construction, standards recommended design for ground accelerations of 6 percent of the acceleration of gravity. These standards were later upgraded to 50 percent.
- *Maintenance/Rehabilitation/Reconstruction*. According to Pollack and Bishop (1989), priority setting dictated that attention should be paid to avoiding auto accidents which had claimed far more lives than earthquake related highway accidents (which had only claimed two lives up to the collapse of the Nimitz Freeway section). Reinforcement of the Nimitz was not ignored, but rather was scheduled for a later phase of the reinforcement program for old roadways. As a result, preliminary reinforcement strengthened one side of the structure and not the other, resulting in an uneven impact when the earthquake struck.
- *Inspection*. Design deficiencies are not usually the focus of inspection programs; whatever weakening had occurred from previous earthquakes, for example the earthquake in 1971, went undetected.

Third, natural hazards affect the ability of transportation to perform the functions that are demanded both in normal times and emergencies. Emergency closures of both access points and networks occur as an outcome of both direct destruction as well as actions on the part of transportation managers to avoid harm to users and damage to the transportation infrastructure that could affect recovery. Severe damage requiring reconstruction will cause very lengthy restoration periods for transportation. Examples of these kinds of disruptions are given below for roads, rail and combinations of the two.

Road closures and recovery

Road closures occur both as an outcome of direct damage to roads and as a deliberate action by government to reduce the consequences of damage by reducing exposure and thereby reducing traffic.

Research has addressed the effect of interdiction on transportation systems as well as the effect of real or simulated catastrophes on the ability of transportation systems to rebound (Baykal-Gürsoy et al. 2009). Examples of interdiction studies include the model developed by Baykal-Gürsoy et al. (2009) to examine the effects of partial and full road closure on rate of service. Other studies have looked at the response of transportation networks during and following catastrophes. One set of studies evaluates roadway characteristics under different assumptions about behavior, for example, the Ozbay and Yazici (2006) research on roadways during evacuation indicates that the special characteristics of demand during an evacuation affect clearance and delay time and cannot be assumed from normal trip generation models. They emphasize the need to model response rate explicitly, and include the behavior of evacuees before a message to evacuate is issued (called "shadow evacuation") and after an evacuation message is issued. In connection with the effect of messages both formal and informal on population movement, Zimmerman and Sherman (2011) examined the influence of information from others around them during the September 11, 2001 World Trade Center attacks on whether people left the area immediately or lingered, and the modes of transportation they used to leave.

Earthquakes   The Loma Prieta and Northridge earthquakes illustrate the extensive, widespread damage that earthquakes can create, limiting the ability of not only normal movement but also the movement of emergency services.

During the Loma Prieta earthquake of October 17, 1989 there was extensive bridge damage (Yashinsky 1998, pp.8, 11, 12): 20 state bridges ($100,000 in damages), 40 state bridges ($5,000 to $100,000), and 33 city and county bridges.

The year the bridges were built varied. The 20 state bridges with the most damage were built from 1936 to 1986.

There was extensive road damage, and hence closures, from poor soil, landslides and rocks, though it did not exceed the cost of bridge damages (Yashinsky 1998, pp.165, 166): ten state routes, 49 local roads and seven other roads and tunnels. Yashinsky (1998, p.167) identifies 12 miles along State Highway 17 closed for 32 days as being one of the lengthier closures. Local residents were allowed to use the roads.

The Association of Bay Area Governments (ABAG 2003) produced estimates of the actual number of road closures in the Loma Prieta and Northridge earthquakes.

In addition, ABAG (2011) estimated that 5,219 road closures would occur for future earthquakes, based on direct earthquake effects only, across nine Bay Area counties out of the 58 counties in California and covering three plate faults. Organized by county, Alameda County accounted for the highest number of closures, with 45 percent of the total. They present data by fault also.

Hurricanes   As reported by Zimmerman (2010; US NOAA various years), during Hurricane Floyd (1999), the average duration of road closures in Florida where 12 counties were affected was about 14 hours, and in North Carolina where 14 counties were affected the average closure was about ten hours. Both states were directly hit by the Hurricane. Road closures in Georgia (from traffic only), where ten counties were affected, averaged 30 hours (Zimmerman 2010; based on US NOAA, Post Storm Assessment Review for Hurricane Floyd, various years).

In Vermont, massive destruction of roads during Hurricane Irene isolated many communities in the state. Estimates cited from state officials were that 118 road segments and 24 state bridges were closed (Burlington Free Press 2011). By the following Friday (September 2, 2011) 84 of the roads had reopened and 15 had limited access (Burlington Free Press 2011). Temporary roads were built in the interim.

The extent of damage to transportation infrastructure after Hurricane Ike is included in the recovery cost which was estimated at $131.8 million (The State of Texas, 2008, p.2).

During transport network closures or other conditions where people lack access, equity issues have arisen. The prevalence of disadvantaged populations, particularly the elderly, in areas prone to hurricanes was analysed by Zimmerman et al. (2008) based on NOAA road closure data and US Census socioeconomic data. During Hurricane Floyd, the average percentage of elderly in counties affected by Hurricane Floyd was always somewhat greater than the average percentage statewide of elderly in the states in which those counties were located:

Florida: 17.4 percent versus 16.8 percent statewide;
Georgia: 11.5 percent versus 9.6 percent statewide, and
North Carolina: 12.7 percent versus 12.1 percent statewide.

In general, those states were frequently hit by hurricanes. From 1851 to 2010, for example, the total number of hurricanes that hit Florida, North Carolina, and Georgia was 114, 51 and 23 respectively (Blake et al. 2011, p.21).

TRB (2008) identified a number of critical disruptions of road transportation from Hurricanes Katrina and Rita that illustrate some of the mechanisms by which transportation systems can be damaged from hurricanes, for example, storm surges and rapid water movement lifted bridges off their piers (TRB 2008, p.112). Estimated costs to repair highways and bridges totaled $800 million and two bridges alone accounted for three-quarters of the cost (computed from TRB 2008, p.108). TRB (2008, p.82) identified a number of attributes of the road transportation infrastructure related to redundancy that enabled truck traffic to resume operations during the 2005 hurricanes and the 1993 Mississippi floods by being able to be rerouted over different roads and through other hubs (TRB 2008, p.106).

Transit shutdowns and recovery
The vulnerability of transit systems depends on the type of hazard and the location relative to potential damages.

Earthquakes   In earthquakes, rails run the very serious risk of having rail lines distorted, moved, and cracked depending on the severity of the earthquake and the proximity of the equipment to earth movement. Overhead electrical lines held by catenaries are also vulnerable to rupture if ground connections are compromised. When signs of earthquakes appear, trains typically will reduce speed, and this occurred, for example, during the earthquake that hit the northeast US on August 23, 2011 (Achenbach 2011). In instances of sustained ground motion and the threat of aftershocks, more extensive action may be called for, such as shutting down the service and where possible rolling trains to the nearest stations. During the Loma Prieta earthquake, the steel tube structure of the Bay Area Rapid Transit system suffered no damage at all, though some highway tunnels were damaged (Yashinsky 1998, p.176).

The experience of Washington, DC during the August 2011 earthquake reflects the widespread impacts on and recovery of one of the most extensive and complex rail systems in the country. Although the magnitude of the earthquake was reported by the US Geological Survey as being about 5.8 at the epicenter in Virginia, it was somewhat less in the Washington, DC area. The account provided by the *Washington Post* staff (2011) details much of the immediate impact and recovery the day of the earthquake:

- The immediate reaction of the Metro was to operate at slower speeds (common in earthquakes), for example, at 15 mph, which continued through the evening while train crews inspected the infrastructure because of signal malfunctions.
- Extensive crowding of stations occurred from people trying to board trains and special handling was put in place in the form of holding passengers at gates.
- Amtrak trains were halted, awaiting tunnel and track inspections.
- By the evening, much of the service was restored though with reported delays of one to two hours.
- Commuter rail experienced delays due to the need to meet FTA rest requirements for train operators.

Hurricanes and flooding   In hurricanes, movement of water, the impact of wind, and the effects of projectiles damaging transport facilities are common threats. In the case of Hurricane Irene in late August 2011, the New York metropolitan area took risk aversive action using weather guidelines and shut down mass transit about a half day prior to the approach of the storm. The MTA chairman indicated that the train system could not operate where sustained winds exceeded 39 mph.

Flooding is a critical disruptive element for rail transportation systems in hurricanes. Major shutdowns of mass transit systems have occurred as a result of flooding in cities (Zimmerman 2005). Both above and below ground trains are threatened by flooding. During Hurricane Ike, the State of Texas estimated that "12 of its 21 buses, two of its five para-transit vans and all four rail trolleys" were flooded (The State of Texas 2008, p.22). The State indicated that virtually no funding was available to cover the costs. Damage to rail administrative offices, track and trains were estimated to cost $628,000 (The State of Texas 2008, pp.22–3). Hurricane Irene caused the disruption of numerous segments of Amtrak's rail line resulting in a lengthy recovery time. In advance of the storm, Amtrak reported canceling numerous trains along its major east coast routes over the weekend (August 27–8, 2011) (Amtrak 2011), and the Washington to New York corridor was not back in operation until a few days after the storm, due to extreme flooding in some of the segments. All it can take is one small disabled segment to disable an entire system if there are no alternative routes.

Bridge scour, which became a national issue after the collapse of the Schoharie Bridge in New York State (National Transportation Safety Board (NTSB) 1988), had been a serious cause of the destruction of rail lines as well as roads. In 1997 an Amtrak train passing over Bridge 504.1 south near Kingman, Arizona, derailed, and the apparent contributing factors were washing out of the track bed from a severe storm and flash flooding event that overwhelmed the crushed rock or rip rap protecting the track (NTSB 1998). Some other historic, examples of extensive rail damage from natural hazards, reported by NTSB, occurred on April 1, 1946 (Alaska), March 28, 1964 (Alaska), April 29, 1965 (Seattle, Washington), and February 9, 1971 (San Fernando, California).

According to TRB (2008, p.106) rail carriers were able to cope with both the 2005 hurricanes and the Mississippi floods of 1993, where some carriers were able to reroute trains on to little used track or shared with other carriers, and also shift operations to different carriers.

Urban rail systems have tracked the time it takes to recover from extreme storms that result in flash flooding, and the ranges reported, for example, for New York City, tend to be within a few hours to a day (MTA 2007).

Road and rail shutdowns combined

Very often, if roads shut down, rail systems may shut down also reducing or eliminating the availability of any transportation alternatives. The snowstorm of December 26, 2010 in the New York City area illustrates this. According to various reports, a combination of an extreme record weather condition, delayed storm warnings and a lack of preparedness led to catastrophic failures of both the road and rail systems within the City, as Kluger (2011) reports. The NOAA National Weather Service reported about 26 inches of snow in Central Park, ranking sixth in a century, accompanied by blizzard conditions. Although information on the oncoming storm was received, the warnings about the actual magnitude of the storm became available in what the City considered insufficient time for adequate response. There were an estimated 650 buses stranded and 500 people spent the night in subway cars (Kluger 2011, p.1). The City's snow clearance facilities and manpower were insufficient, since truck operators could not access the vehicles, communication systems were unavailable to identify where vehicles were located, and a complex procurement system did not support rapid acquisition of alternative equipment and services. This situation, coupled with stranded vehicles, resulted in the roads becoming impassable for days. Ultimately, the City had learned from experience as it faced other snowfalls in 2011 as well as Hurricane Irene, and changed many of the ways it handled its transportation system to reduce the impact on its users.

Debris Accumulation

Debris accumulation is a major impediment in the recovery of all forms of transportation after natural hazards and accidents, regardless of the type. Debris becomes a hazard in itself because it can cause fires, create flooding, and become an attractant for rodents and other vermin and disease vectors. It also takes the path of least resistance, which is usually a roadway, often blocking roadways especially when floodwaters move it. Debris can become projectiles in high winds. It can produce secondary damage if it results in collapses and landslides. These forces can be so powerful that they can cause a major source of death, injury and destruction. During recovery, the removal of debris can become an industry in itself with equipment to break it up, dewater it, haul it away, and dispose of it (see Table 6.1).

As in the case of natural hazards and accidents, debris accumulation after a terrorist attack can prove formidable and becomes a disaster in its own right. In New York City, according to the NYC Office of Emergency Management, the accumulation of debris after the collapse of the Towers and other buildings amounted to 1.6 million tons. NYC was fortunate to have access to piers in order to remove much of the debris by barge. This involved expediting permits to open up piers for marine transport,

Table 6.1   Examples of debris generated by selected natural hazards

Location	Event	Date	Estimated amount of debris
In millions of cubic yards:			
Galveston, TX (Houston area)	Hurricane Alicia*	August 1983	2
Mecklenburg Cty, NC	Hurricane Hugo	September 1989	2
Metro-Dade Cty, FL	Hurricane Andrew	August 1992	43
Kauai, HI	Hurricane Iniki	September 1992	5
Los Angeles, CA	Northridge Earthquake	January 1994	7
Upper Texas Gulf Coast, Texas**	Hurricane Ike	September 13, 2008	25
Haiti***	Earthquake	January 2010	20
Joplin, MO****	Tornadoes	April 2011	2.5
Alabama (Tuscaloosa, etc.)****	Tornadoes	Spring 2011	4.8
In millions of tons:			
Gulf States	Hurricane Katrina	August 2005	22
Japan*****	Earthquake and tsunami	March 11, 2011	27

Sources: The second through fifth entries are summarized from US EPA (1995), *Planning for Disaster Debris*, Washington, DC, USA: US EPA. Gulf State estimates for Hurricane Katrina and NYC 9/11 estimates are government estimates.

*   Rudolph P. Savage, Jay Baker, Joseph H. Golden, Ahsan Kareem and Billy R. Manning (1984), *Hurricane Alicia Galveston and Houston, Texas, August 17–18, 1983*, Washington, DC, USA: National Academies Press, pp.136–7, available at http://www.csc.noaa.gov/hes/docs/postStorm/H_ALICIA_GALVESTON_ HOUSTON.pdf.

**   The State of Texas, Office of the Governor, Division of Emergency Management (December 2008), 'Hurricane Ike Impact Report – December 2008', p.47, available at http://www.fema.gov/pdf/hazard/hurricane/2008/ike/impact_report.pdf.

***   Tacoma Perry (February 2011), 'Ga. Tech engineers turn Haiti rubble into resource', available at myfoxatlanta.com, http://www.myfoxatlanta.com/dpp/news/ local_news/Ga.-Tech-Engineers-Turn-Haiti-Rubble-into-Resource-20110208-am-sd.

****   John Schwartz (August 2011), 'Long after natural disasters, the cleanup grinds on', *The New York Times*, available at http://www.nytimes.com/2011/08/05/us/05debris. html?_r=1&hp.
The Alabama number is the estimate that USACE had removed.

***** Ken Belson (July 2011), 'In tsunami-torn city, seaside playgrounds become debris dumps', *The New York Times*, available at http://www.nytimes.com/2011/07/10/ world/asia/10sendai.html?_r=1&scp=1&sq=Sendai%20Japan&st=cse.
The World Trade Center attacks of September 11, 2001 generated an estimated 1.6 million tons of debris.

enabling the debris to be deposited in Fresh Kills landfill, which had already been closed. The existence and availability of construction firms in the area provided much of the equipment to accomplish that monumental task. Debris removal occurred through May of 2002, ahead of schedule and under budget, according to the NYC Office of Emergency Management.

TRANSPORTATION ACCIDENTS

Accidents in transportation systems range from small inconveniences created by a vehicle that goes out of service on a roadway or rail line to massive network disruptions. Disruptions are either direct due to a disabling of a link or node, or indirect, produced by a service such as electric power having an outage that is vital to transportation functioning. Although the origins of accidents that disrupt transportation are different from those that originate from natural hazards, many of the consequences are similar, as are the reactions to the emergencies that occur.

Whether or not the severity of some of the consequences of accidents is associated with the prior condition of the structures is often difficult to assess. The federal government maintains ongoing condition inventories and reports of transportation infrastructure condition. For highways, this is undertaken by the FHWA (US DOT, FHWA 2010). Post-accident investigations are the responsibility of the National Transportation Safety Board for road and rail, as well as other transportation infrastructure such as marine facilities and pipelines.

Rail Failures

Rail disruptions have numerous causes including weather, equipment malfunction, and any combination of those. They usually reflect the dependencies of rail on other vital infrastructures, such as electric power, stormwater drainage, and computer control systems. When these other systems fail, they can produce catastrophic failures on rail transit.

Stormwater drainage problems and flash flooding can overwhelm drainage, and have one of the largest impacts on rail transit systems, as they do on roadways. Zimmerman (2005) provided examples of cases where flooding disrupted transit services in some large cities. There are many ambitious stormwater management programs underway, such as the New York City "Green Infrastructure Plan", and the Philadelphia plan described in

Chapter 4 that incorporate stormwater management for roadways and parking lots, and potentially for rail lines.

The Long Island Railroad is one of the largest commuter lines in the US, and exemplifies how failures in single components can ripple throughout a large part of the system, affecting thousands of people. When incidents occur they are usually at unique points in the system where there is a single control point or a single rail line. Disruptions can spread over a very large area and take a long time to resolve. In the winter of 2007, the LIRR experienced five incidents that were so serious that they were investigated by the MTA Office of the Inspector General (2007). What starts as a natural hazard can be combined with an accident to produce greater consequences. According to an MTA (2011, p.2) report, on September 29, 2011 a lightning strike disabled a signal system, which disabled trains between the Jamaica Station and Penn Station, New York. While attempting to rectify the problem, an operator through a programming error disabled about 17 trains which were stranded and nine others that were standing to the east of Jamaica. Several other incidents compounded the problem, such as police action, causing a third rail power outage. Service was restored the next morning. The LIRR experienced a double natural hazard and accident condition on August 23, 2010 when excessive precipitation caused cables to short and cause an accidental fire in a control tower at a choke point in the system (Jamaica station where ten out of the 11 lines come together), disabling service in the entire system for a few hours (Grynbaum 2010). Finally, within a few years of these events, a new computer system controlling signaling became disabled, causing massive outages in the LIRR system (Grynbaum 2010). These episodes illustrate the role of network properties in producing extreme consequences, given a transit system with a few critical nodes that have numerous interconnections.

Highway Bridge Failures

Highway bridge failures are particularly critical since they are often unique links in a road network. Natural hazards often contribute to the destruction of highway bridges, as they do for transportation infrastructure discussed earlier. Yet, in a number of cases of bridge failures, weather might have played an initiating role, but was not considered the major factor in a catastrophic collapse. Similarly, age may have contributed, but not always.

Many factors contribute to the extreme collapses of bridges and overpasses. The destruction of some of the smaller structures is primarily considered to be weather-related, such as flooding.

Collisions are identified as a source of damages to bridge components. The National Transportation Safety Board (NTSB) (1994) study notes that from the National Highway Traffic Safety Administration (NHTSA) Fatal Accident Reporting System "The NHTSA estimates that annually 1,000 trucks and buses (10,000 pounds gross weight or greater) collide with bridge structures." One notable accident occurred involving a marine vessel when on September 22, 1993 a tow boat hit the piers supporting a rail line, resulting in the derailment of a rail line and the death of 47 out of 210 people in the train (NTSB 1994, p.22). Where collisions are a factor in the destruction of a bridge, the time of day has been known to contribute to accidents involving vehicle collisions, including collisions with structures such as bridge supports. The accident report for the collision and ultimate destruction of bridge/overpass supports in Evergreen, Alabama, in 1993 pointed out the vulnerabilities created by nightshifts because of greater fatigue and sleep deficit (NTSB 1994, p.12 citing Teaps and Monk (1987) and McDonald (1984)) in support of this type of condition.

Bridge age is considered a factor in the rating of the condition of bridges, though it is not clearly a factor in the most catastrophic failures. The National Bridge Inventory provides the distribution of bridges by age in the National Highway System (US DOT, FHWA 2008, Chapter 11). According to the FHWA National Bridge Inventory from 1800 through 2005 (Zimmerman et al. 2009):

- The largest number of bridges was built between the 1950s and 1970s.
- The structural deficiency and obsolescence rating clearly increases with age, signifying increasing deterioration over time.
- The percentage of bridges where the superstructure was rated poor or worse also increased with age.

Although age is related to the structural and functional condition rating of a bridge, it is not clearly related to whether it has collapsed or not, which an analysis of bridge age and date of collapse shows.

There were over 600,000 bridges in the United States according to the National Bridge Inventory through 2010. Although a small proportion of these have experienced catastrophic failures the impacts have been extensive. The National Transportation Safety Board (NTSB) records of bridge collapses (which focus on major collapses usually involving loss of life) indicate that for over two dozen massive bridge collapses that the NTSB has investigated since the NTSB began operation in the mid-1960s, age was not a clear or consistent factor in the collapses. Age was available for about two dozen of the bridges that collapsed.

Table 6.2   Age of all bridges and age of collapsed bridges at date of
collapse

Bridge age	All bridges* (%)	Collapsed bridges** (%)
Under 20 years old	20.5	30.4
20–30	10.7	17.4
31–40	25.3	30.4
41–50	27.9	4.4
51–70	10.4	17.7
>70	5.2	0.0

Sources:
* Calculated from the National Bridge Inventory for National Highway System bridges only.
** Calculated from data compiled from National Transportation Safety Board bridge collapse reports.

- About two-thirds of the bridges that collapsed were open for operation in the 1950s or 1960s.
- Only four bridges that had collapsed, or about a fifth of the group, were built in the 1920s or 1930s.

The NTSB reports as a whole tend to attribute collapses to design flaws or maintenance (though design protocols that were in force at the time may have been followed). Of the 23 bridges for which age was available, the correlation between age and date of accident was not strong ($r=0.2$).

Table 6.2 compares the age of the collapsed bridges to the age of all bridges in the US in 2006. While less than a third of all bridges were 30 years old or younger in 2010, almost half of the collapsed bridges were in that age category. About the same percentage of all bridges and bridges that had collapsed were greater than 50 years old. However, none of the bridges that had collapsed was older than 70 years old, whereas in the entire inventory about 5 percent was in that category.

Two bridge collapse cases illustrate the complexity of factors that go into such events. While natural hazards play an initial factor in some collapses, a combination of other underlying causes was a significant contributing factor. These cases illustrate how it is not one cause, but a number of them either in combination or that go unnoticed or not acted on, that create the environment for collapse.

Case 1. The Mianus Bridge, I-95, Greenwich, Connecticut (NTSB 1984). A 100 foot section of the Mianus Bridge fell into the Mianus River on June 28, 1983 at 1:30 am, resulting in three deaths and three injuries. If it had occurred during the day, the number of casualties could have been enormous. The bridge is a major link along the New York to Boston corridor. Pre-event conditions included an Annual Average Daily Traffic (AADT) of 90,000 vehicles and a higher accident rate than typical for such a bridge. Drainage blockages, lack of regular painting, and a thinner pin cap thickness in its assembly allowed water penetration, contributing to its deterioration; maintenance and oversight procedures were not sufficient to detect the problem (NTSB 1984; Zimmerman 1999). Standards did not prevail that could have prevented the pre-event conditions from occurring.

Case 2. The Minneapolis Bridge (I-35 W Bridge), Minneapolis, Minnesota (NTSB 2008). The Minneapolis Bridge collapsed on August 1, 2007 into the Mississippi River, killing 13 people and injuring 121 (Federal Communications Commission (FCC) 2008, p.9). According to the National Transportation Safety Board (2008, p.6), the Minnesota Bridge that collapsed was built in 1967. Part of the bridge's main span fell into the river below (NTSB 2008, p.xiii). The NTSB concluded that design, inspection, and construction practices that did not take into account the ability of the bridge to sustain the loads contributed to the collapse.

THE ROLE OF TRANSPORTATION IN EMERGENCIES

Emergencies from whatever cause create several major interrelated demands on transportation that distort transport networks. It is imperative that transportation planning and operations take these critical points into account given the ongoing threats from natural hazards and accidents that are occurring. One such demand is the evacuation of people out of an affected area, where evacuation is the decision. Another is for the movement of goods and services, including emergency personnel into the affected area. Connected to both the movement of people, goods and services is the removal of debris out of an area where considerable devastation has occurred that was described earlier, and transport plays a key role in this. A third need is maintaining equity in the distribution of services before, during and after a crisis. A fourth is building in sufficient flexibility in legal and administrative arrangements to accommodate unusual conditions by means of emergency exemptions.

Transportation and Evacuation

Transportation is obviously key to the movement and accommodation of people, supplies and emergency vehicles in often unforeseen ways. Jim Defede recounts how the Town of Gander, Newfoundland accommodated the planes that landed on September 11, 2001 after air traffic was shut down, and how this reflects the adaptability of a transportation network to a crisis. Defede notes that ground transportation played a crucial role in transporting the thousands of passengers to their accommodations and moving supplies to them (Defede 2002).

Evacuation depends on the type of hazard, its suddenness and unexpectedness and the ability of people to be forewarned. It also depends on what type of response is called for, such as shelter-in-place versus movement to a shelter or other areas, self-evacuation or organized evacuation, mandatory or voluntary evacuation, and the nature of the people requiring evacuation. All of these options affect transportation in different ways.

Earthquakes are among the most sudden and least predictable hazards. In the earthquake that affected Washington, DC on August 23, 2011, people largely self-evacuated at the same time, overwhelming transportation facilities. As reported in the media (Fox News and Associated Press 2011), road and rail systems were jammed as people tried to leave the area, in addition to the 19 evacuation routes and train services slowing to avoid damage. The ultimate reaction of public services to relieve some of the congestion was placing police officers on traffic duty, moving train services into a rush hour mode earlier, lifting carpooling restrictions, and altering traffic signals (Fox News and Associated Press 2011).

This contrasts with the evacuation of low lying areas in the New York area in advance of Hurricane Irene in late August 2011 involving about one million people in New Jersey, 400,000 on Long Island, and about 370,000 in New York City and hundreds of thousands elsewhere (Severson et al. 2011). Even with public transportation systems deliberately stopping, massive roadway congestion was not typically reported given the length of time over which the evacuation occurred. Instances where there is not much warning for evacuation can produce massive traffic jams. Litman (2006, p.7) notes that during Hurricane Rita, the evacuation of about three million people in the Houston area caused traffic congestion that people were not prepared for, for example, taking four to five hours to traverse 50 miles. Models did not anticipate the large numbers (Litman 2006, p.8). Hurricane Ike was the third costliest storm (Harris County 2009, p.1) – and involved a mandatory evacuation of 245,000 people – less than the number of people evacuated in NYC during Hurricane Irene. Within the upper Texas coast Hurricane Ike had the highest storm surge since 1915 (Harris County 2009, p.2).

As much as transportation enables people to move quickly away from a hazard, it can also trap people. Fatalities often result from people relying on personal vehicles for self-evacuation involving a rapid escape. There are numerous examples, but here are a few:

- Of the 46 deaths covering 13 US states and eight in the Caribbean that were estimated to have occurred during Hurricane Irene and reported by the Associated Press (2011), nine were automobile or road related.
- Of the estimated 10–20 deaths during Hurricane Alicia in 1983, Savage et al. (1984, p.134) reported four incidents involving cars including a collision of a vehicle with a tree, a tree falling on an evacuating family's car, a tree falling on a car during an effort to move a car, and various objects hitting a car during a storm.
- In the tornado that struck Joplin, Missouri in 2011, the US Department of Commerce, National Oceanic and Atmospheric Administration (2011, p.9) noted a Joplin Globe survey that initially reported that though most (54 percent) of the deaths occurred in residences, in 14 percent of the fatalities people had gotten into their vehicles or were otherwise outside.

Even where transportation routes to carry people out of a disaster are available, traffic reduces the effectiveness. As described above, during Hurricane Rita, where response to the hurricane was quicker than it was during Hurricane Katrina, congested transportation routes and a shortage of fuel limited the ability to use those routes (Litman 2006).

The effectiveness of public transport vehicles in evacuations depends on the extent to which sources of delay can be overcome. One is accommodating passengers with luggage which tends to reduce vehicle capacity for passengers by at least half (Litman 2006, p.9). A second is being deployed in areas where they are needed. A third is being able to obtain the cooperation of drivers. A fourth is roadway congestion, described above, and competition from supply vehicles.

Many solutions have been tried to move large numbers of people in emergencies. One is to reverse lanes moving traffic in the direction away from disastrous conditions, called contraflow (Urbina and Wolshon 2003). Drawbridges, where they exist, can be placed in a lock down position to increase the flow of traffic as one was during Hurricane Andrew (Post, Buckley, Schuh & Jernigan, Inc. 1993, p.5-5) and extensively in Hurricane Floyd (Post, Buckley, Schuh & Jernigan, Inc. 2000). Another is to use high occupancy vehicles in dedicated lanes (Litman 2006, p.13). Another is to rely on mass transit to the extent possible, since it can move larger numbers of people quickly. Litman (2006, p.13) estimates that one lane can accommodate 15,000 passengers per hour for bus travel and light rail can accommodate 20,000 per hour. Another effective way to handle this is obviously to evacuate ahead of time where that is possible and supported. Areas have "clearance times" which indicate how long it will take to move a certain number people along the transport routes available, and this provides a guide to the timing of evacuation. Clearance times can vary dramatically depending on location and road conditions. For example, for Hurricane Andrew, Post, Buckley, Schuh & Jernigan, Inc. (1993, p.5-1 and 5-3) give a range of seven to 24 hours. For Hurricane Floyd the estimates ranged from ten to 48 hours (Post, Buckley, Schuh & Jernigan, Inc. 2000, Table 5-1).

Moving Goods and Services

The nature of urban form influences the ability of transportation systems to respond adequately to emergencies. Suburban fringes typically have different constraints on their road systems than urban areas. They have often grown up around small centers with narrow street systems that cannot accommodate increased growth. Trowbridge et al. (2009) analysed the response times for emergency medical service (EMS) and ambulance arrival delays as a function of the degree of sprawl of an area for motor vehicle crashes reported under the Fatal Analysis Reporting System. Using Ewing et al.'s (2003) county-level sprawl index and controlling for weather conditions and construction, they found a significant association between increased sprawl and increased response time and ambulance arrival delay. They offer as possible explanations the greater difficulty of covering a larger area with limited resources. Moreover, suburban development is usually characterized by narrow street systems with less capacity to absorb surges created by evacuation or the movement of emergency services. Emergency services by definition are faced with a high degree of uncertainty, though some natural hazards are enabling a certain level of predictability. For example, Bassil et al. (2011, p.830) reported in a summer 2005 study in Toronto, Canada that during heat extremes the number of ambulance calls increased with temperature, for instance, calls increased by about a third with a one degree centigrade increase in maximum temperature. This has been noted as a potential impact of climate change (Madrigano et al. 2012).

Maintaining Equity

Issues of race and class in the context of exposure to and recovery from disasters have a very long history, originating most recently in the twentieth century as the environmental justice movement that had connections to the civil rights movement (Zimmerman 1994a). Fothergill et al. (1999) review many of the reasons why race and ethnicity are critical factors in disasters.

Vulnerable populations are particularly dependent on transportation in disasters and many have fewer options than those without such restrictions. Access to vehicles and escape routes during Hurricane Katrina illustrates this point.

Although being in vehicles during a hurricane can be dangerous to life, access to vehicles prior to the onset of a hurricane is critical to being able to leave a threatened area. Wright and Bullard (2007, p.190) noted that many of the more vulnerable people caught in Hurricane Katrina in New Orleans did not own cars: African Americans in New Orleans had relatively less access to cars, with over a third not owning a car compared to a fifth of all households in hurricane disaster areas, and 8 percent nationwide.

Public transit was another option, since about a quarter of the people in New Orleans rely on public transportation. School buses often relied upon to move large numbers of people in disasters were not available during Hurricane Katrina since the areas where they were stored were flooded, bus drivers were often not available, and plans for deployment were not clear. Litman (2006, p.5, citing Preston 2005) portrays the bus capacity in New Orleans as follows:

> The city had approximately 500 transit and school buses, a quarter of the estimated 2,000 buses needed to evacuate residents who wanted transport (even more buses would have been needed to carry all residents who needed transport, since under emergency conditions it is unrealistic for a bus to carry 50 passengers). However, if given priority in traffic, buses could have made multiple trips out of the city during the 48-hour evacuation period, and even evacuating 10,000 to 30,000 people would have reduced emergency shelter overcrowding. (Preston 2005)

Another problem is the availability of bus drivers. Even in advance of Hurricane Katrina, researchers had already identified the difficulty of evacuating large numbers of people, particularly the poor from the New Orleans area (Kendra et al. 2008; Wolshon 2002).

The availability of transportation does not always imply access. The equity issues that arose during Hurricane Katrina included the lack of access to routes of escape over the Danziger Bridge. Other equity issues in connection with Hurricane Katrina have been analysed extensively in terms of vulnerability and disparities in vulnerability within the Gulf region (Wright and Bullard 2007; Cutter et al. 2006) and in connection with natural hazards in general (Cutter and Finch 2008).

Overcoming Legal Impediments and Emergency Exemptions

Provisions exist to adapt some rules and regulations that safeguard the environment to emergency needs during and following a disaster that may conflict with environmental needs. These exemptions and waivers extend across a wide range of situations and legislation; a few examples of those that pertain particularly to transportation and how they were used in specific emergencies created by natural hazards and accidents are presented below.

A wide range of waiver provisions pertaining to the environment are allowed for statutes under the jurisdiction of the US EPA. In addition, McCarthy and Copeland (2006, p.CRS-2) identify waivers under the Robert T. Stafford Disaster Relief and Emergency Assistance Act regarding restrictions on conditions for dispensing financial assistance. Waiver provisions also exist for NEPA regulations, in particular for debris management (Luther 2006, p.CRS-1).

Clean Air Act and transport fuel

The US EPA in coordination with the US DOE and the states allows waivers from fuel restrictions under the Clean Air Act Section 211(c)(4)(C). These usually pertain to waivers from Reid Vapor Pressure (RVP), ethanol, Reformulated Gasoline (RFG) and other fuel requirements such as sulfur content. Many have been issued in connection with flooding and pipeline shutdowns due to hurricanes or other extreme weather conditions to prevent shortages of gasoline supplies. The waivers occur for a confined period of time and a limited geographic area (US EPA September 2011).

Between 2005 and 2010 a total of 47 waivers were granted, plus a nationwide waiver in 2005 in connection with Hurricane Katrina. Most of the waivers granted in 2005 were in connection with Hurricane Katrina. In 2011 through September, there were two exemptions. One was granted during Hurricane Irene, to Pennsylvania. It was a short-term exemption (20 days) from Clean Air Act requirements by the EPA for the use of certain types of gasoline, since the Buckeye pipeline was flooded and shut down. This involved going to 9.0 psi from the required 7.8 psi low RVP in a six county area in the Pittsburgh–Beaver Valley area of Pennsylvania (US EPA September 2011; US EPA September 12, 2011).

Clean Water Act and water discharges

The Clean Water Act regulates the discharge of water and other materials into navigable waterways. Section 404 covers dredge and fill permits administered by the US Army Corps of Engineers, and exemptions were granted following Hurricane Katrina (McCarthy and Copeland 2006). Permits issued under the National Pollutant Discharge Elimination System of the Clean Water Act and its delegations to state agencies also directly allow for emergency exemptions. Both permits could potentially be applicable to certain transportation-related conditions such as clearing water and debris from roadways and rail lines during and after flooding, and for transportation facility reconstruction following a disaster. These kinds of permits are typically exempt in emergencies, for example, such exemptions were granted for the dewatering and related discharge activities following Hurricane Katrina (McCarthy and Copeland 2006, CRS-3, CRS-4).

Environmental review

Exemption provisions under NEPA were covered in Chapter 5. Emergency exemptions granted under NEPA for the rebuilding of Lower Manhattan following the World Trade Center attacks were also covered in Chapter 5. Analogous exemptions for long-term reconstruction following Hurricane Katrina were also considered (McCarthy and Copeland 2006, CRS-7). For more immediate response and recovery stages, exemptions were granted following the World Trade Center attacks that are also potentially relevant to natural hazards and accidents. A pier was opened up on the west side of Manhattan in order to expedite the shipment of debris out of the area, and a section of the Fresh Kills landfill which had been closed was reopened to accept the debris.

Other transportation-related waiver possibilities

The National Infrastructure Advisory Council (2009, pp.29–31) identified provisions for truck size and weight restrictions on highways as potential areas for waivers in emergencies.

CONCLUSIONS: INCREASING THE RESILIENCE OF TRANSPORTATION INFRASTRUCTURE

Ultimately, the question of how to improve the resiliency of transport structures to withstand the impact of natural hazards and accidents arises as a central theme in management, the sciences and engineering. Many solutions are commonly put forth and extensively tested relating to design, adaptation to local environmental and social conditions, operations, materials and the like. Though these areas are well-known, instances occur where they fell short of what was needed to avert a catastrophe.

Problem Areas

A number of engineering and operational conditions arise in transportation accidents. Meyer (2008) suggests solutions needed for subsurface conditions, materials specifications, cross sections and standard dimensions, drainage and erosion, structures and location engineering. Meyer (2008) notes that impacts affect materials, supply chains, research and development efforts for new technologies, and geographic areas that are indirectly affected by a specific area they are not in proximity with. In addition, infrastructure usage is critical to its endurance and resilience to the additional stresses posed by climate change and other environmental conditions. The positive side, as Meyer (2008) points out, is that the lifetime of infrastructure enables replacement to account for design modifications in light of new threats.

Subsurface conditions are influenced by soil moisture or saturation in the case of heavy precipitation (Meyer 2008). This condition occurred in the Mississippi Floods of 1993 (Zimmerman 1994b). Liquefaction can occur during earthquakes (Meyer, 2008, p.5), weakening the stability of the subsurface supporting infrastructure, which occurred in the San Francisco earthquake. Waste piles can also weaken substructures.

Materials specifications are given in codes and professional protocols and are often difficult to alter (Meyer, 2008, p.6). The stability and strength of transportation materials are influenced by environmental conditions. For example, the resistance of road beds, particularly on bridges, to deformation is diminished by the density of traffic, the weight of vehicles, and the idling time of the vehicles on bridges producing compression (Zimmerman 1996).

With respect to cross sections and standard dimensions, Meyer (2008, pp.6–7) points out that vertical bridge clearances in the Gulf Coast were often too low and storm surges resulted in bridge decks floating off the supporting structures.

Drainage and erosion underscore the fact that managing water plays a critical role in ensuring the resilience of transport infrastructure. Inadequate drainage played a key part in the Mianus Bridge collapse in Connecticut, where impaired drainage ditches allowed water to spill over the sides of the bridge and come in contact with steel support structures. That together with insufficient protection of the steel from rusting contributed to the failure of key structural supports (NTSB 1984).

Some Solutions

As with climate change, historical records are being exceeded in some areas of natural hazards and accidents with considerable implications for transportation infrastructure and its users.

These vulnerabilities suggest the following strategies commonly identified as a means of protecting transportation infrastructure against catastrophic failures – in some cases modifying the design of transportation networks, the materials, and how they are used. What is emphasized here is solutions that intersect with those that achieve or are compatible with environmental needs. Many others were discussed in connection with adaptation and planning for climate change in Chapters 3 and 4.

Better materials and design are a growing area of emphasis. Hardening structures with better and more water- and vibration-resistant materials is presenting new and innovative solutions. For bridges, Zoli has developed an innovative solution by reducing the weight of the bridge and increasing their flexibility and blast resistance to withstand hazardous conditions (MacArthur Foundation 2009). Ultra-high performing concrete is a growing field, and barriers, where all else fails, tend to be a simple solution to resist the impacts of floodwaters, where they work. In rebuilding, Perry (2011) has suggested using debris following a disaster as a source of building material.

Operational flexibility is often overlooked as a means to adapt to hazardous conditions. Many have already been mentioned, such as contraflow (Urbina and Wolshon 2003), where the direction of a roadway is reversed. Contraflow was invoked in Hurricane Rita to enable people to use roadways that moved in the direction of Houston. Rail flexibility that enables tracks to be realigned and trains to travel over alternative routes was used in the aftermath of 9/11. This versatility is also important for security.

The success of overcoming many of the limitations of alternative transport technologies that involve vehicular transport – limited distances or ranges and speeds that electric vehicles can achieve, for example – is the ability to store energy to extend battery life. This in turn requires materials, many of which are not found in the US and are concentrated in a few locations outside the US; however, new sources are being discovered. The value of overcoming obstacles to and shortcomings of electric vehicles, is exemplified by the fact that electric vehicles were the main vehicles used to enter emergency areas after the Japanese earthquake of March 11, 2011 when gasoline was in short supply for traditional vehicles (Belson 2011).

Many solutions to natural hazard disasters and accidents that affect transportation support security needs as well, which the next chapter addresses.

REFERENCES

Achenbach, J. (2011), 'Zoo mystery: how did apes and birds know quake was coming?', *The Washington Post* online, available at http://www.washington-post.com/national/health-science/zoo-mystery-how-did-apes-and-birds-know-quake-was-coming/2011/08/24/gIQAZrXQcJ_story.html?hpid=z2.

Amtrak (August 2011), 'News release: Amtrak cancels more east coast trains in advance of Hurricane Irene, service reductions on Saturday, no service on Sunday', Washington, DC, USA: National Railroad Passenger Corporation.

Associated Press (September 1, 2011), 'Hurricane Irene blamed for at least 46 US deaths', available at http://www.oregonlive.com/newsflash/index.ssf/story/hurricane-irene-blamed-for-at-least-46/81ecc8c3ac48483db54dfa3040a5a591.

Association of Bay Area Governments (April 2003), excerpts from 'Riding out future quakes', available at http://www.abag.ca.gov/bayarea/eqmaps/eqtrans/pastex.html.

Association of Bay Area Governments (May 2011), 'Expected transportation losses in an earthquake', available at http://quake.abag.ca.gov/transportation/.

Bassil, K.L., D.C. Cole and R. Moineddin et al. (2011), 'The relationship between temperature and ambulance response calls for heat-related illness in Toronto, Ontario, 2005', *Journal of Epidemiology and Community Health*, **65**, 829–31.

Baykal-Gürsoy, M., W. Xiao and K. Ozbay (2009), 'Modeling traffic flow interrupted by incidents', *European Journal of Operational Research*, **195** (1), 127–38.

Belson, K. (July 2011), 'In tsunami-torn city, seaside playgrounds become debris dumps', *The New York Times*, available at http://www.nytimes.com/2011/07/10/world/asia/10sendai.html?_r=1&scp=1&sq=Sendai%20Japan&st=cse.

Belson, K. (May 2011), 'After disaster hit Japan, electric cars stepped up', *The New York Times*, available at http://www.nytimes.com/2011/05/08/automobiles/08JAPAN.html?hpw (accessed November 21, 2011).

Bender, M.A., T.R. Knutson, R.E. Tuleya, J.J. Sirutis, G.A. Vecchi, S.T. Garner and I.M. Held (2010), 'Modeled impact of anthropogenic warming on the frequency of intense Atlantic hurricanes', *Science*, **327**, 454–8.

Blake, E.S., C.W. Landsea and E.J. Gibney (August 2011), 'The Deadliest, Costliest, and Most Intense United States Tropical Cyclones from 1851 to 2010 (and other frequently requested hurricane facts)', NOAA Technical Memorandum NWS NHC-6, available at http://www.nhc.noaa.gov/pdf/nws-nhc-6.pdf.

Bouchon, M., H. Karabulut, M. Aktar, S. Ozalaybey, J. Schmittbuhl and M-P. Bouin (2011), 'Extended nucleation of the 1999 Mw 7.6 Izmit earthquake', *Science*, **331**, 877–80.

Bourque, L.B., J.M. Siege, M. Kano and M.M. Wood (2007), 'Morbidity and mortality associated with disasters', in H. Rodriguez, E.L. Quarantelli and R.R. Dynes (eds), *Handbook of Disaster Research*, New York, NY, USA: Springer, pp.97–112.

Burlington Free Press (September 2011), 'Heavy equipment is used Friday to clear debris from Vermont 100 near Pittsfield in the wake of flooding triggered by Tropical Storm Irene', available at http://www.burlingtonfreepress.com/.

Centers for Disease Control and Prevention, *Natural Disasters & Severe Weather*, available at http://emergency.cdc.gov/disasters/.

Cutter, S.L. and C. Finch (2008), 'Temporal and spatial changes in social vulnerability to natural hazards', PNAS, **105** (7), 2301–6.

Cutter, S.L., C.T. Emrich, J.T. Mitchell, B.J. Boruff, M. Gall, M.C. Schmidtiein, C.G. Burton and G. Melton (2006), 'The long road home: Race, class, and recovery from Hurricane Katrina', *Environment*, **48** (2), 9–20.

Defede, J. (2002), *The Day the World Came to Town: 9/11 in Gander, Newfoundland*, New York, NY, USA: Harper.

Emanuel, K., R. Sundararajan and J. Williams (2008), 'Hurricanes and global warming', *Bulletin of the American Meteorological Society*, **89** (3), 347–67.

Ewing, R., R. Pendall and D. Chen (2003), 'Measuring sprawl and its transportation impacts', *Travel Demand and Land Use*, Transportation Research Record No. 1831, 175–83.

Federal Communications Commission (November 2008), *Emergency Communications during the Minneapolis Bridge Disaster*, Washington, DC, USA: Federal Communications Commission.

Federal Emergency Management Administration (FEMA) (December 2008), *Hurricane Ike Impact Report*, US Department of Homeland Security and Federal Emergency Management Administration, available at http://www.fema.gov/pdf/hazard/hurricane/2008/ike/impact_report.pdf (accessed February 3, 2009).

Federal Emergency Management Administration (FEMA) (February 2012), 'Declared disasters by year or state', available at http://www.fema.gov/news/disaster_totals_annual.fema.

Fothergill, A., E.G.M. Maestas and J. DeRouen Darlington (1999), 'Race, ethnicity and disasters in the United States: a review of the literature', *Disasters*, **23** (2), 156–73.

Fox News and Associated Press (August 2011), 'Magnitude 5.8 earthquake hits Virginia, sends shock waves throughout East Coast', available at http://www.foxnews.com/us/2011/08/23/magnitude-58-earthquake-hits-virginia-sends-shock-waves-throughout-east-coast/.

Grynbaum, M.M. (August 2010), 'Some service restored on L.I.R.R.', *The New York Times*, available at http://www.nytimes.com/2010/08/24/nyregion/24lirr.html.

Guha-Sapir D., F. Vos and R. Below with S. Ponserre (2011), 'Annual Disaster Statistical Review 2010: The Numbers and Trends', Brussels: Centre for Research on the Epidemiology of Disasters (CRED), available at http://www.undp.org.cu/crmi/docs/cred-annualdisstats2010-rt-2011-en.pdf.

Harris County Office of Homeland Security and Emergency Management (March 2009), *Harris County Hurricane Ike After Action Report*, Harris County, Texas, available at http://www.newsrouter.com/NewsRouter_Uploads/67/HarrisCounty_HurricaneIke_AAR_Final_03_30_2009.pdf (accessed April 3, 2009).

Holzer, T.L. (ed.) (October 1998), *Professional Paper 1551 – Strong Ground Motion and Ground Failure*, US Geological Survey, available at http://earthquake.usgs.gov/regional/nca/1989/papers.php.

International Strategy for Disaster Reduction (ISDR) (2010), '2010 disasters in numbers', available at http://www.unisdr.org/files/17613_rectoversodisasters2010.pdf.

Kendra, J., J. Rozdilsky and D.A. McEntire (2008), 'Evacuating large urban areas: challenges for emergency management policies and concepts', *Journal of Homeland Security and Emergency Management*, **5** (1), article 32.

Kluger, B.L. (December 2011), *NYC Transit's Response to December 2010 Blizzard*, Albany, NY, USA: State of New York.

Knutson, T.R., J.J. Sirutis, S.T. Garner, G.A. Vecchi and I.M. Held (May 2008), 'Simulated reduction in Atlantic hurricane frequency under twenty-first-century warming conditions', *Nature*, available at www.nature.com/naturegeoscience (accessed May 21, 2008).

Litman, T. (2006), *Lessons from Katrina and Rita: What Major Disasters Can Teach Transportation Planners*, Victoria, BC, Canada: Victoria Transport Policy Institute.

Luther, L. (March 2006), *NEPA and Hurricane Response, Recovery, and Rebuilding Efforts, CRS Report RL33104*, Washington, DC, USA: Congressional Research Service, available at http://www.hsdl.org/?view&did=461710.

MacArthur Foundation (September 2009), Theodore Zoli, Vice President and Technical Director, Bridges, HNTB Corporation, MacArthur Fellow newsletter, available at http://www.macfound.org/site/c.lkLXJ8MQKrH/b.5458047/k.9B7A/Theodore_Zoli.htm.

Madrigano, J., P. Kinney and J. Trtanj (2012), 'Public Health', in W. Solecki and C. Rosenzweig et al. (eds), *U.S. Cities and Climate Change: Urban, Infrastructure, and Vulnerability Issues*, Review Draft, New York, NY, USA.

McCarthy, J.E. and C. Copeland (February 2006), *Emergency Waiver of EPA Regulations: Authorities and Legislative Proposals in the Aftermath of Hurricane Katrina*, Washington, DC, USA: Congressional Research Service, available at http://www.cnie.org/NLE/CRSreports/06Mar/RL33107.pdf.

Metropolitan Transportation Authority (MTA) (September 2007), 'August 8, 2007 storm report', New York, NY, USA: Metropolitan Transportation Authority, available at http://www.mta.info/mta/pdf/storm_report_2007.pdf.

Metropolitan Transportation Authority (MTA) (October 2011), 'Preliminary review September 29, 2011 lightning strike at Jamaica', New York, NY, USA: MTA.

Metropolitan Transportation Authority, Office of the Inspector General (2007), *Response to LIRR Service Disruptions, Winter 2007*, available at http://mtaig.state.ny.us/assets/pdf/08-03.pdf.

Meyer, M.D. (2008), *Design Standards for US Transportation Infrastructure: The Implications of Climate Change*, available at http://onlinepubs.trb.org/onlinepubs/sr/sr290Meyer.pdf.

National Highway Traffic Safety Administration, 'Fatal analysis reporting system (FARS)', available at http://www.nhtsa.gov/FARS.

National Infrastructure Advisory Council (July 2009), 'Framework for dealing with disasters and related interdependencies', available at http://www.dhs.gov/xlibrary/assets/niac/niac_framework_dealing_with_disasters.pdf.

National Oceanic and Atmospheric Administration (NOAA) (undated website), National Weather Service–National Hurricane Center, 'Storm surge overview', available at http://www.nhc.noaa.gov/ssurge/index.shtml.

National Oceanic and Atmospheric Administration (NOAA) (undated website), National Weather Service–National Hurricane Center, 'Tropical cyclone climatology: Return periods', available at http://www.nhc.noaa.gov/HAW2/english/basics/return.shtml.

National Oceanic and Atmospheric Administration (NOAA) Satellite and Information Service, National Climatic Data Center (2012), Billion Dollar US Weather/Climate Disasters, available at http://www.ncdc.noaa.gov/img/reports/billion/timeseries2011.pdf.

National Oceanic and Atmospheric Administration, US Department of Commerce (undated web page), available at www.noaa.gov. (Use search window to find information.)

National Research Council, Committee on Hydrologic Science (2011), *Global*

Change and Extreme Hydrology: Testing Conventional Wisdom, Prepublication Copy, Washington, DC, USA: The National Academies Press.

National Transportation Safety Board (1984), *Highway Accident Report: Collapse of a Suspended Span of Interstate Rte 95 Highway Bridge over the Mianus R. Greenwich, CT. 6/28/83*, Washington, DC, USA: National Transportation Safety Board.

National Transportation Safety Board (NTSB) (1988), *Highway Accident Reports: Collapse of New York Thruway (I-90) Bridge over the Schoharie Creek, near Amsterdam New York, April 5, 1987*, available at http://www.ntsb.gov/investigations/summary/HAR8802.htm.

National Transportation Safety Board (1994), *Highway Accident Report. Tractor-Semi-trailer Collision with Bridge Columns on Interstate 65, Evergreen, Alabama, May 19, 1993*, available at http://www.ntsb.gov/investigations/summary/HAR9402.htm.

National Transportation Safety Board (1998), *Railroad Accident Report Derailment of Amtrak Train 4 Southwest Chief on the Burlington Northern Santa Fe Railway near Kingman, AZ August 9, 1997*, NTSB/RAR-98/03, available at http://www.docstoc.com/docs/7229505/Abstract-NTSB-RAR.

National Transportation Safety Board (NTSB) (2008), *Highway Accident Report: Collapse of the I-35W highway bridge, Minneapolis, MN, August 1, 2007*, available at http://www.ntsb.gov/doclib/reports/2008/HAR0803.pdf.

Ozbay K. and M.A. Yazici (2006), 'Analysis of network-wide impacts of behavioral response curves for evacuation conditions', proceedings of the 2006 IEEE Intelligent Transportation Systems Conference, Toronto, Canada, September 17–20, 2006.

Perry, T. (February 2011), 'Ga. tech engineers turn Haiti rubble into resource', available at http://www.myfoxatlanta.com/dpp/news/local_news/Ga.-Tech-Engineers-Turn-Haiti-Rubble-into-Resource-20110208-am-sd.com.

Pielke, R.A., Jr., J. Gratz, C.W. Landsea, D. Collins, M.A. Saunders and R. Musulin (2008), 'Normalized hurricane damage in the US: 1900–2005', *Natural Hazards Review*, **9** (1), 29–42, available at http://sciencepolicy.colorado.edu/admin/publication_files/resource-2476-2008.02.pdf.

Pollack, A.W. and K. Bishop (November 1989), 'The highway collapse: some columns and some assumptions were weak', *The New York Times*, p.28.

Post, Buckley, Schuh & Jernigan, Inc. (1993), *Hurricane Andrew Assessment: Review of Hurricane Evacuation Studies Utilization and Information Dissemination*, Tallahassee, FL, USA: US Army Corps of Engineers and Federal Emergency Management Agency Region IV, available at http://www.csc.noaa.gov/hes/docs/postStorm/H_ANDREW_ASSESSMENT_REVIEW_HES_UTILIZATION_INFO_DISSEMINATION.pdf.

Post, Buckley, Schuh & Jernigan, Inc. (2000), *Hurricane Floyd Assessment: Review of Hurricane Evacuation Studies Utilization and Information Dissemination*, Tallahassee, FL, USA: US Army Corps of Engineers Mobile and District and Federal Emergency Management Agency Region IV, available at http://www.csc.noaa.gov/hes/docs/postStorm/H_FLOYD_ASSESSMENT_REVIEW_HES_UTILIZATION_INFO_DISSEMINATION.pdf.

Preston, B. (2005), 'Less than a mile from the dome', *Junk Yard Blog*, available at http://junkyardblog.net/archives/week_2005_08_28.html.

Savage, R.P., J. Baker, J.H. Golden, A. Kareem and B.R. Manning (1984), *Hurricane Alicia Galveston and Houston, Texas, August 17–18, 1983*, Washington,

DC, USA: National Academies Press, available at http://www.csc.noaa.gov/hes/docs/postStorm/H_ALICIA_GALVESTON_HOUSTON.pdf.

Schott, T., C. Landsea, G. Hafele, J. Lorens, A. Taylor, H. Thurm, B. Ward, M. Willis and W.T. Zaleski (undated website), 'The Saffir-Simpson Hurricane Wind Scale', National Weather Service, National Hurricane Center, available at http://www.nhc.noaa.gov/sshws.shtml.

Schwartz, J. (August 2011), 'Long after natural disasters, the cleanup grinds on', *The New York Times*, available at http://www.nytimes.com/2011/08/05/us/05debris.html?_r=1&hp.

Severson, K., D. Barry and C. Robertson (2011), 'Hurricane Irene pushes north with deadly force', *The New York Times*, August 27, available at http://www.nytimes.com/2011/08/28/us/28hurricane-irene.html?hp.

The State of Texas, Office of the Governor, Division of Emergency Management (December 2008), *Hurricane Ike Impact Report*, available at http://www.fema.gov/pdf/hazard/hurricane/2008/ike/impact_report.pdf.

Transportation Research Board, Division on Earth and Life Studies (2008), *Potential Impacts of Climate Change on US Transportation: Special Report 290*, Washington, DC, USA: The National Academy of Sciences, available at http://onlinepubs.trb.org/onlinepubs/sr/sr290.pdf (accessed August 2009).

Trowbridge, M.J., M.J. Gurka and R.E. O'Connor (2009), 'Urban sprawl and delayed ambulance arrival in the US', *American Journal of Preventive Medicine*, **37** (5), 428–32.

Urbina, E. and B. Wolshon (2003), 'National review of hurricane evacuation plans and policies: a comparison and contrast of state practices', *Transportation Research Part A*, **37**, 257–75.

US Department of Commerce, National Oceanic and Atmospheric Administration, National Weather Service, Central Region Headquarters (July 2011), *NWS Central Region Service Assessment Joplin, Missouri, Tornado – May 22, 2011, Kansas City, MO*, available at http://doh.sd.gov/Prepare/Hospital/Documents/Joplin_tornado.pdf.

US Department of Transportation, Federal Highway Administration, Federal Transit Administration (2010), *2010 Status of Nation's Highways, Bridges, and Transit: Conditions and Performance*, available at http://www.fhwa.dot.gov/policy/2010cpr/index.htm.

US Department of Transportation, Federal Transit Administration (undated website), National Transit Database 2009, available at http://www.ntdprogram.gov/ntdprogram/; http://www.ntdprogram.gov/ntdprogram/data.htm.

US Environmental Protection Agency (1995), *Planning for Disaster Debris*, Washington, DC, USA: US Environmental Protection Agency.

US Environmental Protection Agency (September 2011), 'Civil enforcement – fuel waivers', available at http://www.epa.gov/compliance/civil/caa/fuelwaivers/.

US Environmental Protection Agency (12 September 2011), News Brief (HQ): 'EPA approves emergency fuel waiver for Pennsylvania', Washington, DC, USA: US EPA.

US Geological Survey (USGS) (2009a), Earthquake Hazards Program, Measuring the Size of an Earthquake, available at http://earthquake.usgs.gov/learn/topics/measure.php.

US Geological Survey (USGS) (2009b), The Modified Mercalli Intensity Scale, available at http://earthquake.usgs.gov/learn/topics/mercalli.php.

US National Oceanic and Atmospheric Administration (various years), *Post*

Storm Assessment Review for Hurricane Floyd, available at http://www.csc. noaa.gov/hes/docs/postStorm/H_ANDREW_ASSESSMENT_REVIEW_HES_ UTILIZATION_INFO_DISSEMINATION.pdf.

Washington Post staff (August 2011), 'Earthquake throws commuting into chaos', available at http://www.washingtonpost.com/blogs/dr-gridlock/post/metro-limits-train-speeds-conducts-inspections/2011/08/23/gIQAMxyFZJ_blog.html? hpid=z1.

Webster, P.J., G.J. Holland, J.A. Curry and H-R. Chang (2005), 'Changes in tropical cyclone number, duration, and intensity in a warming environment', *Science*, **309**, 1844–6.

Wilson, S.G. and T.R. Fischetti (May 2010), 'Coastal population trends in the US: 1960–2008', available at http://www.census.gov/prod/2010pubs/p25-1139.pdf.

Wolshon, B. (2002), 'Planning for the evacuation of New Orleans', *Institute for Transportation Engineers Journal*, **72** (2), 44–9.

Woo, G. (1999), *The Mathematics of Natural Catastrophes*, London, UK: Imperial College Press.

Wright, B. and R.D. Bullard (2007), 'Washed away by Hurricane Katrina, rebuilding a "new" New Orleans', in R.D. Bullard (ed.), *Growing Smarter*, pp. 189–211.

Yashinsky, M. (1998), *The Loma Prieta California Earthquake of 1989 – Highway Systems*, available at http://pubs.usgs.gov/pp/pp1552/pp1552b/ and http://pubs. usgs.gov/pp/pp1552/pp1552b/pp1552b.pdf.

Zimmerman, R. (1994a), 'Issues of classification in environmental equity: How we manage is how we measure', *Fordham Urban Law Journal*, **XXI** (3), 633–69.

Zimmerman, R. (1994b), 'After the Deluge', *The Sciences*, **34** (4), 18–23.

Zimmerman, R. (1996), 'Global warming, infrastructure, and land use in the metropolitan New York area: prevention and response', in D. Hill (ed.), *The Baked Apple? Metropolitan New York in the Greenhouse*, New York, NY, USA: New York Academy of Sciences, pp.57–83.

Zimmerman, R. (1999), 'Planning and administration: frameworks and case studies', in J. Ingleton (ed.), *Natural Disaster Management*, Leicester, UK: Tudor Rose, pp.225–7.

Zimmerman, R. (2005), 'Mass transit infrastructure and urban health', *Journal of Urban Health*, **82** (1), 21–32.

Zimmerman, R. (January 2010), 'Transportation protection and recovery in an age of disasters', Transportation Research Board 89th Annual Meeting, Washington, DC, USA.

Zimmerman, R. and M. Sherman (2011), 'To leave an area after disaster: How evacuees from the WTC buildings left the WTC area following the attacks', *Risk Analysis*, **31** (5), 787–804.

Zimmerman, R., C.E. Restrepo, B. Nagorsky and A.M. Culpen (2007), *Vulnerability of the Elderly During Natural Hazard Events*, proceedings of the Hazards and Disasters Research Meeting, Boulder, CO, USA: Natural Hazards Center, July 11–12, 2007, pp.38–40, available at http://www.colorado.edu/ hazards/workshop/hdrm_proceedings.pdf.

Zimmerman, R., C.E. Restrepo, J.S. Simonoff, Z.S. Naphtali and A.M. Culpen (2008), *Transportation, Natural Hazards and Access for the Elderly*, unpublished manuscript.

Zimmerman, R., C.E. Restrepo and J.S. Simonoff (2009), *The Age of*

Infrastructure in a Time of Security and Natural Hazards, presented at the 2009 Department of Homeland Security (DHS) Aging Infrastructure Workshop, New York, NY, USA July 21–23, 2009, and forthcoming in the DHS workshop proceedings.

7.   Security

PUBLIC CONCERN ABOUT TERRORISM AND TERRORISM INCIDENTS

The magnitude of concern over the threat of terrorism has persisted in the US at least since the September 11, 2001 attacks and subsequent terrorist attacks and threats throughout the US and the world. The findings of the Pew Research Center January 2011 political survey (Pew Research Center 2011, p.1) show that:

- Seventy-three percent of the surveyed public felt that terrorism ("Defending the US against terrorism") was among the top policy priorities to be addressed by the government.
- Terrorism ranked as the third concern following the economy and jobs.
- Terrorism consistently ranked at least third over the ten-year period, and ranked first in 2006 and 2007 following the Madrid and London bombings (Pew Research Center 2011, p.6).
- The 2010 level of 80 percent for concern about terrorism was only exceeded by the levels in 2002 and 2003 of 83 percent and 81 percent respectively (Pew Research Center 2010, p.2) which were the years immediately following the September 11, 2001 attacks.
- The 2011 level of 73 percent, though still the third ranking priority, represents a drop of 7 percent over the 2010 level, and is the lowest percentage over the 2001–2011 time period (Pew Research Center 2011, p.6), probably reflecting the greater concern over the economy, jobs and the deficit.
- There is a considerable bipartisan split in the issue with republicans rating terrorism concerns higher than the democrats (Pew Research Center 2011, p.10).

The results of different polls, however, are not consistent with one another but still support a majority expressing concern. A *USAToday*/Gallup poll found a reduction from 62 percent in its May 2011 poll to 38 percent in its August 2011 poll for Americans thinking a terrorist attack would be very or somewhat likely in the next few weeks (Saad September 2011). Gallup suggested that the captures of major terrorist figures were a possible explanation for the decline in interest. Immediately following September 11, 2001, the percentages were close to 60 percent. This supports the potential influence of immediacy and proximity of events on public attitudes. Federal Signal's 2011 nationwide survey found that most people feel less safe than they did prior to the September 11, 2001 attacks, yet Federal Signal reports that a third (34 percent) felt that public safety was not a high priority (Federal Signal 2011). The Federal Signal 2010 Public Safety survey revealed a high degree of concern for natural hazards and terrorism, reporting those areas as being of greatest concern to two-thirds of the respondents (Federal Signal 2010).

TERRORISM TRENDS

Trends in terrorism in the US and worldwide differ, according to the National Consortium for the Study of Terrorism and the Responses to Terrorism (cited henceforth as START) Global Terrorism database (START 2011a). According to START findings, in the US the trend shows an increase in attacks per year from 1991 to 1995 and generally a decline from 1995 to 2010 (START 2011a, p.2), whereas worldwide attacks decreased per year prior to 2001 and have been increasing per year from 2001 to 2010 (START 2011a, p.4). The concentration of attacks by location within the US generally follows population concentration as does the concentration of transportation facilities and their usage. START tracked the location of attacks at the state level from 1991 to 2010. START found that in the pre- and post-2001 periods, California led the rest of the states with 15 percent and 24 percent of the attacks respectively and New York ranked second with 7 percent and 6 percent of the attacks in the two periods respectively (START 2011a, p.3).

Seventy-one percent of the 68 known attacks in the Arabian Peninsula from 2004 to 2010 occurred in 2010 (48 attacks) and the highest number prior to that during that period was eight in 2008 (START 2011b, p.1). Although transportation was not listed as a target, 7 percent of the attacks during that period occurred against utilities (START 2011b, p.2), with which transportation has connections. Between 1991 and 2010 START identified 17 groups including Al-Qa'ida and affiliated groups that have been responsible for many of the attacks (START 2011b, p.3).

Meleagrou-Hitchens (2011 pp.83–90) attributes a large number of incidents from individuals and groups affiliated with and influenced by Anwar al-Awlaki of Al-Qa'ida's Yemen operation, who was reported killed on September 30, 2011.

In the 2012 report from START for the period 1970 to 2008, LaFree and Bersani (2012, p.15) report the continued decline of terrorism events in the US but a significant percentage of events that are fatal in some years in the period 2000–2008. The report also shows events and fatalities over the entire period were geographically clustered in the largest cities. New York (Manhattan), Los Angeles, Miami-Dade, San Francisco and Washington, DC, all with key transit centers, accounted for about a third of events and fatalities, and there were also concentrations in some of the suburban and rural areas surrounding other urban areas.

Risk Management Solutions, Inc. (RMS 2011, p.8) uses its database to track trends, and notes that since 2007 Jihadi plots have been increasing in the US. The RMS (2011, p.5) report particularly identifies transportation as an important target, and reflects what they see as a move toward smaller weapons and softer targets.

Transportation has been a key target of terrorism partly because it provides the major connector for people, goods and services, and places, and often involves highly dense connection points or links. In the decade prior to September 11, 2001 rail or buses accounted for an estimated 42 percent of all terrorist attacks worldwide (Howitt and Makler, 2005, p.1, citing US Congress 2004). Other figures are higher. The US Department of Transportation (DOT) Federal Transit Administration (FTA) cites a figure of 58 percent based on 1998 data for the proportion of all terrorist attacks that target transportation (Leung et al. 2004, p.963, citing FTA). Yet, within the transportation sector, much of the earlier security legislation tended to focus on aviation and maritime security rather than roads or rail, in spite of the concentration of incidents in these sectors outside the US in the mid-1990s and again in the mid-2000s. Given the evidence for transportation as a potential target for terrorist attacks, Bier et al. (2008) used transportation in terms of bridge traffic and air departures as one measure of target attractiveness for urban areas as a means of illustrating how priorities among cities might be set for budget allocation.

VULNERABILITY

An understanding of what makes transportation vulnerable to terrorism is a prerequisite to potentially reducing the incidence and consequences of terrorist attacks. Many factors contribute to the vulnerability of transportation facilities and their users. Leung et al. (2004, pp.969–70), for example, established a detailed risk management based system for bridge attributes that improve resiliency.

Three factors contributing to vulnerability are described below:

concentration of facilities and users, population concentration, and dependencies and interdependencies for transportation and other infrastructure.

Concentration of Facilities and Users

One attribute is the concentration of users and transportation infrastructure along travel routes, which varies according to the type of transportation. A few findings from earlier chapters demonstrate this.

For rail transit, 68 percent of passenger travel on heavy rail systems occurs on New York City Transit's system and 38.1 percent of passenger travel on commuter rail systems is accounted for by two of the New York area's Metropolitan Transportation Authority (MTA) systems, the Long Island Railroad (LIRR) and Metro North. As shown in Chapter 2, the concentration of heavy rail transit infrastructure is similar to the concentration of passenger travel. New York City Transit's subway system, for example, accounted for 45 percent of the stations and 37 percent of track mileage in the United States. The LIRR, one of the largest commuter rail lines in the country, has ten out of 11 of its lines going through one station, the Jamaica Station, and when an outage occurs there, the whole system is disabled (Grynbaum 2010).

Road travel is concentrated along a few routes in the US. Moreover, points of congestion are concentrated as well, which draw a large number of travelers. A few intersections within major urban areas account for most of the congestion; about half of the top twenty five most congested corridors were located in California and New York (INRIX, Inc. 2011), and Schrank et al. (2011, p.42) similarly reported that of the 15 very large urban areas with greater than three million in population, three of the highest ranking areas for hours of delay for auto riders were in California and one was in New York.

Freight transport patterns reflect another form of concentration. There are many points of concentration and congestion for both road and rail based truck or train transport of freight. The trailer or container on flatcars travels most frequently along a route that extends from ports along the Pacific Coast through Chicago and then to New York (US DOT, FHWA 2010, Figure 3-15). Trucks that carry freight over long distances tend to concentrate "on major routes connecting population centers, ports, border crossings, and other major hubs of activity. Except for Route 99 in California and a few toll roads and border connections, most of the heaviest traveled routes are on the Interstate System" (US DOT, FHWA 2010, Figure 3-5). The PricewaterhouseCoopers (PwC) (2011, p.7) report notes that the Hong Kong–Shenzhen area or freight cluster accounts for

14.8 percent of both container and air freight, and if a disruption occurred there, the impact could be large. Other points where concentration occurs in supply chains that they identify are in Central America, the Middle East and Asia. They also point out that 90 percent of the world's trade occurs through 39 gateway areas (PwC 2011, p.12). Freight movement by product type also shows that numerous entities can be tied to a single product. The PwC (2011, p.29 citing Russell and Saldanha 2003) report indicates that for any given product 25 entities are involved in its movement.

Population Concentration

Savitch (2008) finds that two significant factors influence how severe a terrorist attack will be: population and population density. Savitch (2008) defines severity as "unrelenting violence coupled with the cumulative damage caused to human life" and can be measured as "frequency of incidents" and "fatalities and injuries caused by the attacks" (Savitch 2008, p.22). Savitch identifies the following specific measures from research examples: (1) an increase of one million in population increases the severity score by 4.85 points and (2) an increase of 1,000 people per square kilometer increases the severity score by one point (Savitch 2008, p.24). Savitch (2008, p.24) observes that terrorist attacks have occurred equally in cities in both developed and developing countries. If the population and population density relationship holds true, this could mean that cities in the developing countries are more likely to be targets of terrorist attacks. For Savitch, the density relationships do not imply density reduction policies for cities (Savitch 2008, p.148–53).

Cutter et al. (2003) explore a wide range of spatial analytical techniques in order to identify population distribution as well as other attributes relevant to understanding vulnerability to terrorism.

Dependencies and Interdependencies

Transportation is dependent on and interdependent with other kinds of infrastructure and activities. Thus, if another infrastructure upon which transportation depends is susceptible to attack or destruction from other means, then transportation is also likely to feel the impacts of that destruction as well. The strongest dependencies are on electric power and telecommunications. When electric power, for example, is physically disabled, transportation facilities are likely to be severely affected. The 2003 northeastern US and Canada blackout cascaded down into the transportation sector very severely. The recovery of the subways and roads in New York City took much longer than electric power given the need to readjust system components (Zimmerman and Restrepo 2006).

Although this was not a terrorist attack, the consequences were in many ways similar.

PHYSICAL TERRORIST ATTACKS

The prominence of attacks on surface rail systems was underscored in a 2010 Mineta Institute report: "Terrorists see public surface transportation as a killing field . . . when it comes to wholesale killing, trains and buses offer easily accessible concentrations of people" (Jenkins et al. 2010, p.3).

PricewaterhouseCoopers' (PwC) (2011) analysis of the US National Counterterrorism Center (NCTC) Worldwide Incidents Tracking System (WITS) for transportation found a gradual increase in supply chain attacks, and an overwhelming proportion of those attacks were on vehicles such as cars and trucks. If those are eliminated, PwC (2011, p.12) found a steady increase in trains and subway attacks with the exception of a decline between 2007 and 2008.

Public Transportation

The threat against transit from terrorism is real. Even though the US has not experienced actual incidents that could be ascribed to terrorists, numerous terrorist threats and plots have occurred. Stoller (2010) summarizes evidence of terrorist plots from September 11, 2001 through 2010 as consisting of six transit plots in the US and the foiling of four simultaneous bomb plots against Washington, DC Metro stations in October 2010, and one using explosives against the NYC system in 2009.

The Mineta Institute and START routinely publish the incidence of such attacks on rail systems. START (2010, pp.6–7) in its review of the London transit bombings, reported that out of a total of 4,382 attacks on transportation between 1970 and 2008 (recorded on the START Global Terrorism Database) those that involved transportation peaked in 1995 and 1996 at about 8 percent, and the peak was followed by a decline in the percentage until 2008 when there was a large jump, but it did not exceed the peak of about a decade earlier. These percentages are lower than those cited earlier by government agencies.

The START (2010, p.6) report findings also indicate further that during a 15-year period between March 1995 and March 2010 a total of 12 separate incidents against transit in nine countries resulted in 876 deaths and 9,780 injuries. The number of injured in relation to the number killed is not correlated. Over half of these 12 attacks occurred in the summer.

Of the dozen attacks listed between 1995 and 2010, three occurred in the mid-1990s, three in the early 2000s, five in the mid-2000s and one in 2010. Deaths ranged from seven (Paris in 1995) to 259 (Angola in 2001), and injuries ranged from 20 (Manila in 2000) to 5,500 (Tokyo in 1995) (START 2010, p.6).

The 2010 Mineta study of 181 deliberate derailments showed that 144 of them occurred since January 1996 (Jenkins et al. 2010, p.3) and 170 since January 1, 1970 (Jenkins et al. 2010, p.11). About a third occurred in South Asia (with India accounting for a fifth of all of them) and a fifth occurred in Europe (Jenkins et al. 2010, p.13). Their initial study included 900 attacks (Jenkins 1997).

Attacks on rail systems appear to be episodic; 1995 seemed to be a major year with the Sarin attacks on the Tokyo subway, the derailment of the Sunset Limited in Arizona, and a number of attacks in France. The Armed Islamic Group, or GIA, was held responsible for: the July 26, 1995 attack in the RER metro station in France in which eight were killed and dozens injured, the placement of a bomb in a TGV on August 17, 1995 that never exploded, a bomb explosion in an RER commuter train on October 17, 1995 injuring 30, and a number of other explosions that occurred in public places (Jenkins et al. 2010, p.5 citing news coverage from *The Herald* (Glasgow) August 1995, *The Independent* (London), August 1995 and the *Chicago Sun-Times*, October 1995).

Jenkins et al. (2010, p.16) judge the overall success rate as 58 percent for 47 derailed trains out of 81 attempts with bombs. Using mechanical means, the rate was 86.4 percent for 19 successful derailments out of 22 attempts. The impact in terms of deaths is also a significant factor in judging the severity of these attacks. Jenkins et al. (2010, p.17) point out that in 33 out of their set of 181 events, 955 people were killed.

Location of attacks
The location of attacks is significant for the deployment of protection strategies. In general, both the nodes – stations and trains – appear to be a common location of attacks given the number of people potentially affected and the fact that link or rail attacks may have more uncertain impacts. In the 1997 study, 27 percent of the attacks were located in subways and or trains, 13 percent were in subway and train stations, and 8 percent were on rails (Jenkins 1997, p.106).

The 2010 study found that 10.5 percent of all surface transportation attacks resulted from derailments (Jenkins et al. 2010, p.11). They also found that over half (53.6%) attacked trains and over a quarter (28.2%) attacked rail lines (Jenkins et al. 2010, p.16). In the period from 1920 to 1970 they found that derailments accounted for about three-quarters of the attacks and the majority of injuries, concluding that "Today, terrorists kill passengers" (Jenkins et al. 2010, p.11).

Preparations to reduce likelihood of occurrence and severity of consequences

Taylor et al. (2006) trace the history of concern about and preparations for terrorist attacks citing case studies and surveys, and also report on their own survey of transit agencies. They report on a 1997 survey of 60 agencies (42 respondents) that identified concern but little preparation for an attack, and a 2002 US Government Accountability Office (GAO) survey of 200 agencies (155 responses) that identified concern, awareness of attacks, and the beginnings of preparations (Taylor et al. 2006, p.4). Their survey in 2004 found that a substantial portion had experienced attacks and the preparations and plans had progressed over what was found in the earlier GAO survey (Taylor et al. 2006, pp.6, 9). Rail systems were more likely to be active in their preparations.

A number of solutions to minimize the risk of an attack have been put forward. For example, an American Public Transportation Association (APTA) working group suggested numerous ways to detect anomalies and intrusions (APTA 2010). Closed-circuit television (CCTV) and other optical means can also provide detection, but after the event, as was the case in the London bombings.

The US DOT FTA (2003, p.115) guide identified a wide range of preventive measures, primarily from the experiences of specific transit agencies, such as the Washington Metropolitan Area Transit Authority (WMATA). The WMATA security systems described in the guide addressed "supporting columns, entrances, exits, and pathways, lighting and maintenance, security devices", and security and other personnel issues. Many of the efforts identified also support safety needs, such as eliminating, redesigning or relocating areas that can serve as hiding places by, for example, reducing the number of columns, improving lighting to enhance surveillance, straightening passageways, and relocating bathrooms and litter bins (US DOT FTA 2003, p.115).

The Taylor et al. (2006) study explored the use of four central security strategies for transit: policing, structural measures, public education and design, and found that policing and structural measures were important both before and after September 11, 2001, but design increased in importance thereafter.

Recovery from attacks

The reaction of transit systems in terms of transit ridership was analysed following the September 11, 2001 attacks (Zimmerman et al. 2006;

Zimmerman and Simonoff 2009). The results for NYC transit were that although ridership was initially slow in the first day or two (primarily because of mandatory shutdowns of the systems) it rebounded gradually and soon regained levels characteristic of the normal pattern (with some instability) within two weeks. The Long Island Railroad (LIRR) showed a weak effect over a few months, NJ Transit ridership increased after an initial drop, possibly picking up ridership from other lines, and the Port Authority TransHudson (PATH) experienced massive drops that were sustained through 2002. Redistribution of ridership among stations, primarily for the PATH and NYC transit occurred due to the destruction of stations in the area. Many of the observed patterns are consistent with psychological literature on how people behave when faced with unusual stress.

Roads and Surface Transportation Vehicles

Roadways are vulnerable to terrorism. However, in contrast to transit, the attacks are more decentralized given the nature of the road networks. The mechanisms are usually different also, involving an individual or two, for example, in the case of sniper attacks. Sniper attacks would typically not be classified as terrorism though they often produce similar public reactions and can have similar motives. The Washington, DC area beltway sniper attacks in October 2002 were notable in terms of where they occurred (in the capital city and in a relatively densely populated area), the randomness, and duration and geographic spread of the occurrences both before and during the DC area killings. Most occurred along or in the vicinity of roadways or adjacent roadway facilities such as gas stations and parking lots, and the threat was significant enough that people were said to have avoided roadway travel as much as possible.

One of the stated motives of the perpetrator, who was quoted at the trial, was to train children for terrorism (*The New York Times* 2006) and to shut the country down (Urbina 2006). The impacts were far wider than the size of the geographic areas in which the incidents occurred, resulting in heightened security in public buildings and even lock downs (Wikipedia, accessed January 27, 2012). Before the sniper and his accomplice were caught, about a dozen and a half shootings had occurred over a three month period in five states, resulting in almost a dozen deaths and six wounded (Wikepedia, accessed January 27, 2012).

Bridges are a potential target of terrorists (as they have been in wartime), given the significance and often uniqueness of the linkages they provide, thus enlarging the impact. Bridge attacks have typically involved explosives placed at points on the structure that are likely to do the most damage. Attack strategies also influence the magnitude of the damages.

Gordon et al. (2005) modeled the impacts of an attack scenario of the Los Angeles–Long Beach ports and found that those impacts were magnified by simultaneous attacks on access bridges.

CYBER-ATTACKS

While the number of physical terrorist attacks has been declining in the US, the number of cyber-attacks has been growing (Symantec Corporation 2011). These attacks occur through the computer control systems and communication systems and other information technologies that are being used with increasing frequency. Wilson (2005, pp.6–7) acknowledges the numerous and variable kinds of considerations that go into defining cyber terrorism, such as the motive, the way in which information technologies are used, and the consequences. Ultimately the common denominator, according to Wilson (2005, p.7) is destruction of facilities that provide information or destruction of the information itself (information technology as a target), or the use of information for destructive purposes (weaponization). Wilson (2005, pp.2–3) identifies three types of attacks: physical attacks against computer components, attacks that are electronic, for example an electromagnetic pulse that overloads a facility, or the introduction of destructive code. The consequences of attacks may be indirect. A notable example of physical attacks affecting telecommunication infrastructure indirectly is the September 11, 2001 attacks on the World Trade Center (WTC) in New York City that resulted in a major disabling of telecommunications worldwide, though this was not the direct target of the attacks. Gorman (2005, pp.12–13, citing FCC reports) notes that "Verizon alone had to replace 1.5 million voice circuits, 4.4 million data circuits, and 19 SONET rings" and Internet service providers lost "112,000 private branch exchange trunks, and 11,000 fiber lines".

Trends in cyber-attacks appear to support a growing threat regardless of the way the trends are measured. Symantec Corporation (2011, p.6), for example, points to the following in its 2010 trends report for changes between 2009 and 2010: a 93 percent increase in web attacks, 6,253 new vulnerabilities recorded, over one million bots controlled, 260,000 data breaches from hacking, and a 42 percent increase in vulnerabilities among mobile operating systems. The USDHS (2012, p.20) cited US-CERT FY2006 to FY2010 trends showing an increase of cyber incidents from 5,503 to 41,776. Transportation systems are potentially vulnerable to a lot of these given their growing use of and dependency on information technology. The increase in cyber-attacks, particularly in infrastructure systems such as transportation, may in part be due to the increasing use of information technologies, reliance on security systems, and reliance on computerized controls that are ubiquitous, isolated (security systems may not be subject to surveillance), and remote that can be accessed at considerable distances that separate the perpetrator from the target.

Concentration plays a key part in cyber vulnerability, as it does in the case of vulnerability to physical attacks. Perrow (2007, p.250) emphasizes that Microsoft provides 90–95 percent of the users of operating systems. Starting with the Internet, Domain Name Systems (DNS) servers are operated at 13 centers (root-servers.org). In 2002 most of the 13 backbone computers or root servers that provide email and web addresses from numeric codes were disabled in what may have been one of the largest attacks; other root server outages occurred in July 1997 and February and August of 2000 (*The New York Times* 2002; Vixie et al. 2002; ICANN 2007). Although not specifically associated with cyber-attacks, these events do point to serious vulnerabilities from concentration and transport systems and their users are also at risk.

Cyber Connectivity and Transportation Vulnerability

Computer and communication technologies have grown in their ability to support and promote automobile and rail travel. Yet this integration has not been without its downsides. Vulnerabilities exist, many of which are not specific to transportation alone but affect that sector.

A 2009 survey of 600 infrastructure executives in IT and security worldwide was conducted to identify sources of cyber vulnerability in infrastructure (Baker et al. 2010, p.41). Results identified distributed denial of service (DDOS) on domain name servers as among the most expensive, costing about $6 million per day for a major attack (Baker et al. 2010, p.3). The transportation sector ranked as being the least satisfied with resources to combat the problem (Baker et al. 2010, p.14). One transportation official suggested not connecting Supervisory Control and Data Acquisition (SCADA) systems to the internet (Baker et al. 2010, p.23).

Cyber-attacks that occur against other types of infrastructure upon which transportation is dependent can have severe impacts on transportation. One example was the 2003 northeast and Canada blackout, which at one time was suspected to be associated in part with a cyber-attack. A computer was initially disabled from a software bug which in turn disabled both audio and visual alarm systems, and thus operators were not aware of the condition of the northeast Ohio shared line (Poulsen February 2004, April 2004; NERC 2004).

Vulnerability through electric power systems upon which transportation depends can occur through Supervisory Control and Data Acquisition

(SCADA) systems. SCADA systems provide information feedback to operators and also the ability to control processes directly (Wilson 2005, p.10). Transportation systems are relatively dispersed and SCADA systems are an attractive means of connecting them to central control systems. SCADA systems are widespread in the electric power industry upon which transportation depends. Slay and Miller (2008, p.75) note that in the US 270 utilities are using SCADA systems (citing Fernandez and Fernandez 2005) which amounts to about 80 percent of the US's power systems. Thus, any systematic attack on SCADA systems could result in massive outages and disruptions to the other activities that depend on electric power. Many have argued that SCADA systems lack security, primarily because they link to outside systems or have an open architecture without the usual security protections, thus enabling access through remote locations. In some cases they can cover very large areas that increase the likelihood of intrusion. They are apparently susceptible not only to hacking but also to worms and viruses, due to their connections to other systems (Slay and Miller 2008 p.76).

Transportation infrastructure, like other infrastructure, is increasingly dependent on the use of cellphone technology in order to communicate and dispatch orders and other messages. The growth in cellular technology has been very dramatic. According to the 2010 Cellular Telecommunications and Internet Association (CTIA) semi-annual survey of the wireless industry, between 1985 and 2010, the number of estimated connections for all uses increased almost 1000-fold (889 times), from 340,000 to 303 million and the number of cell sites increased by almost 300 times (276 times) from 913 to 253,086 sites (CTIA 2010 p.2). Interestingly, this reflects a growing centralization and hence vulnerability, since if one computes the number of connections per cell site using CTIA data from 1985 to 2010, the connections per cell site grew from 373 to 1,197. The dependency on this type of technology produces vulnerabilities in emergencies as common experience and recent studies have shown that cellphone connections become jammed at the outset of an emergency.

Cellular technology is but one example of information technologies that are showing a dramatic growth with the potential for affecting transportation should breaches in those systems occur. Hilbert and Lopez (2011), for example, trace the dramatic increase and transformation in numerous kinds of information technologies in computing and communication capacity for storing, telecommunicating and broadcasting. Shrobe (2011) traces the growth in desk top and notebook PCs and smart phones, which clearly estimates the takeover of smartphones in 2012. The same rapid growth appears for mobile data traffic (Cisco Systems 2011) and bandwidth (Telegeography 2011).

Beyond the general growth in the use of information technology, the US Department of Transportation (2009, p.2-18) has identified a dozen or more areas in which information technologies are deployed in 75 municipalities and this deployment has grown for most uses since 1997. Those uses in which half or more of the systems have deployed the technology since 2006 are: electronic toll collection, dispatch of emergency vehicles, bus electronic fare collection, fixed transit vehicle automatic locators, control of signalized intersections, and the provision of on-call service for freeway drivers (US DOT, 2009, p.2-18).

Roads and Automobiles

Conventional vehicles
The introduction and proliferation of computerized controls in cars are thought to be introducing significant points of vulnerability. The vulnerabilities potentially exist all throughout the life cycle of road vehicles.

Computers now provide not only amenities but also safety features for automobile travel through a myriad of sensors. Within vehicles, these detect defects in automobile components, such as tires and engines. They enable the speed of windshield wipers to adjust to the intensity of rainfall, thus freeing up the driver to pay more attention to driving. "Connected Vehicle Technology", which enables communication among vehicles to provide connectivity to warn against adverse driving conditions is considered to be a way of avoiding accidents (Belcher 2011).

The increase in the use of sensors has been considered to be a vulnerability as is the use of computerized controls for vehicle breaking (Markoff 2010; Koscher et al. 2010).

McMillan (2011) noted the potential for hackers to open locked cars and start them as a vulnerability when using mobile phones and laptops. McMillan underscored vulnerabilities that Koscher et al. (2010) noted, namely vulnerabilities created by external connections used in cars that have not been secured. McAfee (2011, p.6) cites studies that point to the ability to read radio frequency identification (RFID) tags used for tire pressure monitoring to track a vehicle's travel pattern, and also point to the use of wireless devices to disable vehicles. Beyond these theoretical demonstrations are some actual known accounts of tampering involving remote access through wireless devices to disable cars and the use of a GPS system to track and report driver behavior (McAfee 2011 p.7).

Intrusions into infrastructures other than transportation have occurred in ways that could also pose a threat to transportation. One way is where an external computer, usually a laptop or a radio transmitter, has been used to cause massive infrastructure malfunctions. Attacks on water and sewage processing systems, for example, have been known targets using this type of intrusion approach (US GAO September 2007, p.7).

Direct access to computer controls has been another means of intrusion. This can be illustrated by examples of attacks on road systems as distinct from attacks on vehicles. Road signaling systems, for example, have been targets of attack to disrupt traffic. Traffic lights in Los Angeles were hacked in August 2006 by employees, apparently related to a labor protest, who gained access to the computers controlling the signal lights. Four intersections were affected and traffic jams resulted (US GAO September 2007, p.7; Los Angeles County District Attorney's Office 2007).

New vehicle technologies: driverless vehicles

Driverless vehicles are being developed which will make extensive use of computers. Guizzo (January 2012) has reported on the one developed in France as well as Google's new robot car (Guizzo, October 2011). Many personal rapid transportation (PRT) vehicles depend heavily on computers, for example, those that have been developed in Masdar, Abu Dhabi. Scaling up the technology has been a challenge.

Freight traffic

Road and rail based freight transportation is particularly vulnerable to breaches in cyber security given the very large number of parties involved in the transfer and other types of handling and the number of transfer points for a single product (PwC 2011, p.29). Presumably perpetrators could potentially take advantage of areas of concentration to produce the greatest damage from either a cyber or physical attack or a combination of both.

Information technologies are used widely in freight shipments for example for the control of inventories, the deployment of transportation resources (Transportation Research Board (TRB) 2003, p.15), the overall routing and tracking of movements of shipments (TRB 2003, p.19), control of the speed of movement, and identifying vehicle location through the use of transponders (TRB 2003, p.23). TRB (2003, pp.2–4) identified three different kinds of cyber-attacks that could affect freight transport – denial of service where computer access to the web and control systems would be breached, alteration of transportation operating systems in a way that could cause the release of hazardous materials during transport, and the movement of weapons of mass destruction via information systems. TRB (2003, p.3) notes for hazardous material spills that an attack could take control of railroad switches and signals and cause a spill of hazardous material shipments. To illustrate the potential magnitude of that problem, they cite that an estimated 800,000 such freight shipments occur in the US each day.

A number of detection devices are suggested not unique to transportation to identify cyber intrusions, such as sensors, authenticated and encrypted radio frequency identification (RFID) tags (TRB 2003, p.31), wireless tracking systems, and digital authentication for shippers (TRB 2003, p.7). The very large proliferation of these devices, the fact that they are embedded, and are often open to communication with outside entities with relatively little security creates the threat.

Public Transit

Computerized control and communication systems are now widely used in transit systems. As described by APTA (2010), they are used for locating and managing the movement of trains and automated breaking and signaling systems for example, which are among the most important security features of rail transit for safety (APTA 2010 p.3). Computerized controls are also used to maintain the integrity of ventilation, lighting, and drainage (APTA 2010, p.7) which are especially critical in subsurface structures. Computerized communication systems are also used for emergency communications, monitoring and detection of intrusion (CCTV) (APTA 2010, p.4). Vulnerability and the susceptibility to both physical and cyber-attacks can arise through any number of dozens of different computer and communication systems depending on the design.

The following stories and case studies from rail transit illustrate the consequences of cyber-attacks.

Deliberate attacks
In 2003, the CSX railway signaling and other control systems were disabled at the CSX's Jacksonville, Florida, headquarters in 2003 by the "Sobig virus". There were delays in passenger and freight train service over a four to six hour period, and Amtrak was affected also (APTA 2010, p.21).

In 2007, the Polish tram hack attack was a case in which switching points along a rail track were altered by a 14-year-old in Lodz, Poland, resulting in injuries and derailments (APTA 2010, p.21).

The Bay Area Rapid Transit (BART) was the target of several hacker attacks beginning on August 14, 2011 which was portrayed as being politically motivated. The US DHS TSA (2011) provided the account of the attacks. BART and the Fullerton Police Department experienced a hacking attack on August 14, 2011 from a hacker-activist group, called "Anonymous", apparently in retaliation for BART police action against homeless men. According to the account the BART system had to shut down its marketing website that is used to draw users to the system, since the attack resulted in the personal information of website users to be unprotected as reported by the US DHS, Transportation Security Administration (TSA) (2011). The original account from the *LA Times* indicated that the attack was motivated by BART's intent to affect cell service to prevent a protest from occurring. The account also indicated that the California Office of Traffic Safety shut down its website, and that attack was to object to California's political climate (Barnard 2011). *The New York Times* (Elinson 2011) reported the events as beginning on August 14, 2011 against the BART marketing site, and the attack released passenger email addresses and passwords. This was in response to a shutdown by BART of its cellphone and wireless services because of an impending protest. Another attack happened on August 17, 2011 against the Police Officers Association website and as in the first attack personal information (this time on the policemen) was released.

The motives behind deliberate attacks are varied and often not known. The BART attack was motivated by social/political activism. Motives for others are unclear. Cyber-attacks against other kinds of infrastructure are more common, and yield somewhat more information on motives.

Computer control failures (unintentional)
Breaches in communication capacity and capability have been the source of a number of other mishaps and signal vulnerabilities that could be taken advantage of by cyber-attackers. Consequences of deliberate and accidental breaches can be similar. Some anecdotes are noteworthy in the transportation sector.

According to an account by Daniels (2003) on August 20, 2003, the entire CSX transportation system was shut down in 23 states due to the inoperability of a computer system responsible for monitoring signals and train movements. Amtrak trains were also affected. The system was restored in part using manual overrides, such as faxing of train orders (Daniels 2003).

The New York area transit was affected on May 25, 2006 when 112 Amtrak trains and 45 NJ Transit trains were disrupted by a four-year-old computer part that failed to relay an order to restore electric power to one of the six substations providing power to the Amtrak system after electricity had been reduced for maintenance, according to news media accounts. Amtrak took actions to manage such situations by having substations manned during peak hours, not reducing power capacity for maintenance, and having spare locomotives available to move stalled trains (Wald 2007; Associated Press 2007).

Communication failures

In August 2006, 4,000 people were evacuated and a couple of dozen people and a number of firefighters were injured in a New York City subway fire, largely attributed to delayed communications. Subway operators could not reach radio dispatchers for five minutes and radio dispatchers were delayed 13 minutes in getting messages to emergency rescue workers due to the lack of a dedicated radio frequency and the fact that different radio frequencies were being used (WABC News January 2007).

Communication failures between police and fire officials have been extensively reviewed by McKinsey & Co. in connection with the September 11, 2001 attacks. Although these did not directly affect the transportation systems, they are equally applicable to emergencies in those systems. An editorial in *The New York Times*, citing an inspector general's report, noted the lack of progress five years later in developing an emergency communication system (*The New York Times* 2007). A progress report by the 9/11 commission similarly pointed to a lack of progress in communications connecting emergency responders in particular (Rockwell 2011).

Some massive accidents have shown significant lapses in communications. The Gulf Oil spill, relevant as a type of infrastructure connected to transportation, is one such case where communication failures were multidimensional (National Commission on the BP Deepwater Horizon Oil Spill and Offshore Drilling 2011). According to the Commission upper level executives initially did not provide adequate communications to the public during and immediately following the event. The measures for the extent and seriousness of the spill were numerous and not often consistent making communication difficult.

In Minot, North Dakota on January 18, 2002 a spill from a rail car released 240,000 gallons of anhydrous ammonia and a toxic cloud resulted. According to Klinenberg (2007) no public announcements reached the citizens of Minot since the one public radio system was broadcasting pre-recorded programs.

Communication successes

In Bhopal, December 1984, according to Ali (2004) communication warnings may also have enabled trains to be used to move people out of the area and prevent trains from entering Bhopal, India at the time of the release of methyl isocyanate, thus preventing many more deaths. The train operator noticed the toxic odors and acted quickly to control a train in order to avoid the effects. Although this is related to an industrial accident it also serves as a practice in terrorist incidents.

According to accounts by the US DOT, Volpe Center (2003) and Jenkins and Winslow (2003) in New York City on September 11, 2001, communication averted adverse consequences such as deaths in trains in the area at the time of the attack by allowing train operators time to roll back trains or not have them start on what would have been a perilous journey. They report that within a minute of the first plane hitting the north tower a train operator alerted the control center of MTA of an explosion and emergency procedures began. Within six minutes PATH began emergency procedures.

Improvements in communications in transit have been occurring in New York City. Neuman (2007) provides one recent example related to communication systems in the L line connecting Brooklyn and Manhattan, although he notes that the sound and signage system did not meet with a very positive response despite the large investment.

Also, since 2010, the NYC system has expanded an electronic system that alerts passengers in stations how long a train will take to arrive. MTA has installed electronic or LED countdown clocks also known as the Public Address Customer Information Screens (PA/CIS) system that carries messages as well as train schedules. The MTA indicated in mid-2011 that the goal by December 2011 was signs at 193 stations and the status as of August 2011 was that the clocks were installed at 163 stations with 139 on numbered lines and 24 on the L line – one at every station (MTA 2011).

After the London train bombings in 2005, CCTV enabled the authorities to initially track the perpetrators and finally apprehend them, though it was not able to avoid the attack.

INSTITUTIONAL MECHANISMS FOR PHYSICAL AND CYBER SECURITY

US Federal Government Programs

Transportation is one of over a dozen critical infrastructure sectors that have received considerable attention and protection by the federal government. Although most of the attention has occurred since the September 11, 2001 attacks, major federal efforts have been underway since the mid-1990s, after the 1993 attack on the World Trade Center in New York. Security has been one of a number of high priority criteria for ranking transportation infrastructure for some time. For example, the

Transportation Equity Act for the 21st Century (TEA-21) (US DOT 1998; Leung et al. 2004, p.967) identified security as one of the priorities in a number of provisions. Security is identified related to cargo security across borders (1119c(2)) and in the scoping of the metropolitan planning process (1203f(1)B) (US DOT 1998, pp.65, 77).

Below is a summary of some of the key federal developments that affect critical infrastructures, including transportation.

1996   Executive Order 13010
1997   President's Commission on Critical Infrastructure Protection
1997   US Department of Commerce Critical Infrastructure Assurance Office
1998   Presidential Decision Directive (PDD) 63
2001   USA Patriot Act Section 1016
2002   Homeland Security Act of 2001 (P.L. 107-296)
2002   National Strategy for Homeland Protection
        Homeland Security Presidential Directive 5
2003   Homeland Security Presidential Directive (HSPD) 7 and 8
2003   National Strategy for the Physical Protection of Critical Infrastructures
2004   National Incident Management System (NIMS)
2006   US DHS National Infrastructure Protection Plan (NIPP)
2007   Sector-Specific Plans (17 Infrastructure Sectors), Including Transportation
2008   National Response Framework
2009   US DHS National Infrastructure Protection Plan (NIPP) Revision
2010   Sector-Specific Plan revisions (the transportation plan was revised in 2010)
2011   National Preparedness Guidelines (PPD-8).

Source: Updated from Zimmerman (2006).

Federal executive orders, not specifically listed above, have also addressed transportation along with other infrastructure. As of April 8, 2011, there were 25 presidential directives for homeland security beginning on October 29, 2001 (US DHS April 2011). These were preceded by many other actions, and were also accompanied by many programs and plans.

The NIPP and sector-specific plans for infrastructure protection
The NIPP (US DHS 2009) is the framework used to carry out the Homeland Security Presidential Directive 7 (HSPD-7), Critical

Infrastructure Identification, Prioritization, and Protection of December 13, 2003. The NIPP appeared in its initial form in 2006 and was updated in 2009. As an essential part of the NIPP, a sector-specific plan (SSP) was developed for each of the sectors, including transportation. Many of the sector-specific plans appeared in 2007, with updates in line with the 2009 NIPP appearing in 2010. In 2009, 2010, and 2011 by proclamation, the President designated one month (December) as "Critical Infrastructure Protection Month". The NIPP is the framework by which critical infrastructure is secured. Moreover in 2011, the President by proclamation also underscored the need for preparedness.

The Sector-Specific Plan (SSP) for transportation systems was first produced in May 2007 (US DHS May 2007), and amended in 2010 (US DHS 2010).

The incorporation of transportation as a priority occurred in many forms prior to these operating procedures and programs – in executive orders, directives, and other mechanisms – that address infrastructure in general.

Cyber security planning
The NIPP and the Sector-Specific Plans that accompany it have also incorporated cyber security into critical infrastructure protection and the protection of other assets of national significance.

The US GAO (October 2007) evaluated all of the Sector-Specific Plans (SSPs) at that time in order to ascertain their coverage of cyber security along 30 different criteria. The GAO account revealed uneven coverage. The two areas that the GAO indicated were not addressed in the transportation SSP were: that in assessing risk, no screening process was described for cyber issues; and for research and development for protection, no existing projects were identified that could address gaps and goals (US GAO October 2007 p.44). Six areas were also identified as only being partially addressed.

A Transportation Cybersecurity Control Systems Roadmap (Transportation Roadmap) is a ten-year program being developed by the DHS Control Systems Security Program (CSSP) and the Transportation Security Administration (TSA). It will use roadmaps from other infrastructure areas as a guide (US DHS June 2011, p.2).

Cybersecurity legislation was introduced by the US House of Representatives on November 30, 2011 (H.R. 3523) and the US Senate on February 14, 2012 (Cybersecurity Act of 2012, S. 2105).

US Federal Funding

In the early years following the September 11, 2001 attacks, funding for transportation security tended to emphasize air travel security rather than roads and rail. As Howitt and Makler (2005, p.5) point out two pieces of legislation in 2004 aimed at transit failed to become law: the Public Transportation Terrorism Prevention Act and the Rail Security Act in 2004. A number of the mainstream transportation laws have incorporated security, but security competes with other funding priorities.

US DHS Homeland Security Grant Programs

Federal funding for transportation comes from a number of sources through the homeland security grant programs (HSGP), which consist of five programs (US DHS, FEMA (undated website)). Two that are most directly related to transportation are the Urban Area Security Initiative (UASI) and the State Homeland Security Program (SHSP).

The Urban Area Security Initiative (UASI) goes to urban areas through the states, and the FY 2011 funding was $662,622,100 (US DHS FEMA undated website). The stated purpose is: to provide "funding to address the unique planning, organization, equipment, training, and exercise needs of high-threat, high-density urban areas, and assists them in building an enhanced and sustainable capacity to prevent, protect against, respond to, and recover from acts of terrorism. Per the 9/11 Act, states are required to ensure that at least 25 percent (25%) of UASI appropriated funds are dedicated towards law enforcement terrorism prevention activities." (US DHS, FEMA undated website). Thirty-one high risk areas are funded. "The 11 highest risk urban areas, designated Tier I urban areas, were eligible for $540,696,100. The remaining 20 high risk urban areas, designated Tier II urban areas, were eligible for $121,926,000. Funds were allocated based on DHS' risk methodology and effectiveness" (US DHS, FEMA undated website).

The State Homeland Security Program (SHSP) supports state agencies in planning, enforcement and related functions to combat terrorism.

The other three programs under the HSGP are Operation Stonegarden (OPSG), the Metropolitan Medical Response System (MMRS), and the Citizen Corps Program (CCP) ((US DHS, FEMA undated website).

The Infrastructure Protection Program (IPP), Transit Security Grant Program (TSGP)

There are several grant programs that target transportation emergencies directly. The Transit Security Grant Program (TSGP) is one of the five programs under the Infrastructure Protection Program (IPP), and the funds go directly to the transit agencies.

The TSGP funds transit agencies based on a priority system (US DHS, May 2011, p.6):

DHS has identified critical infrastructure assets of national concern through the Top Transit Asset List (TTAL). Critical infrastructure assets are those vital to the functionality and continuity of a major transit system and their incapacitation or destruction would have a debilitating effect on security, national economic security, public health or safety, or any combination thereof . . . With the creation of the TTAL, DHS can now target funding to the remediation of those assets on the list in an informed and risk-based approach.

The authority for grants under the TSGP originates under Section 1406 of the Implementing Recommendations of the 9/11 Commission Act 2007 (Public Law 110-53) (hereafter 9/11 Act) and the Department of Defense and Full-Year Continuing Appropriations Act, 2011 (Public Law 112-10) (US DHS May 2011, p.5).

The eligible systems are listed on a Top Transit Asset List (TTAL) (US DHS May 2011, Table 7, p.24). In FY 2011, $200,079,000 was made available under the TSGP and is the largest of the infrastructure protection

Table 7.1   US Department of Homeland Security funding for transit security

From FY06 through FY11 the TSGP reported the following funding levels:

	Intracity	Additional Amtrak portion
	(in dollars)	
2006*	131,000,000	7,243,000
2007*	250,500,000	13,400,000****
2008*	356,100,000	25,000,000
2009*	348,000,000	25,000,000
2010**	253,000,000	20,000,000*****
2011***	200,079,000	19,960,000
Total	1,538,679,000	110,603,000

Sources:
*   US GAO (2009) TSGP, p.7, available at http://www.gao.gov/new.items/d09491.
        pdf. Unadjusted for inflation; FY2009 is target only.
**   US DHS (December 2009), FY 2010 Preparedness Grant Programs Overview.
        TSGP. Washington, DC, USA: US DHS, pp.3–6, available at http://www.dhs.gov/
        xlibrary/assets/grants_tsgp_overview_fy2010.pdf.
***   US DHS (May 2011), Fiscal Year 2011, Transit Security Grant Program, Guidance
        and Application Kit Section I – Application and Review Information, p.12,
        available at http://www.fema.gov/pdf/government/grant/2011/fy11_tsgp_kit.pdf.
****   Includes both a base and a supplemental amount.
*****   US DHS (December 2009), Fiscal Year 2010, Transit Security Grant Program,
        Guidance and Application Kit, Washington, DC, USA: US DHS, p.7, available at
        http://www.tsa.gov/assets/pdf/fy10_tsgp_guidance.pdf.
        http://www.fema.gov/government/grant/hsgp/.
About a half billion was granted under the program between FY03 and FY07.

programs, amounting to 85 percent of the IPP funds (US DHS May 2011, p.12). For FY 2011, a dozen systems are listed as being an asset on the DHS TTAL (see Table 7.1).

Tier I funding goes to the high risk areas, and the cities identified for this level of funding are Atlanta, Boston, Chicago, Los Angeles, the National Capital Region, New York, Philadelphia, and the San Francisco Bay Area. The distribution to these areas from 2006 to 2010 is provided by the US Department of Homeland Security, Transportation Security Administration (2010). These are all high population and high volume transportation areas.

FY 2010 TSGP Grants awards total $253.4 million, with $226.1 million awarded to Tier I regions. Final allocations for 2010 are at US Department of Homeland Security (TSA 2010). For previous years (figures are not aggregated the same way as in Table 7.1):

- "FY 2009 grant awards total $312 million. In FY 2009, both the Freight Rail Security Grant Program (FRSGP) and the TSGP Tier II program were awarded their entire target allocations of $15 million and $36.6 million respectively, due to an increase in the quantity and quality of applications. Thus, TSGP Tier I received their target allocation of $312 million and not any additional funds from FRSGP and Tier II like in FY2008" (US DHS, TSA 2009).
- "In Fiscal Year (FY) 2008, TSGP provided $333.2 million to owners and operators of transit systems (passenger rail, intracity bus, and ferry systems) in Tier I regions" which included "Atlanta, Boston, Chicago, Los Angeles, the National Capital Region, New York, Philadelphia, and the San Francisco Bay Area" (US DHS, TSA 2008).

A strong relationship exists between TSGP funding (aggregated between 2003 and 2007) (US DHS May 2007) and passenger trips obtained from the National Transportation Database (NTD) (US DOT, FTA undated web page) for about three dozen urban areas with major transit systems. Passenger trips are one measure of transit use and hence potential exposure and risk. The relationship between funding and transit trips is extremely strong with a correlation coefficient of 0.94. Another measure of transit system use, passenger miles (not shown), also revealed a very strong relationship with TSGP funding, with a correlation coefficient of 0.95. The New York area, represented by the New York City/Northern New Jersey, Jersey City/Newark areas is the outlier. When the New York area is removed, the relationship is slightly lower but still strong between TSGP funding for the rest of the cities, with correlation coefficients of

0.83 and 0.85 for passenger trips and passenger miles respectively. The relationship between TSGP funding and the size of the service area population is in a positive direction but is much weaker. For example, the correlation is 0.36 when the New York outlier is eliminated.

Disaster assistance

FEMA also provides disaster assistance to supplement other coverage or where no coverage exists. It is primarily for housing but covers damaged vehicles as well (FEMA http://www.fema.gov/assistance/process/individual _assistance.shtm).

In disasters other than terrorism, the US DHS provides financial support for transportation. For example, after Hurricane Katrina, the DHS provided transportation assistance (US DHS 2006). The program was called "LA Moves". It coordinates with services under the Statewide Emergency Transportation Plan and the agencies involved in transport. FEMA funds various programs at 100 percent funding. The funds are for the maintenance of and expansion of fixed routes, the replacement of damaged vehicles and other transportation services, and the provision of bus services.

US DOT funding programs

The American Recovery and Reinvestment Act (ARRA) of 2009 (Recovery Act) provides funding to the states. Under ARRA, through September 30, 2010, a total of 1,072 grants were made for transit totaling $8,778,730,416 (US DOT, FTA 2010). Railroads received another $9 billion and highways and bridges received $27.5 billion and more for state and local projects (US Congress, House of Representatives 2009).

For transportation emergencies, the US DOT has funding for "Quick Release Emergency Relief Funds" to support repair of transportation structures in major disasters. The funds originate from the Highway Trust Fund and are capped at $100,000,000 per disaster per state. For example, funding was released for the following disasters in 2011:

- June 9, 2011 Alabama tornadoes;
- June 27, 2011 North Dakota flooding, and
- August 31, 2011 Vermont flooding.

The US DOT, FHWA Emergency Relief Program is authorized and funded under the following authorities (US DOT, FHWA 2011):

Description: Congress authorized in Title 23, United States Code, Section 125, a special program from the Highway Trust Fund for the repair or reconstruction of Federal-aid highways and roads on Federal lands which have suffered serious damage as a result of (1) natural disasters or (2) catastrophic failures from an external cause. This program, commonly referred to as the emergency relief or ER program, supplements the commitment of resources by States, their political subdivisions, or other Federal agencies to help pay for unusually heavy expenses resulting from extraordinary conditions.

The applicability of the ER program to a natural disaster is based on the extent and intensity of the disaster. Damage to highways must be severe, occur over a wide area, and result in unusually high expenses to the highway agency. Applicability of ER to a catastrophic failure due to an external cause is based on the criteria that the failure was not the result of an inherent flaw in the facility but was sudden, caused a disastrous impact on transportation services, and resulted in unusually high expenses to the highway agency.

Funds available: $100 million in annual authorization. By law, the FHWA can provide up to $100 million in ER funding to a State for each natural disaster or catastrophic failure that is found eligible for funding under the ER program (commonly referred to as the $100 million per State cap). Also, the total ER obligations for US Territories (American Samoa, Commonwealth of Northern Mariana Islands, Guam, and Virgin Islands) is limited to $20 million in any fiscal year. For a large disaster that exceeds the $100 million per State cap, Congress may pass special legislation lifting the cap for that disaster.

Federal Share: Approved ER funds are available at the pro-rata share that would normally apply to the Federal-aid facility damaged. For Interstate highways, the Federal share is 90 percent. For all other highways, the Federal share is 80 percent. Emergency repair work to restore essential travel, minimize the extent of damage, or protect the remaining facilities, accomplished in the first 180 days after the disaster occurs, may be reimbursed at 100 percent Federal share.

Response Mechanisms

A wide range of innovative strategies have been used for response to and recovery from terrorist attacks ranging from simple operational controls to major reconstruction and redesign efforts. The response of transport systems after September 11, 2001 is illustrative of such strategies.

The September 11, 2001 attacks on the World Trade Center reconfigured surface rail and road transportation services in the New York area. Two of its five major routes were withdrawn due to the destruction of two major PATH hubs (the World Trade Center in Lower Manhattan and Exchange Place in New Jersey). The WTC station was physically destroyed from the collapse of the towers and the Exchange Place station was flooded. PATH routed passengers along three remaining routes two of which were centered at 33rd Street and the third connected Jersey City and Hoboken (APTA 2001, pp.3–4). In Hoboken, service to the Exchange Place location was picked up by light rail – the Hudson–Bergen Light Rail system (at Pavonia/Newport).

The ability to reroute trains also occurred, given the existing design of the NYC subway system. Some trains were converted to shuttles to provide continuous service by bypassing the WTC site into Brooklyn. Much of the response efforts of transit systems to the September 11, 2001 attacks actually had their origins in previous actions (Jenkins and Winslow 2003).

Zimmerman and Simonoff (2009) used monthly ridership data to examine the changes in ridership in New York City and regional rail systems before and after September 11, 2001 (described in detail earlier), and found relatively rapid improvement. No changes in the physical rail systems were apparent; however, very substantial security measures were superimposed upon them for detection and rapid response.

Response in terms of ridership in and around the WTC area was uneven in the late 2000s. The transit stations in the immediate vicinity show uneven trends, largely tracking the 2008 recession and changes in the economy thereafter. Some of the newer projects in the area, however, have been designed to make longstanding improvements. These include the Fulton Street Transit Center and improvements to the South Ferry transportation systems. Much of the TSGP funding has in fact been allocated to the Fulton Street project.

CONCLUSIONS

Physical destruction of transport infrastructure is still the more common form of security breach. Physical threats exist across natural hazard, accident, and deliberate attack conditions. However, the threat of cyber-attacks is likely to increase as transport increases its dependency on information technology and manual overrides are withdrawn. With respect to cyber security, the transportation sector has moved into the information technology age relatively more slowly than most other public infrastructure service sectors; however, it is now rapidly entering that arena.

The dependency of a given type of infrastructure such as transport on other kinds of infrastructure has been increasing in terms of usage, diversity and complexity. Such dependencies present both opportunities and challenges for management who must keep in mind flexible alternatives including manual intervention when electronic systems fail. Direct detection and intervention systems to combat both physical and cyber security problems also have to keep pace with the use of information technologies, and the transportation industry already has begun these efforts (APTA 2010), for example in the areas of intrusion detection systems (US DOT, Federal Railroad Administration 2007), the tracking of movement using

Global Positioning Systems (Colclasure 2010), and explosive detection systems (US GAO July 2010). Moreover, part of the management challenge for security will be to secure the entire transport chain from beginning to end – from acquisition of resources through recycling, and many of these steps can incorporate or integrate environmental considerations.

REFERENCES

Ali, F.M. (2004), 'Forgotten hero of Bhopal's tragedy', BBC Hindi service, in Bhopal, available at http://news.bbc.co.uk/1/hi/world/south_asia/4051755.stm.

American Public Transportation Association (APTA) (2001), 'America under threat: transit responds to terrorism. September 11, 2001. Passenger Transport. Special Report', available at http://www.apta.com/resources/reportsandpublica tions/Documents/911.pdf.

APTA Control and Communications Working Group (2010), 'Securing control and communications systems in transit environments', APTA RP-CCS-1-RT-001-10, Washington, DC, USA: APTA, available at http://www.aptastandards. com/LinkClick.aspx?fileticket=MGtGhaNVcd0%3D&tabid=329&mid=1670& language=en-US.

Associated Press (February 24, 2007), 'Amtrak Blames Outage on Computer Flaw', Associated Press online.

Baker, S., S. Waterman and G. Ivanov (2010), *In the Crossfire: Critical Infrastructure in the Age of Cyber War*, Santa Clara, CA, USA: McAfee, Inc.

Barnard, C. (2011), 'Hacker group anonymous: BART cyber-attacks just the beginning', available at http://latimesblogs.latimes.com/lanow/2011/08/bart-anticipates-more-cyber-attacks-from-anonymous-hackers.html.

Belcher, S. (February 2011), 'Driving toward zero fatalities with connected vehicle technology', ITS America email communication.

Bier, V., N. Haphuriwat, J. Menoyo, R. Zimmerman and A. Culpen (2008), 'Optimal resource allocation for defense of targets based on differing measures of attractiveness', *Risk Analysis*, **28** (3), 763–70.

Cellular Telecommunications and Internet Association (CTIA) (2010), 'CTIA – The Wireless Association 2010 semi-annual wireless industry survey', available at http://files.ctia.org/pdf/CTIA_Survey_Year_End_2010_Graphics.pdf.

Cisco (2011), 'Cisco visual networking index: global mobile data traffic forecast update 2010–2015', available at http://www.cisco.com/en/US/solutions/collateral/ns341/ns525/ns537/ns705/ns827/white_paper_c11-520862.pdf.

Colclasure, R. (2010), 'GPS system helps keep track of busses – video', available at http://www.kfyrtv.com/News_Stories.asp?news=45199 (accessed November 18, 2011).

Cutter, S.L., D.B. Richardson and T.J. Wilbanks (eds) (2003), *The Geographical Dimensions of Terrorism*, New York, USA and London, UK: Routledge.

Cybersecurity Act of 2012, S. 2105, 112th Congress (2012).

Daniels, C. (2003), 'Computer failure shuts down CSX train system', *Miami Herald*, available at http://www.miami.com/mld/miamiherald/news/local/6577053.htm.

Elinson, Z. (2011), 'After cellphone action, BART faces escalating protests', available at http://www.nytimes.com/2011/08/21/us/21bcbart.html?_r=1&hp.

Federal Signal (2010), 'Natural disasters and terrorist threats top Americans' public safety concerns', available at http://www.alertnotification.com/Natural DisastersandTerroristThreatsTopAmericansPublicSafetyConcerns_9119.aspx.

Federal Signal (2011), 'Public safety concerns persist 10 years after 9/11', available at http://www.alertnotification.com/PublicSafetyConcernsPersist10Years After911_9330.aspx.

Fernandez, J. and A. Fernandez (2005), 'SCADA systems: vulnerabilities and remediation', *Journal of Computing Sciences in Colleges*, **20** (4), 160–68.

Gordon, P., J.E. Moore II, H.W. Richardson and Q. Pan (2005), 'The economic impact of a terrorist attack on the twin ports of Los Angeles–Long Beach', in H.W. Richardson, P. Gordon and J.E. Moore II (eds), *The Economic Impacts of Terrorist Attacks*, Cheltenham, UK and Northampton, MA, USA: Edward Elgar, pp.262–86.

Gorman, S.P. (2005), *Networks, Security and Complexity*, Cheltenham, UK and Northampton, MA, USA: Edward Elgar.

Grynbaum, M.M. (August 2010), 'Some service restored on L.I.R.R.', *The New York Times*, available at http://www.nytimes.com/2010/08/24/nyregion/24lirr. html.

Guizzo, E. (October 2011), 'How Google's self-driving car works', available at http://staging.spectrum.ieee.org/automaton/robotics/artificial-intelligence/ how-google-self-driving-car-works.

Guizzo, E. (January 2012), 'French self-driving car takes to the road', available at http://spectrum.ieee.org/automaton/robotics/industrial-robots/french-self-driving-car-takes-to-the-road?utm_source=feedburner&utm_medium=feed &utm_campaign=Feed%3A+IeeeSpectrum+%28IEEE+Spectrum%29.

Hilbert, M. and P. Lopez (2011), 'The world's technological capacity to store, communicate and compute information', *Science*, **332**, 60–65.

Howitt, A.M. and J. Makler (2005), *On the Ground: Protecting America's Roads and Transit Against Terrorism*, Washington, DC, USA: The Brookings Institution.

ICANN (March 2007), Fact Sheet, Root Server Attack on February 6, 2007, available at http://www.icann.org/en/news/announcements/announcement-08mar07-en.htm.

INRIX, Inc. (2010) 2009 scorecard release, available at http://www.inrix.com/ pressrelease.asp?ID=93.

INRIX, Inc. (2011), 'National Traffic Scorecard 2010 Annual Report', available at http://inrix.com/scorecard/.

Jenkins, B.M. (1997), 'Protecting surface transportation systems and patrons from terrorist activities: case studies of best security practices and a chronology of attacks', San José, CA, USA: The Mineta Transportation Institute (MTI), San José, CA, USA: San José State University College of Business, available at http:// transweb.sjsu.edu/MTIportal/research/publications/documents/97-04.pdf.

Jenkins, B.M. and F.E. Winslow (2003), 'Saving city lifelines: lessons learned in the 9/11 terrorist attacks', The Mineta Transportation Institute (MTI), San José, CA, USA: San José State University College of Business.

Jenkins, B.M., B.R. Butterworth and J-F. Clair (2010), 'Off the rails: the 1995 attempted derailing of the French TGV (High-Speed Train) and a quantitative analysis of 181 rail sabotage attempts', San José, CA, USA: The Mineta Transportation Institute (MTI), San José, CA, USA: San José State University College of Business.

Klinenberg, E. (2007), 'Idea lab. Air support', available at http://www.nytimes. com/2007/01/28/magazine/28WWLN_IdeaLab.t.html?ex=1170997200&en=ad2 5153d3c49998f&ei=5070&emc=eta1.

Koscher, K., A. Czeskis, F. Roesner, S. Patel, T. Kohno, S. Checkoway, D. McCoy, B. Kantor, D. Anderson, H. Shacham and S. Savage (2010), 'Experimental security analysis of a modern automobile', 2010 IEEE Symposium on Security and Privacy, available at http://www.autosec.org/pubs/cars-oakland2010.pdf.

LaFree, G. and B. Bersani (January 2012), 'Hot Spots of Terrorism and Other Crimes in the United States, 1970 to 2008', available at http://start.umd.edu/start/ publications/research_briefs/LaFree_Bersani_HotSpotsOfUSTerrorism.pdf.

Leung, M., J.H. Lambert and A. Mosenthal (2004), 'A risk-based approach to setting priorities in protecting bridges against terrorist attacks', *Risk Analysis*, **24** (4), 963–84.

Los Angeles County District Attorney's Office (2007), 'Two city engineers charged with allegedly hacking into city's traffic computer', available at http://da.co. la.ca.us/mr/archive/2007/010507a.htm.

Markoff, J. (2010), 'Cars' computer systems called at risk to hackers', available at http://www.nytimes.com/2010/05/14/science/14hack.html?scp=6&sq= Markoff&st=cse.

McAfee (2011), 'Caution: Malware ahead', available at http://www.mcafee.com/ us/resources/reports/rp-caution-malware-ahead.pdf.

McMillan, R. (2011), '"War texting" lets hackers unlock car doors via SMS', NetworkWorld, available at http://www.networkworld.com/news/2011/072711-war-texting-lets-hackers-unlock.html.

Meleagrou-Hitchens, A. (2011), 'As American as apple pie: how Anwar al-Awlaki became the face of Western Jihad', London, UK: International Centre for the Study of Radicalization and Political Violence, http://icsr.info/publications/ papers/1315827595ICSRPaperAsAmericanAsApplePieHowAnwaralAwlakiBe cametheFaceofWesternJihad.pdf (accessed September 30, 2011).

Metropolitan Transit Authority (MTA) (2011), 'Innovation project: countdown clocks', available at http://www.mta.info/countdwn_clocks.htm (accessed August 14, 2011).

National Commission on the BP Deepwater Horizon Oil Spill and Offshore Drilling (January 2011), *Deep Water: The Gulf Oil Disaster and the Future of Offshore Drilling. Report to the President. Final Report*, available at http://www. oilspillcommission.gov/sites/default/files/documents/DEEPWATER_Reportto thePresident_FINAL.pdf.

The National Consortium for the Study of Terrorism and the Responses to Terrorism (see references listed as START).

Neuman, W. (September 2007), 'New York, Manhattan: C grade for L line', available at www.nytimes.com/2007/09/28/nyregion/28mbrfs-TRANSIT.html (accessed November 21, 2011).

The New York Times (2002), 'Worldwide servers overwhelmed with data: attack briefly cripples Net', available at http://www.nytimes.com/2002/10/24/ news/24iht-a1_24.html?scp=1&sq=October%202002%20internet%20outage&st =cse.

The New York Times (2006), 'Sniper accomplice says mentor had extortion and terror plan', available at http://www.nytimes.com/2006/05/24/us/24malvo.html.

The New York Times (2007), 'Editorial. Communication in the face of terror', available at http://www.nytimes.com/2007/03/29/opinion/29thu2.html?_r=1& oref=slogin (accessed November 21, 2011).

North American Electric Reliability Corporation (2004), 'NERC report on blackout: technical analysis of the northeast blackout', available at http://www.nerc.com/docs/docs/blackout/NERC_Final_Blackout_Report_07_13_04.pdf.

Perrow, C. (2007), *The Next Catastrophe*, Princeton, NJ, USA: Princeton University Press.

Pew Research Center for the People and the Press (2010), 'Public's priorities for 2010: economy, jobs, terrorism, energy concerns fall, deficit concerns rise', Washington, DC, USA: Pew Research Center, available at http://people-press.org/files/legacy-pdf/584.pdf; http://people-press.org/2010/01/25/publics-priorities-for-2010-economy-jobs-terrorism/.

Pew Research Center for the People and the Press (2011), 'Less optimism about America's long-term prospects', Washington, DC, USA: Pew Research Center, available at http://people-press.org/files/legacy-pdf/696.pdf.

Poulsen, K. (February 2004), 'Software bug contributed to blackout', available at http://www.securityfocus.com/news/8016 (accessed April 4, 2010).

Poulsen, K. (April 2004), 'Tracking the blackout bug', available at http://www.securityfocus.com/news/8412 (accessed April 4, 2010).

Pricewaterhouse Coopers (PwC) (2011), 'Transportation and logistics 2030. Vol. 4: securing the supply chain', available at http://www.pwc.com/en_GX/gx/transportation-logistics/pdf/TL2030_vol.4_web.pdf.

Risk Management Solutions, Inc. (RMS) (September 2011), 'Terrorism risk in the post-9/11 era, a 10-year retrospective', Newark, CA, USA: RMS, available at http://sarma.org/Data/news/reports/rms65279terrorismr/sarma.rms.pdf.

Rockwell, M. (2011), '9/11 Commission report card says interoperability and better coordination still needed', available at http://www.gsnmagazine.com/node/24388?c=federal_agencies_legislative.

Saad, L. (2011), 'Americans' fear of terrorism in US is near low point, trust in US government to protect citizens from terrorism remains subdued', available at http://www.gallup.com/poll/149315/Americans-Fear-Terrorism-Near-Low-Point.aspx?version=print.

Savitch, H.V. (2008), *Cities in a Time of Terror – Space, Territory, and Local Resilience*, Armonk, NY, USA and London, UK: M.E. Sharpe.

Schrank, D., T. Lomax and B. Eisele (2011), 'Urban Mobility Report 2010', available at http://tti.tamu.edu/documents/mobility-report-2011.pdf.

Shrobe, H. (2011), 'Secure computer systems', Arlington, VA, USA: DARPA Cyber Colloquim.

Slay, J. and M. Miller (2008), 'Lessons learned from the Maroochy water breach', in E.D. Goetz and S. Shenoi (eds), *Critical Infrastructure Protection*, New York, NY, USA: Springer, pp.73–82.

START (2010), 'Background report: on the fifth anniversary of the 7/7 London transit attack', available at http://www.start.umd.edu/start/announcements/July07_LondonMetroBombing_2010.pdf.

START (2011a), 'Background report: 9/11, ten years later', available at http://www.start.umd.edu/start/announcements/BackgroundReport_10YearsSince9_11.pdf.

START (2011b), 'Background Report: Al-Qa'ida in the Arabian Peninsula (AQAP), Anwar al-Awlaki, and Samir Khan', available at http://www.start.umd.edu/start/publications/br/BR_AQAP_alAwlakiandKhan.pdf.

Stoller, G. (2010), 'Can trains, subways be protected from terrorists?', available at http://www.usatoday.com/money/industries/travel/2010-12-27-railsecurity27_CV_N.htm.

Symantec Corporation (2011), 'Internet security threat report trends for 2010', Volume 16, available at https://www4.symantec.com/mktginfo/downloads/21182883_GA_REPORT_ISTR_Main-Report_04-11_HI-RES.pdf.

Taylor, B.D., C.N.Y. Fink and R. Liggett (2006), 'Responding to security threats in the post-9/11 era: a portrait of US urban public transit', *Public Works Management & Policy*, **11** (1), 3–17.

Telegeography (2011), 'Global Internet Geography, Executive Summary', PriMetrica, Inc. available at http://www.telegeography.com/page_attachments/products/website/research-services/global-internet-geography/0002/4221/telegeography-global-internet.pdf.

Transportation Research Board (2003), 'Cyber security of freight information systems: a scoping study', available at http://onlinepubs.trb.org/onlinepubs/sr/sr274.pdf.

Urbina, I. (2006), 'Washington-area sniper convicted of 6 more killings', available at http://www.nytimes.com/2006/05/31/us/31sniper.html.

US Congress, House of Representatives (2009), 'Summary: American recovery and reinvestment: conference agreement 2/13/09', available at http://www.oregon.gov/ENERGY/docs/HouseSummary02-13-09.pdf?ga=t; http://appropriations.house.gov/pdf/PressSummary02-13-09.pdf.

US Department of Homeland Security (December 2006), 'Transportation services provided to hurricane evacuees, release number: 1603-589', available at http://www.fema.gov/news/newsrelease.fema?id=32547.

US Department of Homeland Security (May 2007), 'Overview: FY 2007 infrastructure protection program final awards', updated for May 10, 2007, Washington, DC, USA: US Department of Homeland Security.

US Department of Homeland Security (2007), 'Transportation Systems. Critical infrastructure and key resources sector-specific plan as input to the national infrastructure protection plan', available at http://www.dhs.gov/xlibrary/assets/nipp-ssp-transportation.pdf.

US Department of Homeland Security (2009), *National Infrastructure Protection Plan (NIPP)*, Washington, DC: US DHS.

US Department of Homeland Security (2010), *Transportation Systems Sector-Specific Plan: An Annex to the National Infrastructure Protection Plan 2010*, available at http://www.dhs.gov/xlibrary/assets/nipp-ssp-transportation-systems-2010.pdf.

US Department of Homeland Security (April 2011), 'Homeland Security Presidential Directives', available at http://www.dhs.gov/xabout/laws/editorial_0607.shtm.

US Department of Homeland Security (June 2011), 'ICSJWG Quarterly Newsletter', available at http://www.us-cert.gov/control_systems/pdf/ICSJWG_Quarterly_Newsletter_June_2011.pdf.

US Department of Homeland Security (2012), *National Preparedness Report*, Washington, DC: US DHS.

US Department of Homeland Security (May 2011), 'Fiscal year 2011: transit security grant program, guidance and application kit section I – application and review information', available at http://www.fema.gov/pdf/government/grant/2011/fy11_tsgp_kit.pdf.

US Department of Homeland Security, Federal Emergency Management Agency

(August 2011), FY 2011 Transit Security Grant Program (TSGP), available at http://www.fema.gov/government/grant/tsgp/.

US Department of Homeland Security, Federal Emergency Management Agency (undated website), 'Homeland Security Grant Program (HSGP)', available at http://www.fema.gov/government/grant/hsgp/#2.

US Department of Homeland Security, Transportation Security Administration (2008), Transit Security Grant Program Tier I FY 2008, Grants Programs 2008, available at http://www.tsa.gov/what_we_do/grants/programs/tsgp_tieri/2008/index.shtm.

US Department of Homeland Security, Transportation Security Administration (2009), Transit Security Grant Program Tier I FY 2009, Grants Programs 2009 available at http://www.tsa.gov/what_we_do/grants/awards/tsgp_tieri/2009/index.shtm.

US Department of Homeland Security, Transportation Security Administration (2010), Transit Security Grant Program Tier I FY 2010, Grants Programs 2010 available at http://www.tsa.gov/what_we_do/grants/programs/tsgp_tieri/2010/index.shtm.

US Department of Homeland Security, Transportation Security Administration (2011), 'BART anticipates more cyber attacks from "Anonymous" hackers', *This Week in Transportation Cyber Security*, **2** (32).

US Department of Transportation (1998), 'Transportation Equity Act for the 21st Century', available at http://www.fhwa.dot.gov/tea21/tea21.pdf.

US Department of Transportation (2009) 2008 Status of the Nation's Bridges, Highways, and Transit Conditions and Performance, Washington, DC, USA: US DOT.

US Department of Transportation (2010), 'FHWA freight facts and figures 2010', available at http://ops.fhwa.dot.gov/freight/freight_analysis/nat_freight_stats/docs/10factsfigures/pdfs/fff2010_highres.pdf.

US Department of Transportation, Federal Highway Administration (2011), 'Emergency relief program is authorized and funded under the following authorities', available at http://www.fhwa.dot.gov/programadmin/erelief.cfm.

US Department of Transportation, Federal Railroad Administration (2007), *Alternative Rail Intruder and Obstacle Detection Systems*, Washington, DC, USA: US Department of Transportation, Federal Railroad Administration, available at http://www.fra.dot.gov/downloads/research/rr0721.pdf.

US Department of Transportation, Federal Transit Administration (2003), 'The public transportation system security and emergency preparedness planning guide', available at http://transit-safety.volpe.dot.gov/publications/security/PlanningGuide.pdf.

US Department of Transportation, Federal Transit Administration (2010), 'ARRA grants through 9/30/10', available at http://www.fta.dot.gov/news/10536.htm.

US Department of Transportation, Federal Transit Administration (undated website), 'National Transit Database', available at http://www.ntdprogram.gov/ntdprogram/.

US Department of Transportation, Volpe National Transportation Systems Center (2003), *Effects of Catastrophic Events on Transportation System Management and Operations. Cross Cutting Study*, Cambridge, MA, USA: US Department of Transportation, Volpe Center.

US Government Accountability Office (September 2007), 'Critical infrastructure protection. Multiple efforts to secure control systems are under way, but challenges remain', available at http://www.gao.gov/assets/270/268137.pdf.

US Government Accountability Office (October 2007), 'Critical infrastructure protection. Sector-specific plans' coverage of key cyber security elements varies', available at http://www.gao.gov/new.items/d08113.pdf.

US Government Accountability Office (June 2009), 'Transit Security Grant Program: DHS allocates grants based on risk, but its risk methodology, management controls, and grant oversight can be strengthened', available at http://www.gao.gov/new.items/d09491.pdf.

US Government Accountability Office (July 2010), 'Technology assessment: Explosives detection technologies to protect passenger rail', available at http://www.gao.gov/new.items/d10898.pdf.

Vixie, P., G. Sneeringer and M. Schleifer (2002), '21 Oct 2002 root server denial of service attack – report', available at http://www.isc.org/f-root-denial-of-service-21-oct-2002; ICANN.

WABC Eyewitness News (2007), 'Blistering report on summer subway fire', available at http://abclocal.go.com/wabc/story?section=local&id=4945419.

Wald, M.L. (2007), 'New parts in old system are cited in Amtrak trouble', *The New York Times*, available at http://www.nytimes.com/2007/02/24/us/24amtrak.html?_r=1&oref=slogin.

Wikipedia, 'Beltway sniper attacks', available at http://en.wikipedia.org/wiki/Beltway_sniper_attacks (accessed January 27, 2012).

Wilson, C. (2005), 'Computer attack and cyberterrorism', Congressional Research Service, available at http://www.dtic.mil/cgi-bin/GetTRDoc?AD=ADA444799&Location=U2&doc=GetTRDoc.pdf.

Zimmerman, R. (2006), 'Critical infrastructure and interdependency', in D.G. Kamien (ed.), *The McGraw-Hill Homeland Security Handbook*, New York, NY, USA: McGraw-Hill, Chapter 35, pp.523–45.

Zimmerman, R. and C.E. Restrepo (2006), 'The next step: quantifying infrastructure interdependencies to improve security', *International Journal of Critical Infrastructures*, **2** (2/3), 215–30.

Zimmerman, R. and J.S. Simonoff (2009), 'Transportation density and opportunities for expediting recovery to promote security', *Journal of Applied Security Research*, **4**, 48–59.

Zimmerman, R. with J.S. Simonoff and H. Arnett (2006), 'Urban infrastructure services in a time of crisis: lessons from September 11th, final report to the National Science Foundation', New York, NY, USA: NYU, Wagner School.

8. Conclusions

The opportunity to rethink multiple objectives for transport, the environment, and security that are extensively networked builds on a very long history in each of these areas. Combining them in ways that achieve synergy or at least acknowledge and reconcile conflict is imperative. The trajectory of the deterioration of environmental conditions so eloquently put forth by Speth (2008) signals a collision between transport and the environment, even though in some areas the environment may be showing some improvement. These environmental conditions are coupled with growing challenges to security. Cities are becoming battlefields. As Savitch (2008) notes, most attacks occur in cities. Yet cities small and large remain always vibrant, given the ability to move within and among them. Thus, transport and the many services it represents help to weave a rich fabric that enables those who inhabit cities to retain their mobility and access in the context of the environment and security.

Transport has an intricate relationship with environment and security. These three systems share key nodes and have links in common that when disrupted can have catastrophic effects. When such catastrophes occur, the individual systems are not only affected but also the connections among them, given how impacts are often transferred among them as the previous chapters have shown.

In times of emergencies, compromises have been made, such as the ability to consume less and reorient behavior in ways that are not only less demanding on the environment but also provide security against a compromised resource. Behavior can change and has changed even in normal times. For example, energy from traditional sources can be conserved to reduce the adverse consequences of emissions and other environmental impacts; however, these objectives can also be accomplished by using independent power sources that are disconnected from the grid, are environmentally sound and secure, and are compatible with the grid. Similar options exist directly for transport, and are becoming more viable such as challenges of new more resilient materials, energy storage, and charging stations for alternative vehicles; new materials and renewable energy use in transit; and overcoming choke points in transport systems overall. Yet, there is a long way to go.

Policies and strategies are emerging with the potential to combine transport, the environment and security so as to magnify the effect of improvements in any single area. The environment, recently dominated by climate change, has led to largely local and fine-grained initiatives aimed at transport that tailor broad policies to local conditions and political climates. Security strategies are also proliferating, and how these options interact to enable transport and environmental networks to co-exist and achieve co-benefits will be challenging. Many examples are explored in this book where the three networks are compatible, and some examples reflect an important beginning.

Renewable energy has been thought about in terms of a portfolio of uses, and a portfolio of new transportation technologies is similarly applicable that accommodates multiple travel modes. An increasing number of types of private vehicles, together with non-motorized forms of travel and the land use and resource networks to support them, provide the diversity and flexibility that are needed to achieve environment and security objectives. Walking reduces energy use from transport and enables people to be dispersed in dense urban environments thus preserving the environment from stress and promoting security while retaining the advantages of density. The ratio of bike stations to transit hubs and surface transportation intersections to promote interconnectivity is high and growing higher as this mode of transportation continues to take off. Transit-oriented development reflects another way to alter the organization of transport and its users through land use.

Streets are an important place in which transport, environment and security networks intersect. They consume a significant portion of the land area of urban areas and regions. The very local scale of streets has meaning for people. At very fine-grained levels, for example, the many innovative strategies to accomplish the multiple functions of streets and accommodate their many new and emerging uses will need to expand. Not only will attention have to be paid to the current use of streets, but also when, where and how they are used, and who uses them. For example, street specialization can allow different uses of streets to vary over time and by purposes. Though these strategies are specific to local areas, they are being shared nationally.

Ecological or wildlife corridors not only protect nature but also if designed with multiple purposes in mind, can reduce the consequences of flooding through stormwater control. They also provide a visible buffer around a transportation corridor if designed right to promote security.

Barriers around bridge footings simultaneously offer security benefits, buffers against accidental collisions, and protection against adverse environmental conditions under ordinary and extreme weather conditions that can undermine a bridge's condition.

Bridge accidents are rare but they teach a lesson in how multiple and interrelated causes can produce a single catastrophe. Often, investing in a single area could avert catastrophe.

Sensor systems can serve dual or multiple purposes of detection for security, to identify adverse conditions and forewarn about imminent accidents, impending congestion, and environmental conditions where the ecology is being threatened by transport practices.

Ventilation points, including those associated with transportation facilities, are highly vulnerable to tampering from a security point of view, can produce adverse health and environmental conditions if they deteriorate, and are subject to inundation and disabling from flooding and airborne debris from natural hazards. Through design and placement these vulnerabilities can be eliminated simultaneously and serve all of those purposes.

Many of these and other initiatives are occurring project by project and place by place, and the popularity is growing. What is left is how these add up, and adopting a systems or life cycle perspective that combines these three networks may answer this question.

Concentration continually poses a key network challenge for transport. Concentration provides efficiencies and economic benefits, and can produce security and protection from environmental risks for transport networks. The analysis of US rail systems reveals a high degree of concentration of the infrastructure and its users in just a few systems nationwide, regardless of what measures are used. Within transport systems, increasing dependence on single nodes and new and existing transport hubs that continue to concentrate people have the potential to produce system-wide damage where a single node is disrupted from whatever cause; however, many systems take advantage of decentralization within what are very concentrated systems. Nodes may need to be decentralized even more in ways that can serve people's needs with alternative routing that retains the benefits of concentration but reduces vulnerability. In the area of security in particular, deliberate attacks on transport take advantage of the concentrated network structure of transport systems, and decentralizing that network but still retaining its density is an important consideration.

The parameters are changing for transportation. Interdependencies are increasing with other activities and services. Transport has a recognizably large dependency on electric power and information technology, and the network structure of those systems influences how secure transport is. Technology choices in the electric power industry will inevitably affect how transportation holds up in light of a full life cycle assessment. Those energy policies may not be within the jurisdiction of transportation decision-makers; however, the choices of energy that transport uses is. Transport's dependency on information technology will continue to grow and the security threats in terms of cyber-attacks are growing with it.

An important principle in avoiding the dilemmas that concentration poses is having more than one way out. Transportation systems have been constructed in highly tethered ways, in the language of network theory, in ways in which only a few links connect multiple nodes, usually linearly, yet multiple modes of travel provide the interconnections. The interaction of extreme weather and other natural hazards increases the potential for disruption and recovery delays. Unfortunately, extensive destruction now can occur at a single point. Interdependencies make this worse.

Many of the transport strategies put forth here detail how they impact climate and other aspects of the environment and security, but the accounting needs to engage a full life cycle assessment perspective while the details are worked out. Security is typically not put into the equation together with these other options, yet the co-benefits are often apparent on a case by case basis. It is important to retain the level of detail for strategies in each of the three areas, acknowledging that reframing and new choices are likely as they come together, and also reflect the broader perspective that co-benefit concepts offer in a networked context.

Following the September 11, 2001 attacks in New York City, the National Research Council (NRC) (2002, pp.214–23) put forward the idea of a layered, dual-use, adaptable approach to transportation security. The first step is combining security with other functions. The return to co-benefits or dual use is underscored by networks. Only in that realm can the interconnections be identified.

For security, the vulnerability of targets can be minimized by disaggregating or decentralizing the targets to minimize the impact and make them less accessible and this can be accomplished while still retaining the viability of dense urban environments.

The lessons that natural hazards, accidents and terrorists' attacks teach is how similar the consequences are for different kinds of catastrophes.

If we are already weak, attacks will be more catastrophic. If we are already dependent, attacks on those interconnections will make matters worse. The need for investment where multiple benefits will occur is critical.

REFERENCES

National Research Council (2002), *Making the Nation Safer*, Washington, DC, USA: National Academies Press.

Savitch, H.V. (2008), *Cities in a Time of Terror*, Armonk, New York, USA and London, UK: M.E. Sharpe.

Speth, J.G. (2008), *The Bridge at the Edge of the World*, New Haven, CO, USA and London, UK: Yale University Press.

Index